The 50 Greatest Players in New England Patriots Football History

Robert W. Cohen

Down East Books
Lanham • Boulder • New York • London

Published by Down East Books
A wholly owned subsidiary of The Rowman & Littlefield Publishing Group, Inc.
4501 Forbes Boulevard, Suite 200, Lanham, Maryland 20706
www.rowman.com

Unit A, Whitacre Mews, 26-34 Stannary Street, London SE11 4AB

Distributed by NATIONAL BOOK NETWORK

British Library Cataloguing in Publication Information Available

Library of Congress Cataloging-in-Publication Data

Cohen, Robert W.
The 50 greatest players in New England Patriots football history / Robert W. Cohen.
pages cm
"Distributed by NATIONAL BOOK NETWORK"--T,p, verso.
ISBN 978-1-60893-452-2 (cloth : alk. paper) — ISBN 978-1-60893-453-9 (electronic) 1. New England Patriots (Football team)—History. 2. Football players—Rating of—United States. I. Title. II. Title: Fifty greatest players in New England Patriots football history.
GV956.N36C54 2015
796.332'640974461—dc23

2015026913

The paper used in this publication meets the minimum requirements of American National Standard for Information Sciences—Permanence of Paper for Printed Library Materials, ANSI/NISO Z39.48-1992.

Printed in the United States of America

Contents

Acknowledgments

I wish to thank Todd Tobias of Talesfromtheamericanfootballleague.com, Aaron Frutman of DGA Productions, MEARSonlineauctions.com, Mainlineautographs.com, Pristineauction.com, George Kitrinos, Keith Allison, Scott Slingsby, Joe Schilp, Jason Thompson, Ronny Leber, Scott Horrigan, Barry Lenard, Karen Cardoza, Cris Yarborough, Jeffrey Beall, Marc Sebes, Sgt. Brian Ferguson of the U.S. Air Force, Beth Hart, and Matt Cordon, each of whom generously contributed to the photographic content of this work.

Introduction

Deion Branch breaks away.
(Courtesy Jason Thompson)

THE PATRIOT LEGACY

Professional football arrived in New England on November 16, 1959, when the newly formed American Football League awarded the circuit's eighth and final franchise to a group of local businessmen headed by former public relations executive William H. "Billy" Sullivan Jr. After holding a public contest to find a suitable name for their new team, Sullivan and his partners settled on the "Boston Patriots," who joined the Buffalo Bills, New York Titans, and Houston Oilers in the AFL's Eastern Division. Meanwhile, the Oakland Raiders, Denver Broncos, Dallas Texans, and Los Angeles Chargers comprised the infant circuit's Western Division.

Forced to compete against the more established National Football League, the AFL struggled to survive its first few seasons, prompting the new league to schedule many of its games for Friday and Saturday nights. Furthermore, with NFL franchises already taking up residence in the cities of Dallas (Cowboys) and Los Angeles (Rams), the Texans and Chargers found it necessary to relocate before long, with the Texans moving to Kansas City in 1963 and renaming themselves the "Chiefs," and the Chargers traveling some 130 miles south to the city of San Diego after just one year in Los Angeles.

Initially entrusted to Lou Saban, who General Manager Ed McKeever named the team's first head coach, the Patriots also had a difficult time gaining a foothold in the New England area, spending their first 10 years playing their home games at four different sites, including Boston University Field, Harvard Stadium, Fenway Park, and Boston College Alumni Stadium. Yet, even as they continued to search for a true identity, the Patriots emerged as one of the AFL's stronger teams after former Boston College head coach Mike Holovak replaced Saban at the helm early in 1961. After posting a record of just 5-9 in their first season, the Patriots compiled an overall mark of 35-17-4 under Holovak from 1961 to 1964, advancing to the AFL title game in 1963, when they lost to the San Diego Chargers by a score of 51-10. Unfortunately, the Patriots posted a winning record just once more during the decade, concluding the first 10 years of their existence with a composite mark of 63-68-9. Still, even though they made the playoffs just once during that time, the Patriots featured some of the league's best players. On offense, Babe Parilli established himself as one of the circuit's top quarterbacks, while center Jon Morris earned All-AFL honors on a multitude of occasions. Powerful fullback Jim Nance led the league in rushing twice and earned AFL MVP honors in 1966, when he became the only player in league history to rush for more than 1,400 yards in a season. Wide receiver/kicker Gino Cappelletti was named league MVP two years earlier and eventually went on to score more points than any other player in AFL history. Meanwhile, the Patriots annually fielded one of the league's most imposing defenses, with linebacker Tom Addison and linemen Larry Eisenhauer, Bob Dee, and Jim Lee Hunt all earning multiple trips to the AFL All-Star Game, and linebacker Nick Buoniconti and tackle Houston Antwine later being named to the AFL's All-Time All-Star Team.

Following the NFL/AFL merger in 1970, the Patriots joined the New York Jets, Buffalo Bills, Miami Dolphins, and Baltimore Colts in the Eastern Division of the American Football Conference. One year later, they moved into newly-constructed Schaefer Stadium, which remained their home for the next 30 years. With Schaefer Stadium being situated in the suburb of Foxboro, Massachusetts, some 22 miles from downtown Boston, the Patriots came to represent a larger geographical area, prompting them to rename themselves the "New England Patriots" prior to the start of the 1971 campaign.

The lack of success the Patriots experienced during the latter portion of the 1960s carried over into the ensuing decade, causing team management to change coaches no fewer than four times between 1968 and 1973, a period during which the franchise compiled an overall record of just 24-60. The Patriots finally returned to prominence in 1976, when they finished 11-3 under former Oklahoma head coach Chuck Fairbanks, earning in the process their first trip to the playoffs in 13 years. However, they subsequently suffered a heartbreaking 24-21 loss to the Oakland Raiders in the first round of the postseason tournament. Fairbanks remained at the helm another two years, leading the Patriots to their first outright division title in franchise history in 1978, before electing to return to the college ranks to coach at the University of Colorado. After losing to the Houston Oilers 31-14 in their first home playoff game ever, the Patriots remained a solid team under new head coach Ron Erhardt the next two seasons, finishing 9-7 in 1979 and 10-6 in 1980. However, they fell to just 2-14 in 1981, prompting the dismissal of Erhardt and the hiring of former SMU head coach Ron Meyer.

As the coaching carousel continued in New England, several exceptional players graced the Patriots' roster. Cornerback Mike Haynes and guard John Hannah gained general recognition as arguably the finest players in the league at their respective positions. Linebacker Steve Nelson helped to anchor the defense, while wide receiver Stanley Morgan went on to establish himself as the most prolific pass-catcher in franchise history. Tight end Russ Francis and running back Sam Cunningham also emerged as stars on offense.

Despite leading the Patriots to a wild-card playoff appearance in 1982, Meyer remained head coach in New England just 2 ½ years, eventually being replaced midway through the 1984 campaign by Raymond Berry, who spent most of his playing career catching passes from fellow Pro Football Hall of Famer Johnny Unitas in Baltimore. Berry subsequently helped stabilize the Pats in his 5 ½ years at the helm, leading them to an overall record of 48-39, two division titles, and their first Super Bowl appearance in 1985, which ended up being a 46-10 mauling at the hands of the powerful Chicago Bears. However, after New England finished just 5-11 in 1989, new Patriots owner Victor Kiam, the Remington Products, Inc. CEO who purchased the team from the Sullivan family on July 28, 1988, elected to replace Berry with Rod Rust, who earlier spent the better part of five years serving as defensive coordinator in New England. With the Patriots finishing just 1-15 under Rust in 1990, Kiam replaced him with Dick MacPherson, who subsequently led the team to an overall mark of 8-24 over the course of the next two seasons. Yet, even though the Patriots found themselves mired in mediocrity much of the time during the 1980s and early 1990s, they continued to produce a number of exceptional players. Julius Adams excelled on the defensive line, Raymond Clayborne did an outstanding job of covering opposing wide receivers from his spot in the defensive secondary, and Andre Tippett emerged as one of the game's most dominant linebackers. Quarterback Steve Grogan developed into the team's leader on offense, while Bruce Armstrong established himself as one of the greatest offensive linemen in franchise history.

The Patriots did not become consistent winners until shortly after St. Louis businessman James B. Orthwein purchased them from Kiam in 1992 and hired former New York Giants head coach Bill Parcells to lead his team. Although the Patriots finished just 5-11 under Parcells in 1993, they developed into one of the AFC's stronger clubs the following year after being purchased by Robert K. Kraft, who prevented the Patriots from being moved to Orthwein's hometown of St. Louis by acquiring them. Closing out the 1994 campaign with seven consecutive wins, the Patriots finished 10-6, to earn their first playoff berth in eight years. Unfortunately, the Cleveland Browns subsequently eliminated them from the postseason tournament when they defeated them by a score of 20-13 in the wild card game.

After going just 6-10 under Parcells the following year, the Patriots rebounded in 1996 by capturing the AFC East title with a record of 11-5, before defeating the Pittsburgh Steelers 28-3 and the Jacksonville Jaguars 20-6 in the playoffs, en route to earning their second trip to the Super Bowl. However, this time the Green Bay Packers thwarted the Patriots' quest for their first world championship, defeating them by a score of 35-21 in Super Bowl XXXI.

Differences with Robert Kraft prompted Parcells to leave New England at the end of 1996, forcing the Patriots' owner to turn to Pete Carroll as his successor. The Patriots advanced to the playoffs in two of the next three seasons under Carroll, making it as far as the Divisional round in 1997, when they lost to the Pittsburgh Steelers by a score of 7-6. Unhappy with his team's mediocre 8-8 showing in 1999, Kraft elected to replace Carroll with Bill Belichick, Parcells' longtime defensive coordinator in New York, who earlier had failed in his one previous stint as a head coach with the Cleveland Browns.

After struggling in their first season under the tight-lipped, somber, and extremely regimented Belichick, the Patriots reached the apex of their sport in 2001, when they captured the AFC East title with a regular-season record of 11-5, before defeating Oakland and Pittsburgh in the Conference playoffs and, finally, the heavily favored St. Louis Rams in Super Bowl XXXVI. A key factor in New England's rise to prominence proved to be the emergence of young quarterback Tom Brady, who replaced an injured Drew Bledsoe behind center early in the campaign. Brady quickly developed into an exceptional team leader and one of the league's top signal-callers, establishing himself before long as the cornerstone around which the team could build.

The Patriots unveiled their new home field in 2002—Gillette Stadium, a 68,436-seat facility located in Foxboro that officially opened its doors to the public on September 9, 2002. Yet, the team ended up taking a step backwards that year, finishing the campaign with a record of just 9-7. Since that time, though, the Patriots have emerged as the NFL's model franchise, advancing to the playoffs in 11 of the last 12 seasons, making five Super Bowl appearances, and capturing three more world championships, defeating the Carolina Panthers 32-29 in Super Bowl XXXVIII, the Philadelphia Eagles 24-21 in Super Bowl XXXIX, and the Seattle Seahawks by a score of 28-24 in Super Bowl XLIX. By winning the Super Bowl at the end of the 2001, 2003, and 2004 seasons, the Pats joined the Dallas Cowboys as the only teams in NFL history to win three Super Bowls in four years. The Patriots are also just the eighth team (and the most recent) to win consecutive Super Bowls. Although their quest for a perfect season ended unceremoniously with a 17-14 loss to the New York Giants in Super Bowl XLII, the Patriots put together one of the greatest seasons in NFL history in 2007, when they posted a regular-season record of 16-0, outscoring their opponents by a margin of 589 to 274 along the way. Their overall mark of 18-1 over the course of the campaign made them just the third team in league history to win 18 of 19 games in a season, enabling them to join the 1984 San Francisco 49ers and the 1985 Chicago Bears on an extremely exclusive list. Meanwhile, the Patriots' total of 125 victories from 2003 to 2012 represents a league record over the course of 10 consecutive seasons. The Patriots also established a league mark by winning 21 consecutive regular-season and playoff games from October 2003 to October 2004.

Although Bill Belichick and Tom Brady have remained the two constants throughout the extraordinarily successful run the Patriots have experienced since the beginning of the 21st century, the team has featured several other exceptional players who have helped keep New England among the NFL's elite. Willie McGinest, Richard Seymour, Vince Wilfork, Tedy Bruschi, Mike Vrabel, Ty Law, Lawyer Milloy, and Jerod Mayo have all made significant contributions on defense at various times. Meanwhile, Troy Brown, Deion Branch, Wes Welker, Randy Moss, and Rob Gronkowski have all proven to be exceptional targets for Brady in the passing game.

In all, the Patriots have won 17 division titles, 8 conference championships, and 4 Super Bowls. Seven Patriot players have had their numbers retired, and 18 former Patriots have been inducted into the team's Hall of Fame. Five members of the Pro Football Hall of Fame spent a significant

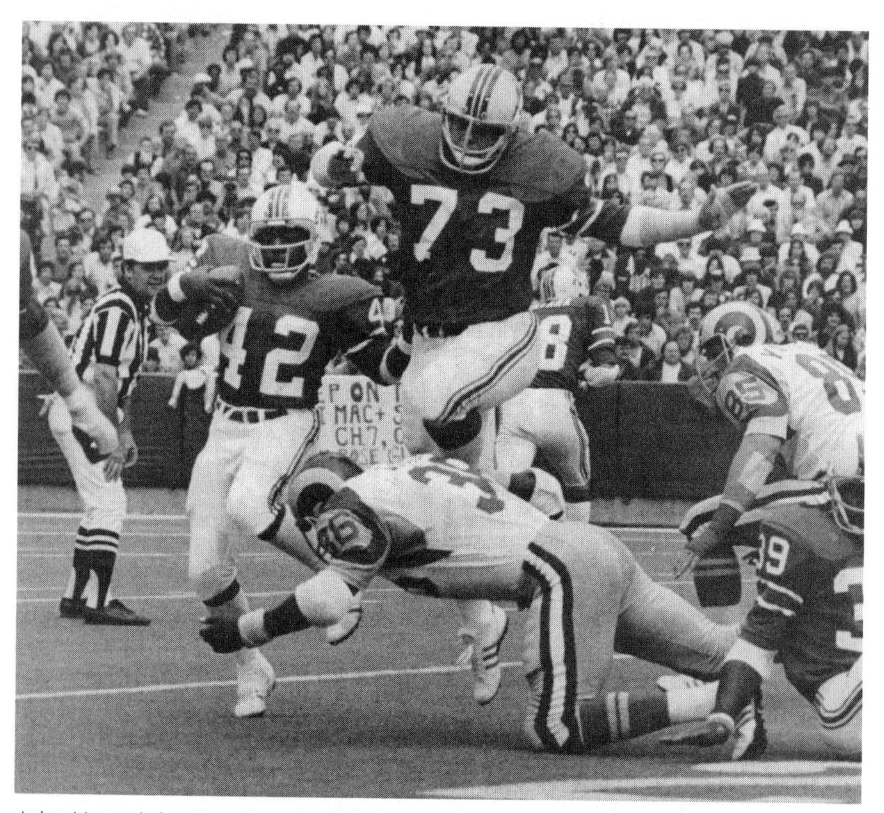

John Hannah leading the way for Mack Herron.
(Courtesy Mears Online Auctions)

amount of time playing for the Patriots—Nick Buoniconti, John Hannah, Mike Haynes, Curtis Martin, and Andre Tippett.

FACTORS USED TO DETERMINE RANKINGS

It should come as no surprise that selecting the 50 greatest players ever to perform for a team with the rich history of the Patriots presented quite a challenge. Even after narrowing the field down to a mere 50 men, I still needed to devise a method of ranking the elite players that remained. Certainly, the names of Tom Brady, Andre Tippett, Gino Cappelletti, John Hannah, Mike Haynes, Stanley Morgan, and Bruce Armstrong would appear at, or near, the top of virtually everyone's list, although the order might vary somewhat from person to person. Several other outstanding performers have gained general recognition through the years as being among the greatest players ever to wear a Patriots uniform. Drew Bledsoe, Sam Cunningham, Kevin Faulk, and Tedy Bruschi head the list of other Patriot icons. But, how does one compare players who lined up on opposite sides of the ball with any degree of certainty? Furthermore, how does one differentiate between the pass-rushing and run-stopping skills of players such as Jim Lee Hunt, Andre Tippett, and Willie McGinest and the ball-hawking and punt return abilities of a Mike Haynes? And, on the offensive end, how can a direct correlation be made between the contributions of Hall of Fame lineman John Hannah and skill position players such as Tom Brady and Wes Welker? After initially deciding who to include on my list, I then needed to determine what criteria I should use to formulate my final rankings.

The first thing I decided to examine was the level of dominance a player attained during his time with the Patriots. How often did he lead the NFL (or AFL) in a major statistical category? Did he ever capture league MVP honors? How many times did he earn a trip to the Pro Bowl or a spot on the All-Pro Team?

I also chose to assess the level of statistical compilation a player achieved while wearing a Patriots uniform. I reviewed where he ranks among the team's all-time leaders in those statistical categories most pertinent to his position. Of course, even the method of using statistics as a measuring stick has its inherent flaws. Although the level of success a team experiences rushing and passing the ball is impacted greatly by the performance of its offensive line, there really is no way to quantifiably measure the level of play reached by each individual offensive lineman. Conversely, the play of the offensive line affects tremendously the statistics compiled by a team's quarterback and running backs. Furthermore, the NFL did not keep an official record of defensive numbers such as tackles and quarterback sacks until the 1980s. In addition, when examining the statistics compiled by offensive players, the era during which a quarterback, running back, or wide receiver competed must be factored into the equation.

To illustrate my last point, rules changes instituted by the league office have opened up the game considerably over the course of the last two decades. Quarterbacks are accorded far more protection than ever before, and officials have also been instructed to limit the amount of contact defensive backs are allowed to make with wide receivers. As a result, the game has experienced an offensive explosion, with quarterbacks and receivers posting numbers players from prior generations rarely even approached. That being the case, one must place the numbers Tom Brady and Drew Bledsoe compiled during their careers in their proper context when comparing them to other top Patriot quarterbacks such as Steve Grogan and Babe Parilli. Similarly, Wes Welker's and Randy Moss' huge receiving totals must be viewed in moderation when comparing them to previous Patriot wideouts Gino Cappelletti and Stanley Morgan.

Other important factors I needed to consider were the overall contributions a player made to the success of the team, the degree to which he improved the fortunes of the club during his time in New England, the manner in which he impacted the team, both on and off the field, and the degree to which he added to the Patriot legacy. While the number of championships and division titles the Patriots won during a particular player's years with the team certainly entered into the equation, I chose not to deny a top performer his rightful place on the list if his years in New England happened to coincide with a lack of overall success by the club. As a result, the names of players such as Jim Nance and Irving Fryar will appear in these rankings.

One other thing I should mention is that I only considered a player's performance while playing for the Patriots when formulating my rankings. That being the case, the names of truly exceptional players such as Curtis Martin and Randy Moss, both of whom had most of their best years while playing for other teams, may appear lower on this list than one might expect. Meanwhile, the names of other standout performers such as Damien Woody and Adalius Thomas are nowhere to be found.

Having established the guidelines to be used throughout this book, we are ready to take a look at the 50 greatest players in Patriots history, starting with number 1 and working our way down to number 50.

1

Tom Brady

(Courtesy Keith Allison)

Tom Brady received stiff competition from John Hannah and Andre Tippett for the number one spot in these rankings, with Hannah providing a particularly strong challenge since he is widely regarded as the greatest guard in NFL history. However, Brady is generally considered to be one of the greatest quarterbacks ever to play the game, with his six AFC championships, four Super Bowl titles, and three Super Bowl MVPs further enhancing his qualifications. Perhaps the strongest argument that can be made on Brady's behalf, though, is the fact that he has manned the most important position on the football field for the better part of the past 14 seasons in New England, making him the most significant figure in the Patriots' extraordinarily successful run during that time. An exceptional leader with a burning desire to win, Brady has been the driving force behind all 12 division titles the Patriots have won with him behind center—the most of any quarterback in NFL history. Add to that his 10 Pro Bowl selections, three All-Pro nominations, two NFL regular season MVP Awards, and career postseason record of 21-8 and Brady became the only possible choice for first-place honors here.

Born in the affluent city of San Mateo, California, on August 3, 1977, Thomas Edward Patrick Brady frequently traveled with his father some 25 miles north to San Franscisco's Candlestick Park during the 1980s, where he cheered on his favorite player, 49ers quarterback Joe Montana. Although Brady lacked superior athletic ability as a youngster, he possessed from the very beginning a competitive spirit and an innate understanding of how to better himself on the playing field, enabling him to excel in youth sports as a catcher in baseball and a quarterback in football. While attending Junipero Serra High School, an all-boys Catholic school in San Mateo, Brady played baseball, football, and basketball, acquitting himself so well as a catcher on the diamond that the Montreal Expos selected him in the 18th round of the 1995 MLB Draft.

Choosing instead to continue pursuing his dream of following in the footsteps of his childhood idol Joe Montana after earning All-State and All-Far West honors as a senior at Junipero Serra, Brady enrolled at the University of Michigan, where he spent his first two years serving as a backup to future NFL quarterback Brian Griese. Growing increasingly frustrated with his backup role, the extremely competitive Brady briefly considered transferring to the University of California, before finally electing to remain at Michigan. Intense and driven, Brady even hired a sports psychologist at one point to help him cope with the anxiety he felt due to his lack of playing time.

Brady finally became the starting quarterback for the Wolverines as a junior, beating out the much-heralded Drew Henson for the job after Griese moved on to the pros. After setting single-season school records for most pass attempts and completions in his first year as a starter, Brady earned All-Big Ten honorable mention honors and was named team captain in his final year at Michigan.

Known for his intelligence and outstanding work ethic while playing for the Wolverines, Brady made a strong impression on Michigan head coach Lloyd Carr, who said, "Tom's a bright guy. He has a good arm, and his teammates look up to him. I think he has the right stuff."

Former NFL linebacker Ian Gold, a teammate of Brady at Michigan, later commented, "He wasn't the greatest athlete, but he was the smartest guy on the field."

Yet, in spite of the many intangible qualities Brady possessed, pro scouts questioned his ability to succeed at the NFL level. Although they admired him for his fearless attitude, exceptional leadership ability, and accurate throwing arm, they at the same time remained unimpressed by his spindly 6'4", 205-pound frame, lack of running speed, and inability to throw the deep ball well. As a result, Brady slipped to the sixth round of the 2000 NFL Draft, where the Patriots selected him with the 199th overall pick.

Angered by the slight, Brady entered the NFL believing he had something to prove, stating years later, "It's never come easy for me. I don't think my mind allows me to rest ever. I have, I think, a chip on my shoulder, and some deep scars that I don't think were healed."

Determined to prove his doubters wrong, Brady arrived at his first NFL training camp 15 pounds heavier and more mechanically sound. He also worked extremely hard over the course of the season at improving his arm strength, impressing his teammates and coaching staff with his dedication, commitment, and intelligence. Nevertheless, with Drew Bledsoe firmly entrenched as the starter in New England, Brady spent his entire rookie season sitting on the bench, appearing in only one game and completing just one of three passes.

Brady's situation changed dramatically the following year, though, after Bledsoe sustained an injury in Week 2 that forced him to the sidelines for the next several weeks. Brady started off slowly after replacing Bledsoe behind center, posting unspectacular numbers as the Patriots won three of their next five games. However, he eventually caught fire, leading the Pats to victory in eight of their last nine contests, thereby keeping Bledsoe on the bench for the remainder of the year, even after he recovered from his injury. Brady finished the season with 11 wins in his 14 starts, passing for 2,843 yards and 18 touchdowns, while also throwing 12 interceptions.

Having led the Patriots to the AFC East title, Brady subsequently passed for 312 yards in his first postseason appearance—a 16-13 overtime win over the Oakland Raiders in a contest that subsequently came to be known as the "Tuck Rule Game." Replaced by Bledsoe after injuring his knee in the first half of the AFC Championship Game against Pittsburgh, Brady returned to action in Super Bowl XXXVI, earning game MVP honors by leading the Patriots to a stunning 20-17 upset win over the heavily favored St. Louis Rams.

The success Brady experienced over the course of the 2001 campaign prompted the Patriots to trade Bledsoe to the Buffalo Bills at season's end, placing the mantle of offensive leadership squarely on the shoulders of the 24-year-old quarterback. Despite playing much of the second half of the 2002 season with a shoulder injury, Brady proved himself up to the challenge, completing 62.1 percent of his passes, for 3,764 yards and a league-leading 28 touchdowns, while tossing only 14 interceptions. However, the Patriots finished the year just 9-7, failing in the process to earn a return trip to the playoffs.

Brady and the Patriots then began an amazing run together that has seen them capture the AFC East title in 11 of the last 12 years, with the only exception being 2008, when Brady missed virtually the entire year after tearing the ACL and MCL in his left knee in Week 1. During that time, the Pats have compiled an overall record of 150-42, posting a mark of 140-37 in the games that Brady has started. In addition to finishing first in their division 11 times, the Patriots have appeared in five Super Bowls and won three more NFL Championships. From 2003 to 2004, New England posted an unprecedented 21 straight victories, also winning at one point a record 10 consecutive playoff games. The Patriots also compiled a perfect 16-0 regular-season record in 2007, making them the first team to go undefeated during the regular season since the NFL instituted a 16-game schedule.

Along with Head Coach Bill Belichick, Brady has remained a constant in New England throughout the period, providing leadership and on-field direction to his teammates, even as the faces around him have continued to change. In discussing Brady, current NFL analyst and former player Ross Tucker, who spent the last of his five pro seasons in New England, says, "'His will . . . or more specifically, the sheer force of his will.' That's the answer I have given every time I have been asked by somebody over the years what makes Tom Brady so special, based upon my time in New England."

Tucker continues, "Yeah, he has 'it' (whatever you want to define that as), but the real question is how 'it' is different from other stars in the league. In Brady's case, there is a passion burning inside him that is uncommon. I don't know if I ever played with another guy on my five teams that possessed his level of determination, and that is truly saying something when talking about the alpha males that make up the NFL."

Tucker concludes, "He has an ability to get the guys around him to play at a level that they themselves didn't even know they were capable of, mainly because they are doing it for him."

Former Patriots teammate Troy Brown echoed Tucker's sentiments when he said, "It doesn't matter whether he's right or wrong. People listen to him. He gives you a look that makes you know if you do what he tells you, it'll be fine."

Brady also made an extremely strong impression on a number of his other former teammates, with Ty Law stating on one occasion, "Tom Brady is the greatest winner in football right now."

In speaking of Brady's drive and determination, Rodney Harrison said, "He wants to be perfect. He wants to win championships."

Meanwhile, Christian Fauria suggested, "He has a presence . . . almost regal-like. It's the same presence of a JFK, someone like that."

A pretty fair passer as well, Brady has compiled exceptional numbers that place him among the NFL's all-time leaders in numerous statistical categories. In addition to ranking fifth all-time in passing yardage (53,258), pass completions (4,551), and touchdown passes (392), he has the fifth-best quarterback rating (95.9) and second-best interception percentage (2.0) in NFL history. He has also thrown for more yards (7,345) and more touchdowns (53) than any other quarterback in postseason history.

Initially considered to be more of a game-manager, Brady rarely placed among the league leaders in any major statistical category his first few seasons, even though he led the Patriots to Super Bowl victories in three of his first four years as a starter. However, after passing for 3,620 yards and 23 touchdowns in 2003, and 3,692 yards and 28 TDs the following year, Brady topped all NFL quarterbacks with 4,110 passing yards in 2005, while also finishing third in the league with 26 TD passes. After posting solid numbers again in 2006 (3,529 yards and 24 TD passes), Brady broke out in a big way in 2007. Given for the first time in his career an outstanding corps of wide receivers that included Randy Moss and Wes Welker, Brady had a season for the ages, leading all NFL quarterbacks with 4,806 yards passing, 50 touchdown passes, a 68.9 completion percentage, and a quarterback rating of 117.2. Brady's fabulous performance, which helped lead the Patriots to a perfect 16-0 record during the regular season, earned him a Pro Bowl berth for the fourth time, his first of two First-Team All-Pro selections, and NFL MVP honors for the first of two times.

After seeing his string of 111 consecutive starts come to an end in Week 1 of the ensuing campaign when he suffered season-ending damage to his left knee, Brady returned in 2009 to begin a new streak that has seen him start the last 96 contests behind center for the Patriots. Fighting through a broken right ring finger and three fractured ribs his first year back, Brady passed for 4,398 yards and 28 touchdowns, en route to earning Pro Bowl and AP Comeback Player of the Year honors. He followed that up by passing for 3,900 yards and a league-leading 36 touchdowns in 2010, while also tossing only four interceptions and topping the circuit with a quarterback rating of 111.0. Brady's outstanding play helped propel the Pats to a 14-2 regular-season record, earning him in the process First-Team All-Pro, AP NFL Offensive Player of the Year, and league MVP honors for the second time each.

Brady subsequently earned Pro Bowl honors for the third of six straight times in 2011 by passing for 5,235 yards and 39 touchdowns, joining in the process Dan Marino, Drew Brees, and Matthew Stafford as the only quarterbacks in NFL history to surpass the 5,000-yard mark, to that point. Although the Patriots ended up losing Super Bowl XLVI to the Giants 21-17, Brady had another outstanding postseason, performing particularly well against Denver in the Divisional Playoff round, when he led the Pats to a 45-10 victory by passing for 363 yards and six touchdowns.

Brady then became the first quarterback to lead his team to 10 division titles in 2012, when his 4,827 yards passing and 34 TD passes helped the Patriots compile a 12-4 record that left them five games ahead of second-place Miami. Meanwhile, the 557 points New England scored over the course of the campaign represented the third highest total in league history. He followed that up by throwing for 4,343 yards and 25 touchdowns in 2013, before leading the Pats to the division title for the 12th time by passing for 4,109 yards and 33 touchdowns this past season. Brady then earned Super Bowl MVP honors for the third time by guiding the Patriots past the Seattle Seahawks in Super Bowl XLIX, directing their offense to 28 points against the NFL's stingiest defense. New England's victory over Seattle enabled Brady to join Joe Montana and Terry Bradshaw as the only quarterbacks in league history to win four Super Bowls. He and Montana are also the only players ever to win the NFL Most Valuable Player and Super Bowl MVP awards multiple times.

Legendary head coach Bill Walsh, who coached Montana in San Francisco, once paid Brady the ultimate compliment when he said, "He's as close to Joe as anyone I've ever seen."

Bill Belichick also had high praise for Brady, stating, "There's no quarterback I'd rather have than Tom Brady. He's the best. He does so much for us in so many ways on so many different levels. I'm very fortunate that he's our quarterback, and what he's able to do for this team. It's good to win with him and all the rest of our players."

In trying to explain the success he has experienced over the course of his career, Brady suggests, "A lot of times, I find that people who are blessed with the most talent don't ever develop that attitude, and the ones who aren't blessed in that way are the most competitive and have the biggest heart."

No one will ever question the size of Tom Brady's heart.

CAREER HIGHLIGHTS

Best Season

Brady performed brilliantly for the Patriots in 2010, earning league MVP and Offensive Player of the Year honors by passing for 3,900 yards, completing 65.9 percent of his passes, and leading all NFL quarterbacks with 36 touchdown passes, a QB rating of 111.0, and a career-best 0.8 interception percentage (he threw only four interceptions all year). Brady had another big year in 2012, when he ranked among the league leaders with 4,827 yards passing, 34 touchdown passes, and a quarterback rating of 98.7, while also completing 63 percent of his passes and throwing only eight interceptions. Brady, though, posted better numbers in 2011, when, in addition to passing for a career-high 5,235 yards, he threw 39 touchdown passes, recorded a quarterback rating of 105.6, and completed 65.6 percent of his passes. Nevertheless, Brady's signature season is considered to be 2007, when he earned NFL MVP and Offensive Player of the Year honors for the first time by leading the Patriots to a perfect 16-0 record during the regular season. With the Patriots breaking the existing league records for most points scored and greatest point differential, Brady also established a new mark for quarterbacks (since broken) by tossing 50 touchdown passes. He also led the league with 4,806 yards passing and a career-high 117.2 quarterback rating and 68.9 completion percentage. Brady's magnificent performance, which ESPN ranked as the greatest passing season of all time in 2013, prompted the Associated Press to name him the Male Athlete of the Year, making him the first NFL player to be so honored since Joe Montana won the award in 1990. The *Sporting News* also named him Sportsman of the Year.

Memorable Moments/Greatest Performances

After struggling somewhat in his first two starts after replacing Drew Bledsoe behind center early in 2001, Brady began to display his wares in Week 5, helping the Patriots overcome a 10-point fourth-quarter deficit to San Diego by leading them to a pair of late scores, the second of which—a three-yard TD pass to Jermaine Wiggins with only 40 seconds left on the clock—knotted the score at 26-26. The Patriots ended up winning the game on a 44-yard Adam Vinatieri field goal four minutes into overtime. Brady concluded the day with 33 pass completions in 54 attempts, for 364 yards and two touchdowns. Brady led the Pats to a 38-17 victory over Peyton Manning and the Indianapolis Colts the following week by completing 16 of 20 passes, for 202 yards and three touchdowns, including a 91-yarder to David Patten, which represented the longest play from scrimmage in franchise history at the time.

Brady threw four touchdown passes for the first time in his career on November 25, 2001, hooking up with Antowain Smith, Troy Brown, Charles Johnson, and Marc Edwards from 41, 8, 24, and 2 yards out, respectively, during a 34-17 win over the New Orleans Saints.

Brady's first postseason contest proved to be a memorable one, as he threw for 312 yards and led the Patriots back from a 13-3 fourth-quarter deficit against Oakland to send the game into overtime, where they won on an Adam Vinatieri field goal after Brady completed eight straight passes. Played in a driving snowstorm, the game created a great deal of controversy due to a play that occurred late in the fourth quarter, when a hit by Oakland cornerback Charles Woodson to Brady created a fumble that the Raiders recovered. However, citing the "tuck rule," which states that any forward throwing motion by a quarterback begins a pass, even if he loses possession of the ball as he is attempting to tuck it back towards his body, the officials overturned the call after watching instant replay, ruling it an incomplete pass instead of a fumble. The Patriots tied the game on a 45-yard Adam Vinatieri field goal shortly thereafter, before winning the contest on a 23-yarder with 6:35 remaining in the first overtime session.

After injuring his knee against Pittsburgh in the AFC Championship Game the following week, Brady again displayed his ability to excel under pressure by leading the Patriots to a 20-17 upset win over the St. Louis Rams in Super Bowl XXXVI. Exhibiting the poise of a veteran, Brady engineered the game-winning drive after gaining possession of the ball at his own 17 yard line, with no timeouts left and only 1:21 remaining in the fourth quarter, putting Adam Vinatieri in position to kick a 48-yard field goal as time expired.

Brady also led the Patriots to a pair of overtime victories in 2002, surpassing 400 yards passing for the first time in his young career during a 41-38 OT win over Kansas City on September 22. Brady concluded the contest with 39 completions in 54 attempts, for 410 yards and four touchdowns. In that year's regular season finale, played at home against Miami on December 29, Brady led the Pats on two late scoring drives that enabled them to overcome an 11-point deficit to the Dolphins with less than five minutes remaining in regulation. After the Patriots tied the score at 24-24 with 1:14 left on the clock, Adam Vinatieri kicked the game-winning 35-yard field goal less than two minutes into overtime. In between those two efforts, Brady provided similar heroics against Chicago on November 10, leading the Patriots to a come-from-behind 33-30 victory over the Bears by mounting two late scoring drives that wiped out an earlier 30-19 deficit. The Patriots won the game when Brady hit David Patten with a 20-yard scoring strike with only 28 seconds left on the clock.

Brady provided Patriots fans with several memorable moments during the 2003 campaign as well, with the first of those coming on October 19, when he combined with Troy Brown on an 82-yard scoring play that gave the Pats a 19-13 overtime win over the Miami Dolphins. Just two weeks later, Brady hit David Givens with an 18-yard scoring strike with only 36 seconds remaining in regulation to give the Patriots a 30-26 win over the Broncos in Denver. However, those heroics merely served as a precursor to the performance he turned in against Carolina in Super Bowl XXXVIII, when he engineered a last-minute drive that enabled Adam Vinatieri to kick a 41-yard field goal with just four seconds remaining in regulation that gave the Pats a 32-29 victory. En route to earning Super Bowl MVP honors for the second time, Brady passed for 354 yards and three touchdowns, establishing in the process a new Super Bowl record by completing 32 passes.

Brady turned in his finest performance of the 2005 campaign in Week 5, leading the Patriots to a 31-28 victory over the Atlanta Falcons by completing 22 of 27 passes, for 350 yards and three touchdowns, including a 45-yard strike to Daniel Graham and a 55-yarder to Bethel Johnson.

Brady's historic 2007 season featured a number of epic performances, including a 388-yard, five-touchdown effort against Dallas in Week 6 and a 354-yard, six-touchdown effort against Miami the following week. The Patriots won those contests by scores of 48-27 and 49-28, respectively. Brady also passed for 373 yards and five touchdowns during a 56-10 thrashing of Buffalo in Week 11.

Yet, Brady experienced arguably his two most memorable moments that year in games that went right down to the wire. With the Patriots seeking to improve their record to 12-0, Brady helped them overcome a seven-point fourth-quarter deficit to the Ravens by leading them on two late scoring drives, with the second of those culminating with an eight-yard TD pass to Jabar Gaffney with only 55 seconds remaining in the fourth quarter. The Pats ended up winning the contest 27-24. Four weeks later, in the regular-season finale against the New York Giants, Brady passed for 356 yards and two touchdowns, in leading the Patriots to a hard-fought 38-35 victory that made them the first team to compile a perfect 16-0 record during the regular season. Brady's 65-yard TD pass to Randy Moss early in the fourth quarter also made him the first quarterback in NFL history to throw 50 touchdown passes in a season.

Although the Patriots ultimately saw their quest for a perfect season come to an end in Super Bowl XLII against the Giants, Brady performed brilliantly in their first-round playoff matchup with Jacksonville, leading the Pats to a 31-20 victory and setting an NFL postseason record by completing his first 16 passes, en route to finishing the day 26-of-28, for 262 yards and three touchdowns.

Brady made his return from season-ending surgery the previous year a triumphant one in 2009, leading the Patriots to a come-from-behind 25-24 victory over Buffalo in the regular-season opener. With the Pats trailing the Bills by a score of 24-13 late in the fourth quarter, Brady hit Ben Watson with a pair of touchdown passes, with the second of those coming with only 55 seconds remaining in regulation. Brady completed 39 of 53 passes on the day, for 378 yards and two touchdowns, en route to earning AFC Offensive Player of the Week honors for the 13th time in his career.

Playing in an early season snowstorm at Gillette Stadium five weeks later, Brady led the Patriots to a 59-0 rout of Tennessee by completing 29 of 34 passes, for 380 yards and six touchdowns, with his five TD passes in the second quarter setting an NFL record for most touchdowns in a single quarter. Brady had another big day later in the year, completing 23 of 26 passes, for 267 yards and four touchdowns, during a 35-7 win over Jacksonville on December 27.

Nearly one year later, on December 6, 2010, Brady led the Patriots to a lopsided 45-3 victory over the Jets by passing for 326 yards and four touchdowns. In the process, he established a new NFL record for most consecutive regular-season wins at home (26).

Brady began the 2011 campaign in style, passing for four touchdowns and a career-high 517 yards during a 38-24 road win at Miami. One of Brady's TD tosses—a 99-yarder to Wes Welker—tied an NFL record for longest play from scrimmage. Brady followed that up by passing for 423 yards and three touchdowns during a 35-21 victory over San Diego just six days later. In the regular-season finale, a 49-21 victory over the Buffalo Bills, Brady passed for 338 yards and three touchdowns, becoming in the process just the fourth quarterback in NFL history (and the third that season) to throw for more than 5,000 yards in a season.

Two weeks later, in New England's first-round playoff matchup with Denver, Brady turned in arguably the finest postseason performance of his career, passing for 363 yards and six touchdowns, in leading the Patriots to a lopsided 45-10 victory over the Broncos. His six TD tosses tied an NFL postseason record previously shared by Oakland's Daryle Lamonica and San Francisco's Steve Young.

Brady had his biggest day of the 2013 campaign on November 3, leading the Patriots to a 55-31 victory over Pittsburgh by passing for 432 yards and four touchdowns.

Brady also led the Patriots to a number of memorable fourth-quarter comebacks in 2013, with the first of those coming against the New Orleans Saints in Week 6. Trailing the Saints 27-23 late in the fourth quarter, Brady engineered a 70-yard scoring drive that ended with a 17-yard TD pass to Kenbrell Thompkins as time expired, giving the Pats a 30-27 win. Nearly two months later, on November 24, the Patriots trailed Denver 24-0 at halftime, before Brady caught fire in the second half, leading his team to 31 unanswered points. After the Broncos sent the game into overtime by scoring a touchdown of their own with just over three minutes remaining in the fourth quarter, Stephen Gostkowski gave the Patriots a 34-31 win by kicking a 31-yard field goal 13 minutes into the overtime session. Brady finished the game 34-for-50, for 344 yards and three touchdowns. Brady provided similar heroics against Cleveland on December 8, leading the Patriots to a pair of touchdowns in the game's final moments to give them a miraculous 27-26 win over the Browns. Trailing Cleveland 26-14 with just 2:43 left in the contest, Brady engineered an 11-play, 82-yard scoring drive that culminated with a two-yard TD pass to Julian Edelman. Regaining possession of the ball following a successful onside kickoff attempt, Brady subsequently needed only 25 seconds to march the Patriots downfield for the game-winning score, which he produced with a one-yard TD toss to Danny Amendola with just 35 seconds left on the clock. Brady finished the day 32-for-52, for 418 yards and two touchdowns.

Brady had his biggest day of the 2014 campaign against the Bears on October 26, leading the Patriots to a 51-23 victory by completing 30 of 35 passes, for 354 yards and five touchdowns, against the porous Chicago defense. He followed that up by passing for 333 yards and four touchdowns during a 43-21 win over the Denver Broncos. Brady had another outstanding game against Detroit on November 23, passing for 349 yards and two touchdowns during a 34-9 victory over the Lions.

Yet, Brady experienced his most memorable moments in 2014 during the postseason, leading the Patriots to their fourth NFL title by posting victories over Baltimore and Indianapolis in the AFC playoffs, before defeating Seattle in the Super Bowl. Particularly effective in the Patriots' 35-31 Divisional Playoff win over the Ravens, Brady brought the Patriots back from two 14-point deficits, putting them ahead for the first time in the contest with only 5:21 remaining in the fourth quarter by hitting Brandon LaFell with a game-winning 23-yard TD pass. Brady finished the day 33-for-50, for 367 yards and three touchdowns. He also scored a fourth touchdown on a four-yard run. After subsequently throwing three more touchdown passes during New England's 45-7 blowout of Indianapolis in the AFC Championship Game, Brady performed magnificently against Seattle in the fourth quarter of Super Bowl XLIX, completing 13 of his final 15 passes, to lead the Patriots to a come-from-behind 28-24 victory. He finished the game with 37 completions in 50 attempts, for 328 yards and four touchdowns, earning in the process Super Bowl MVP honors for the third time in his career.

NOTABLE ACHIEVEMENTS

- Has passed for more than 3,500 yards 12 times, surpassing 4,000 yards seven times and 5,000 yards once (5,235 in 2011).
- Has thrown at least 25 touchdown passes 10 times, topping 30-mark five times and 50-mark once (50 in 2007).
- Has completed more than 60 percent of passes 13 times.
- Has posted quarterback rating in excess of 90.0 eight times, topping 100.0 on three occasions.
- Has led all NFL quarterbacks in: passing yardage twice; touchdown passes three times; completion percentage once; quarterback rating twice; interception percentage twice; and game-winning drives twice.
- Ranks first all-time on Patriots in: passing yardage (53,258); pass completions (4,551); pass attempts (7,168); touchdown passes (392); completion percentage (63.5); quarterback rating (95.9); interception percentage (2.0%); and game-winning drives (46).
- Ranks second all-time on Patriots in games played (209).
- Ranks among NFL all-time leaders in: passing yardage (5th); pass completions (5th); pass attempts (6th); touchdown passes (5th); completion percentage (12th); quarterback rating (5th); interception percentage (2nd); and game-winning drives (3rd).

- Holds NFL career records for: most playoff starts by a QB (29); most division titles won (12); most conference championship game appearances (9); and most conference championship games won by a QB (6).
- Holds NFL career postseason records for: most playoff wins (21); most passing yards (7,345); and most touchdown passes (53).
- Holds NFL career Super Bowl records for: most pass completions; most pass attempts; most passing yards; and most touchdown passes.
- Six-time AFC champion (2001, 2003, 2004, 2007, 2011 & 2014).
- Four-time Super Bowl champion (XXXVI, XXXVIII, XXXIX & XLIX).
- Three-time Super Bowl MVP (XXXVI, XXXVIII & XLIX).
- Two-time NFL MVP (2007 & 2010).
- 2005 *Sports Illustrated* Sportsman of the Year.
- Two-time *Sporting News* Sportsman of the Year (2004 & 2007).
- 2007 NFL Player of the Year.
- 2007 Associated Press Male Athlete of the Year.
- Two-time Associated Press NFL Offensive Player of the Year (2007 & 2010).
- Three-time AFC Offensive Player of the Year (2007, 2010 & 2011).
- 2009 NFL Comeback Player of the Year.
- 10-time Pro Bowl selection (2001, 2004, 2005, 2007, 2009-2014).
- Two-time First-Team All-Pro selection (2007 & 2010).
- 2005 Second-Team All-Pro selection.
- Pro Football Hall of Fame First-Team All-2000s Team.
- Named to Patriots' 50th Anniversary Team in 2009.

2

John Hannah

(Courtesy Pristine Auctions)

Having fallen just short of earning the top spot in these rankings, John Hannah easily warded off a challenge from Andre Tippett for second place on this list. While Tippett gained recognition over the course of his career as one of the premier pass-rushing linebackers in NFL history, Hannah is generally considered to be one of the two or three greatest offensive linemen ever to play the game. Excelling at left guard for the Patriots from 1973 to 1985, Hannah earned 10 All-Pro selections, 11 All-AFC nominations, and nine trips to the Pro Bowl, en route to becoming one of the few players ever to be named to the NFL's All-Decade Team for two distinct 10-year periods. A four-time NFL Players Association Offensive Lineman of the Year, Hannah became the first player to be inducted into the Patriots Hall of Fame in 1991. Hannah's brilliant play also eventually earned him a place in the Pro Football Hall of Fame, spots on the Patriots' 50th Anniversary Team and the NFL's 75th Anniversary Team, and a number 20 ranking on the *Sporting News'* 1999 list of the 100 Greatest Players in NFL History.

Born in Canton, Georgia, on April 4, 1951, John Allen Hannah seemed destined for a career in the NFL when he weighed in at 11 pounds at birth. The son of a former professional football player, Herb Hannah, who played tackle for the New York Giants in 1951, the younger Hannah displayed a predilection for sports at an early age while growing up in Albertville, Alabama. After excelling at football, wrestling, and track for two years at Baylor Prep in Chattanooga, Tennessee, Hannah played his senior season of high school football at Albertville High School, where he graduated in 1969. He subsequently enrolled at the University of Alabama, where, in addition to participating in wrestling, the shot-put, and the discus-throw, he earned All-American honors twice while playing tackle and guard under legendary coach Paul "Bear" Bryant. Eventually named to the University of Alabama All-Century Team, Hannah earned the additional distinction of having Coach Bryant once say of him, "John Hannah is the best offensive lineman I ever coached."

Hannah's stellar play at the collegiate level prompted the Patriots to make him the fourth overall pick of the 1973 NFL Draft. Although he subsequently entered the league with some scouts questioning his ability to adjust from the straight-ahead blocking style employed by Alabama's wishbone offense to the pass-blocking and pulling techniques required by pro guards, Hannah soon allayed any fears the members of New England's coaching staff had, making such a strong impression on them that they immediately awarded him a starting spot on the team's offensive line. Starting his first 13 games as a pro before missing the final contest of the 1973 campaign with a freak leg injury, Hannah quickly established himself as one of the league's top players at his position—a status he maintained for the next 13 seasons.

Standing 6'2" tall and weighing 265 pounds, Hannah possessed only average size for an offensive lineman of his day. However, he played "big," with Patriots coach Ron Erhardt stating on one occasion, "With his attitude, John Hannah could play if he had been five feet two."

New York Jets star defensive lineman Joe Klecko, who had the unenviable task of facing Hannah twice a year, elaborated on the attitude his opponent took with him to the playing field when he said, "John was one of the meaner guys to play against. It's so funny because, off the field, John was a sweetheart . . . When he stepped between the lines he had a different demeanor. He was going to eat your heart out if he could because he wanted to win . . . If you stood in front of him, he was gonna put you in the ground."

Klecko added, "You didn't want to be in front of him because he was coming after you. I just pitied those poor linebackers because he used to just bury them."

Former NFL coach and longtime TV analyst John Madden chimed in, "The thing I always liked about Hannah was that he had the same defensive players' attitude; the same aggression. There is no rule that says an offensive player has to have a milder personality, although most of them seem to."

Hannah also possessed outstanding athleticism and quickness, as well as a powerful lower body that made him very difficult to move. In commenting on some of his adversary's other notable attributes, Klecko suggested, "Being that aggressive, especially on the run, sometimes hurts you in a pass-blocking situation. But Hannah was built like a brick wall. He was very thick from the waist down."

Making Hannah even more formidable was the fact that he employed picture-perfect technique, as noted by Klecko when he stated, "The one thing about him, his feet were always under him. John could actually turn it up inside to where he would always have his feet under him, and he was always under control. The Patriots did a lot with him all because of his athleticism."

After missing the final game of the 1973 season, Hannah began a string of 42 consecutive starts the following year. He then sat out the first three games of 1977 while holding out for a new contract, before beginning another streak of 75 consecutive starts that lasted through the conclusion of the 1981 campaign. During that time, Hannah developed into the NFL's dominant offensive lineman, excelling as a pass-protector, run blocker, and as the pulling guard on sweeps. He also emerged as one of the Patriots' team leaders, often challenging his teammates to demonstrate the same level of commitment to the game that he carried with him throughout his career.

After being named First-Team All-Pro and making the Pro Bowl for the first time in 1976, Hannah failed to be accorded the same honors the following year. However, he made the Pro Bowl in each of his final eight seasons, earned six more First-Team All-Pro selections, and received two Second-Team nominations as well. Hannah also earned the distinction of being named the NFL Players Association's Offensive Lineman of the Year four straight times, from 1978 to 1981.

Hannah's many accomplishments made an extremely strong impression on John Madden, who, when asked on one occasion which player he would take if he were starting an NFL franchise, simply answered, "John Hannah."

The powerful offensive lineman also found himself being greatly admired by *Sports Illustrated*, which dubbed him on the cover of its August 3, 1981, edition, "The Best Offensive Lineman of All Time." Meanwhile, when the *Sporting News* formulated its list of the 100 Greatest Football Players in NFL history in 1999, it placed Hannah at number 20, ranking him behind only Cincinnati Bengals tackle Anthony Muñoz among offensive linemen.

The overall impact that Hannah made on the Patriots can be easily ascertained by viewing the rushing totals the team compiled before and after he left them at the conclusion of the 1985 campaign. With Hannah anchoring their offensive line, the Pats established an all-time NFL record by rushing for 3,165 yards in 1978. They also led the league in rushing in 1982 and 1983. But, after amassing 2,331 yards on the ground and averaging 4.1 yards per carry in 1985, the Patriots rushed for only 1,373 yards and averaged just 2.9 yards per carry the following season.

Yet, in spite of Hannah's greatness on the playing field, he spent much of his career fighting an inward battle to excel while simultaneously trying to remain popular with his teammates. The insecurity Hannah carried with him throughout much of his life prompted him to try to control everything and everyone around him by presenting to others a brash and confident exterior. Nearly 30 years after leaving the game, Hannah detailed the personal demons he faced for much of his adult life in his autobiography entitled *Offensive Conduct: My Life on the Line.* In addition to discussing his professional career and the rampant use of amphetamines and illegal drugs in the NFL during his playing days, Hannah revealed many of the details of his personal life, including the breakup of his first marriage, his estrangement from his children, an egomaniacal approach in the business world, and how he ultimately found religion.

Elected to the Pro Football Hall of Fame in 1991, Hannah later described his mental approach to the game when he said, "Once I got on that football field, it was like a world of its own, and I could just verse myself in that environment. No one could touch me."

Hannah added, "My goal was very simple—I wanted to be the best offensive guard that ever played football. That was it, pure and simple."

Many people feel that Hannah achieved his ultimate goal.

CAREER HIGHLIGHTS

Best Season

Hannah earned consensus First-Team All-Pro honors seven times over the course of his career, including four straight times from 1978 to 1981, seasons in which the NFLPA also named him Offensive Lineman of the Year. Hannah received the additional honor of being named the Seagram's Seven Crowns of Sports Offensive Lineman of the Year in both 1978 and 1980. Since the Patriots finished 11-5 and established a NFL record that still stands by rushing for 3,165 yards in 1978, we'll nominate that as his finest season.

Memorable Moments/Greatest Performances

Hannah anchored a Patriots offensive line that turned in a number of dominating performances, with the first of those coming on October 18, 1976, when the Pats rushed for 330 yards and 4 touchdowns during a 41-7 pasting of the New York Jets. Hannah and his line-mates again performed brilliantly six weeks later, when the Patriots rushed for 332 yards and 3 touchdowns during a 38-14 win over the Denver Broncos. Hannah led New England's line to a similarly dominating performance on September 18, 1983, when the Patriots defeated the Jets 23-13 behind a rushing attack that gained 328 yards and scored 3 touchdowns.

Hannah, though, experienced arguably the most memorable moment of his career on December 15, 1974, when he gave the Patriots an early 7-0 lead over Miami in the regular-season finale by recovering a fumble in the end zone for the only touchdown of his 13 NFL seasons. Unfortunately, the Dolphins eventually overcame a 24-0 deficit to win the contest 34-27.

NOTABLE ACHIEVEMENTS

- Missed only eight games in his entire career, compiling streaks of 42 and 75 consecutive starts at different points.
- 1985 AFC champion.
- Nine-time Pro Bowl selection (1976 & 1978–85).
- Seven-time First-Team All-Pro selection (1976, 1978, 1979, 1980, 1981, 1983 & 1985).
- Three-time Second-Team All-Pro selection (1977, 1982 & 1984).

- Ten-time First-Team All-AFC selection (1974, 1976–81, 1983, 1984 & 1985).
- 1982 Second-Team All-AFC selection.
- Four-time NFL Players Association Offensive Lineman of the Year (1978–81).
- 1984 NFL Alumni Offensive Lineman of the Year.
- NFL 1970s All-Decade Team.
- NFL 1980s All-Decade Team.
- Pro Football Reference Second-Team All-1980s Team.
- Named to Patriots' 50th Anniversary Team in 2009.
- First player inducted into Patriots Hall of Fame (1991).
- Number 73 retired by Patriots.
- Named to NFL's 75th Anniversary Team in 1994.
- Number 20 on the *Sporting News'* 1999 list of 100 Greatest Players in NFL History.
- Elected to Pro Football Hall of Fame in 1991.

3

Andre Tippett

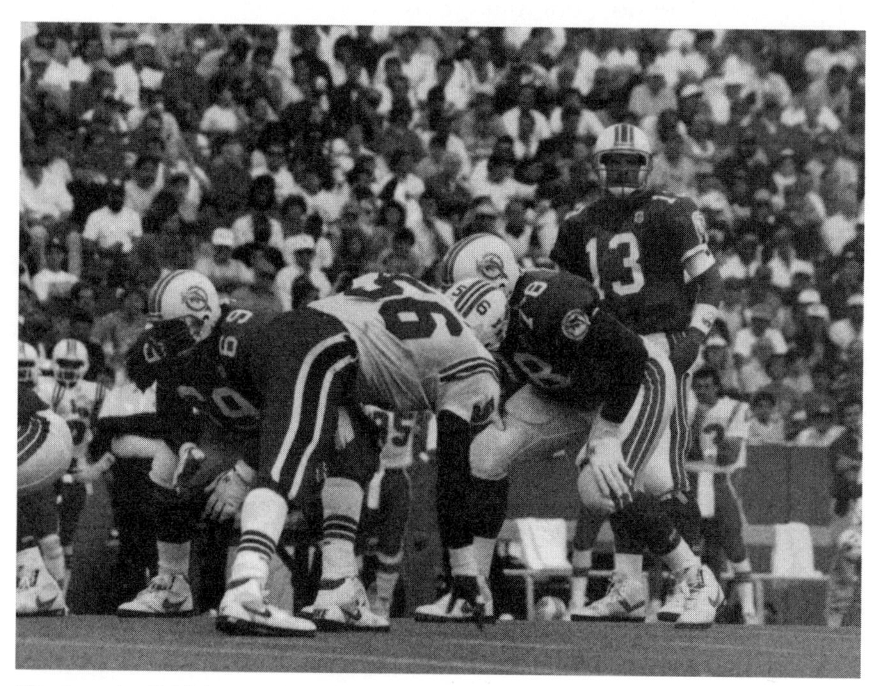

(Courtesy Joe Schilp)

A strong-side linebacker who excelled at rushing the passer, Andre Tippett established himself as the most dominant defensive player in Patriots history during his 12 seasons in New England. The AFC's version of Lawrence Taylor, Tippett recorded double-digit sacks three times over the course of his career, setting an NFL record in 1984 and 1985 by accumulating more sacks over a two-year period (35) than any other linebacker in league history. Tippett's ability to pressure opposing quarterbacks earned him All-Pro honors four times, five Pro Bowl nominations, five All-AFC selections, and recognition as the AFC's Linebacker of the Year three straight times. Also nominated once as the AFC Defensive Player of the Year, Tippett holds the Patriots franchise record for most career sacks (100), earning in the process a spot on their 50th Anniversary Team and a place in their Hall of Fame.

Born in Birmingham, Alabama, on December 27, 1959, Andre Bernard Tippett grew up in Newark, New Jersey, where he attended Barringer High School. Although Tippett never played football until he arrived at Barringer, he made the school's varsity team as a sophomore, being paired on the right side of the defensive line with senior captain Prentice Walker. In discussing the unique qualities possessed by his younger teammate, Walker later said, "He was a guy that didn't really say a lot, but he watched a lot. There was something about him that was special, it really was. Obviously, I was correct."

After graduating from Barringer, Tippett spent one year at Ellsworth Junior College in Iowa, before enrolling at the University of Iowa, where he went on to become one of the elite defenders in school history. In his three years at Iowa, Tippett set the school record for most tackles-for-a-loss in a season (20 in 1980) and earned consensus All-America honors as a senior in 1981. Bill Brashier, who served as Iowa's defensive coordinator during Tippett's time there, said, "We've had several All-Americans, but we've never had an All-American any better than Andre Tippett."

Tippett's exceptional performance at the collegiate level prompted the Patriots to select him in the second round of the 1982 NFL Draft, with the 41st overall pick. Used sparingly by the Patriots as a rookie, Tippett spent most of his first season playing on special teams, before earning a starting job in his second year in the league. Inserted at left outside linebacker by the New England coaching staff during the early stages of the 1983 campaign, Tippett soon began to display the outstanding strength and exceptional quickness for which he eventually became so well noted, amassing a team-leading 8 ½ sacks. He also proved to be an excellent student, heeding the words of veteran linebacker Steve Nelson, who played right next to him in the Patriots' defensive alignment.

Maturing rapidly into the AFC's most dominant linebacker the following season, the 6'3", 240-pound Tippett finished second in the league to Mark Gastineau of the Jets, with 18 ½ quarterback sacks. His extraordinary performance earned him Second-Team All-AFC honors and the first of his five consecutive trips to the Pro Bowl. Tippett followed that up with an equally-productive 1985 campaign in which he helped the Patriots claim their first AFC championship by leading the conference with 16 ½ sacks, en route to earning AFC Linebacker of the Year and consensus First-Team All-Pro honors.

Tippett continued to perform at an extremely high level in each of the next two seasons, making 9 ½ sacks in 1986, despite missing five games due to an injured right knee, before recording an AFC-leading 12 ½ sacks in 1987. Tippett's outstanding play enabled him to earn All-Pro and AFC Linebacker of the Year honors both times.

Yet, as well as Tippett played, he invariably came up short in the comparisons made between him and the incomparable Lawrence Taylor, whose career in New York spanned virtually the same time frame. Certainly, Taylor accomplished somewhat more over the course of his career, winning two NFL championships and one league MVP Award. But he also played in a larger market, for mostly better teams.

Joe Walton, who coached the Jets from 1983 to 1989, weighed in on the inevitable comparisons made between the two men, both of whom wore number 56, when he said, "In our conference, there's no doubt he (Tippett) was the best at the time. . . . Around that time in the '80s, the size and speed of linebackers started to change; they started to be bigger and faster, and more versatile. He and Taylor probably set the standard for what everybody looks for in linebackers today."

Even though injuries forced Tippett to sit out four games in 1988, he appeared in his fifth straight Pro Bowl after making 7 quarterback sacks during the regular season. Tippett also earned First-Team All-AFC and Second-Team All-NFL honors for the final time in his career. A shoulder injury subsequently sidelined Tippett for the entire 1989 campaign, one in which the Patriots finished just 5-11 without him. New England fared no better after Tippett returned to the team in 1990, posting a franchise-worst mark of 1-15, as the linebacker struggled to regain his earlier form, making only 3 sacks in the 13 games in which he appeared.

Tippett spent three more years in New England, accumulating a total of 24 sacks for losing Patriot teams. He retired at the conclusion of the 1993 campaign with 100 career sacks—the most in Patriots history. Tippett also holds franchise records for the most sacks in a season (18 ½ in 1984) and the most fumbles recovered over the course of a career (19). He also forced 17 fumbles. Tippett's total of 18 ½ sacks in 1984 remains the third-highest single-season mark ever posted by an NFL linebacker. He finished either first or second on the Patriots in sacks in each of his final 10 seasons, leading the team in that category six times and placing second the other four times. In addition to his five Pro Bowl selections, four All-Pro nominations, five All-AFC selections, and three straight nominations by the NFL Players Association as the AFC's Linebacker of the Year, Tippett was voted co-Defensive Player of the Year (along with Oakland's Howie Long) by the Newspaper Enterprise Association (NEA) in 1985. The UPI also named him its AFL-AFC Defensive Player of the Year at the end of that same season.

Following his retirement, Tippett assumed a position in the Patriots' front office, working as their Executive Director of Community Affairs—a position he continues to hold. The Massachusetts native is also active in local youth football and coaches a Pop Warner team. Although it took Tippett nearly a decade to be inducted into the Pro Football Hall of Fame once he became eligible, he finally gained admission in 2008. That very same year, a panel of former NFL players and coaches voted Tippett onto *Pro Football Weekly*'s All-Time 3-4 Defensive Team, awarding him a spot alongside fellow linebackers Harry Carson, Lawrence Taylor, and Randy Gradishar, as well as defensive linemen Howie Long, Lee Roy Selmon, and Curley Culp.

CAREER HIGHLIGHTS

Best Season

It could be argued that Tippett had the greatest year of his career in 1984, when he set a Patriots record that still stands by recording 18 ½ sacks. However, he actually had a slightly better all-around season in 1985, earning consensus First-Team All-NFL honors for the first of two times by amassing 16 ½ sacks, forcing 3 fumbles, and recovering 4 others, one of which he returned for a touchdown. In addition to being named First-Team All-Pro, Tippett received AFC Linebacker of the Year honors and was voted the UPI AFL-AFC Defensive Player of the Year. He continued his outstanding play in the postseason, recording 21 tackles and a sack in the Patriots' four playoff games.

Memorable Moments/Greatest Performances

Tippett had the first multi-sack game of his career on December 11, 1983, getting to Los Angeles quarterback Vince Ferragamo twice during a 21-7 Patriots victory over the Rams. He topped that figure in the 1984 regular-season opener, recording 2 ½ sacks of Buffalo quarterback Joe Ferguson during a 21-17 Patriots win over the Bills.

Tippett also had a number of three-sack games over the course of his career, reaching that mark for the first time on September 8, 1985, when he helped lead the Patriots to a 26-20 victory over Green Bay by getting to Packers quarterback Lynn Dickey three times. Tippett recorded 3 sacks in a game five other times, accomplishing the feat on October 20, 1985, against the Jets, November 10, 1985, against the Colts, October 18, 1987, against the Oilers, November 15, 1987, against the Cowboys, and one week later, on November 22, 1987, against the Colts. With the exception of the Cowboys game, each of those contests resulted in Patriot victories. Particularly dominant during the wins over the Jets and Oilers, Tippett earned AFC Defensive Player of the Week honors both times for his exceptional all-around play. In addition to recording 3 sacks against New York, Tippett stopped the Jets three times inside the Patriots' 10-yard line, to help preserve a 20-13 victory. Meanwhile, in leading the Pats to a 21-7 win over Houston, Tippett also defended a pass and blocked a field goal attempt that resulted in a Patriots touchdown when Raymond Clayborn returned it for 6 points.

Tippett recorded a career-high 3 ½ sacks on October 26, 1986, when his constant pressure forced Buffalo quarterbacks Jim Kelly and Frank Reich to throw 4 interceptions during a 23-3 Patriots win over the Bills.

Tippett also twice returned fumbles for touchdowns, scoring the first points of his career on September 29, 1985, when he picked up a loose ball on the opponent's 25-yard line and ran it into the end zone for a score during a 35-20 loss to the Raiders. Tippett scored his other touchdown almost exactly two years later, on September 21, 1987, running with the ball 29 yards after recovering a fumble during a 43-24 loss to the Jets.

Tippett recorded the only interception of his career in the 1991 regular-season opener, picking off a Jeff George pass and returning it 10 yards during a 16-7 win over the Indianapolis Colts.

Despite being plagued by injuries throughout the 1990 campaign, Tippett turned in one of his finest all-around performances in the regular-season finale, recording ½ sack, 10 tackles, and a forced fumble during a hard-fought 13-10 loss to the eventual Super Bowl champion New York Giants.

NOTABLE ACHIEVEMENTS

- Finished in double-digits in sacks three times, topping 15-mark twice.
- Led AFC in sacks three times.
- Finished second in NFL in sacks three times.
- Holds Patriots career record with 100 sacks.
- Holds Patriots single-season record with 18 ½ sacks in 1984.

- Holds NFL record for most sacks by a linebacker in consecutive seasons (35 from 1984–1985).
- 1985 AFC champion.
- Five-time Pro Bowl selection (1984, 1985, 1986, 1987 & 1988).
- Four-time First-Team All-AFC selection (1985, 1986, 1987 & 1988).
- 1984 Second-Team All-AFC selection.
- Two-time First-Team All-Pro selection (1985 & 1987).
- Two-time Second-Team All-Pro selection (1986 & 1988).
- Three-time AFC Linebacker of the Year (1985, 1986 & 1987).
- 1985 Newspaper Enterprise Association (NEA) co-Defensive Player of the Year.
- 1985 UPI AFL-AFC Defensive Player of the Year.
- NFL 1980s All-Decade Team.
- Pro Football Hall of Fame All-1980s Second Team.
- Named to Patriots' 50th Anniversary Team in 2009.
- Inducted into Patriots Hall of Fame in 1999.
- Elected to Pro Football Hall of Fame in 2008.

4

Gino Cappelletti

(Courtesy Mainline Autographs)

Nicknamed "Mr. Patriot" for his lengthy association with New England's entry into professional football, Gino Cappelletti remains arguably the most recognizable figure in Patriots history. Spending most of his adult life serving the Pats in one capacity or another, Cappelletti starred on the playing field for 11 seasons, before transitioning into the broadcast booth, where he became even more of an iconic figure by serving as the team's radio color analyst for another 32 years. Cappelletti also spent three seasons on the sidelines coaching New England's special teams.

Nevertheless, it is primarily on the strength of his playing career that Cappelletti earned the fourth spot in these rankings. An exceptionally versatile player, the Minnesota native excelled at wide receiver and kicker during his time in Boston, establishing himself in 1960 as the only player in professional football history to run for a 2-point conversion, throw a pass for a 2-point conversion, catch a pass, intercept a pass, and return a punt and a kickoff in the same season. Over the course of his 11 seasons in Boston, Cappelletti earned five Pro Bowl nominations and led the league in scoring five times, en route to becoming the AFL's all-time leading scorer. He also continued to hold down the top spot in Patriots' history until 2005, when Adam Vinatieri finally surpassed him. More than 40 years after he appeared in his last game, Cappelletti remains among the team's all-time leaders in several other statistical categories as well. Cappelletti's extraordinary list of accomplishments eventually earned him a spot on the Patriots' 50th Anniversary Team and a place in the team's Hall of Fame.

Born in Keewatin, Minnesota, on March 26, 1934, Gino Raymond Michael Cappelletti attended the University of Minnesota after graduating from Keewatin High School. A quarterback and placekicker in college, Cappelletti saw very little action his first three years at Minnesota, serving as a backup to All-American QB Paul Giel, kicking extra points, and rarely attempting field goals. Cappelletti finally began to garner a significant amount of playing time as a senior in 1954, when he took over from Giel behind center and led the Gophers to a 7-2 record, earning in the process All-Big 10 Second-Team honors.

After going undrafted by the NFL in 1955, Cappelletti travelled north to Canada, where he spent the next two years playing quarterback in the ORFU (Ontario Rugby Football Union). Drafted into the U.S. Army late in 1956, Cappelletti spent the next year-and-a-half out of football, before returning to Canada in 1958. After two more years north of the border, Cappelletti elected to try out for the Boston Patriots when the AFL established itself as a separate entity prior to the start of the 1960 campaign.

Although Cappelletti initially made the Patriots' roster primarily as a placekicker, he proved to be somewhat deficient in that area at first, converting only 8 of 21 field goal attempts as a rookie. Fortunately for Cappelletti, he did a solid job after the Pats inserted him at right cornerback, tying for the team lead with 4 interceptions. Continuing to display his tremendous versatility, Cappelletti moved to the offensive side of the ball in his second season, making 45 receptions for 768 yards and 8 touchdowns from his split-end position. He also improved dramatically as a kicker after the team's new quarterback, Babe Parilli, became his holder, converting a league-leading 17 field goals, en route to topping the circuit with 147 points scored.

Cappelletti had another solid season in 1962, catching 34 passes for 479 yards and 5 touchdowns, converting 20 of 37 field goal attempts, and finishing second in the league with 128 points scored. He then began in 1963 a string of four consecutive seasons in which he led the AFL in scoring, tallying a total of 113 points, on 22 field goals, 35 extra points, and 2 touchdowns, in the first of those campaigns. Cappelletti also nearly equaled his previous year's output by making 34 receptions for 493 yards.

Cappelletti reached his zenith in 1964, when, after being shifted to flanker, he scored 7 touchdowns and established career highs with 49 receptions and 865 receiving yards. Cappelletti also kicked a league-leading 25 field goals, en route to topping the circuit with a career-best 155 points scored. His exceptional all-around performance earned him unanimous league MVP honors, with both the AP and UPI naming him their AFL Player of the Year. Cappelletti followed that up by leading the league in scoring in each of the next two seasons as well, amassing a total of 251 points in 1965 and 1966. He also made a total of 80 receptions, accumulated 1,356 receiving yards, and scored 15 touchdowns over the course of those two campaigns.

Although Cappelletti lacked great running speed and possessed only average athletic ability, he had outstanding hands, superb instincts, and a tremendous "feel" for the game that enabled him to evolve into quarterback Babe Parilli's favorite receiver over time. In fact, the duo worked so well together that their ability to synchronize their actions on the playing field eventually earned them the nickname "Grand Opera." The two men's symbiotic relationship extended onto special teams, with Cappelletti posting one of the league's three best field goal percentages in four of the seven seasons that Parilli remained his holder.

After making 35 receptions for 397 yards and 3 touchdowns in 1967, Cappelletti assumed a lesser role the following year, before serving the Patriots exclusively as a placekicker his final two seasons. He retired at the conclusion of the 1970 campaign with career totals of 292 receptions, 4,589 receiving yards, 42 touchdowns, 176 field goals, 342 PATs (points after touchdowns), and 1,130 points. Cappelletti ended his career having scored more points and kicked more field goals than any other AFL player. He also ranks among the league's all-time top 10 receivers in receptions and reception yardage. Cappelletti's 155 points in 1964 and 147 points in 1961 give him two of the top five scoring seasons in AFL history. From 1961 to

1966, he averaged 9.5 points per game. No other player in the history of professional football has averaged more points per contest over a six-year period. One of only 20 men to play in all 10 AFL seasons, Cappelletti further distinguished himself by being one of only three players to appear in every game for his team during the league's 10-year existence.

Following his retirement, Cappelletti turned to broadcasting, spending 1972–1978 doing color commentary on Patriots radio broadcasts. He then served as the team's special teams coach from 1979 to 1981, before returning to the broadcast booth in 1982. Cappelletti subsequently spent the better part of the next 30 years announcing Patriots games with his longtime partner Gil Santos, before announcing his retirement at the conclusion of the 2011 campaign. During that time, Cappelletti further endeared himself to the fans of New England, who came to refer to him affectionately as "The Duke."

Upon learning of Cappelletti's decision to retire, Patriots chairman and CEO Robert Kraft stated,

> There will never be another Gino Cappelletti. In our 52-year history, Gino served as a player, coach or color analyst for 45 of those seasons. I remember watching him play as an original Boston Patriot in 1960. He quickly became one of the biggest stars of the fledgling American Football League. He retired as the league's all-time leading scorer and deserves special recognition, not just for being one of the pioneers of the AFL, but for creating the foundation from which our franchise was built. He has been a great ambassador for the Patriots over a career that spanned six decades. His legend has grown since he retired as a player, as generations of Patriots fans have grown up listening to him provide insight and analysis of many of the most memorable games in franchise history. While he may be stepping down as a broadcaster, he will always be a Patriots ambassador and will remain one of the most iconic figures in franchise history.

Patriots head coach Bill Belichick added:

> Going back to his days as one of the all-time great players, Gino has been such a fixture, so it is hard imagining not working with him on a regular basis. I have been fortunate to enjoy Gino's presence and share experiences that extend well beyond the game. Around the team, he wasn't just a broadcaster but was—and remains—truly part of the team, respected by players and coaches for representing everything

good about sports. Gino is a class act, one of the true gentlemen of the AFL and NFL, and I am proud to have been associated with him every week of my career as Patriots head coach.

CAREER HIGHLIGHTS

Best Season

Cappelletti had a big year in 1961, when he made 45 receptions for 768 yards and 8 touchdowns, kicked a league-leading 17 field goals, and topped the circuit in scoring for the first of five times by tallying 147 points. He also performed extremely well in 1965, catching 37 passes, placing among the AFL leaders with 680 receiving yards and a career-high 9 touchdowns, and leading the league with 132 points and a 62.96 field goal percentage. However, Cappelletti had his signature season in 1964, when he made 49 receptions for 865 yards and 7 touchdowns, scored a league-record 155 points, and converted 25 of 39 field goal attempts, for a career-best 64.10 field goal percentage, en route to earning AFL MVP honors.

Memorable Moments/Greatest Performances

Cappelletti ironically had the first big day of his pro career on defense, intercepting Oakland quarterback Tom Flores three times during a 27-14 loss to the Raiders on October 16, 1960.

Cappelletti kicked three field goals in one game for the first time in his career on September 23, 1961, doing so during a 23-21 victory over the Bills in Buffalo. Cappelletti's final score, a season-long 46-yarder in the fourth quarter, provided the winning margin. He also made 4 receptions for 73 yards on the day. Cappelletti followed that up the very next week by having a hand in 24 of the 30 points the Patriots scored during a 37-30 loss to the New York Titans. In addition to kicking three extra points and another three field goals, he made a 32-yard touchdown reception and completed his only pass as a professional, hooking up with running back Larry Garron on a 27-yard TD score off a fake field goal attempt.

Cappelletti turned in his first 100-yard receiving game on October 13, 1961, making 6 receptions for 131 yards and 1 touchdown during a 31-31 tie with the eventual AFL champion Houston Oilers.

Cappelletti proved to be the difference in Boston's 26-16 victory over the Oakland Raiders on October 26, 1962, scoring 20 of the Patriots' 26 points, on 4 field goals, 2 extra points, and a 13-yard TD reception. He kicked another 4 field goals just two weeks later during a 33-29 win over the Broncos in Denver.

Cappelletti had another huge day against the Broncos on October 18, 1963, tallying 22 points during the Patriots' 40-21 home win over Denver. In addition to kicking 4 field goals and converting 4 extra points, Cappelletti connected with Babe Parilli on a 24-yard TD pass. He finished the game with 5 receptions for 95 yards.

Cappelletti also came up big in the 1963 AFL Eastern Division Playoff Game against the Buffalo Bills, leading the Patriots to a 26-8 victory by making 4 receptions for 109 yards and kicking 4 field goals.

Cappelletti went through a torrid stretch early in his MVP season of 1964, becoming one of only two AFL kickers to convert at least 4 field goal attempts in three straight games. He began his exceptional run on September 20, when he established a new career high by kicking 5 field goals during a 33-28 victory over the San Diego Chargers. The following week, Cappelletti helped the Pats improve their record to 3-0 by converting 4 three-pointers during a 26-10 win over the New York Jets, connecting on 3 of those from more than 40 yards out. Cappelletti subsequently kicked a career-high 6 field goals during a 39-10 blowout of the Denver Broncos on October 4.

Although the Jets gained a measure of revenge against the Patriots later in 1964, defeating them 35-14 on October 31, Cappelletti had one of the biggest days of his career as a pass receiver, making 7 catches, for 147 yards and one touchdown. The very next week, Cappelletti's 4 field goals helped the Pats defeat the Houston Oilers 25-24, with his 42-yarder late in the fourth quarter providing the margin of victory. Cappelletti turned in another huge effort the following week, leading the Patriots to a 36-28 win over the Buffalo Bills by making 3 touchdown receptions and scoring 24 points. He again proved to be the difference one week later, when he made 5 receptions for 96 yards, scored the Pats' only touchdown on a 25-yard pass from Babe Parilli, and kicked 2 field goals—one from 51 yards out—during a 12-7 victory over the Denver Broncos.

Cappelletti led the Patriots to a 22-6 win over the San Diego Chargers on October 31, 1965, by scoring 20 points, on 2 touchdowns and 2 field goals. However, he topped that performance in the regular-season finale, scoring 2 touchdowns and kicking 4 field goals, en route to setting an AFL record by amassing a total of 28 points during a 42-14 rout of the Houston Oilers.

NOTABLE ACHIEVEMENTS

- Caught more than 40 passes three times.
- Averaged more than 17 yards per reception three times.
- Scored more than 100 points six times.
- Led AFL in: points scored five times; field goals made three times; and field goal percentage once.
- One of only 20 men to play all 10 AFL seasons.
- One of only three men who appeared in every game their team played in the AFL.
- Holds AFL record for most points scored (1,100).
- Ranks among Patriots' all-time leaders in: points scored (3rd); touchdowns scored (tied-8th); touchdown receptions (5th); pass receptions (10th); receiving yardage (8th); and field goals made (3rd).
- 1963 AFL Eastern Division champion.
- Five-time AFL Pro Bowl selection (1961, 1963, 1964, 1965 & 1966).
- Four-time Second-Team All-AFL selection (1961, 1963, 1964 & 1966).
- 1964 AFL MVP.
- Member of Patriots' 1960s All-Decade Team.
- Named to Patriots' 50th Anniversary Team in 2009.
- Number 20 retired by Patriots.
- Inducted into Patriots Hall of Fame in 1992.

5

Stanley Morgan

(Courtesy Mainline Autographs)

Spending all but one of his 14 NFL seasons in New England, Stanley Morgan left behind a legacy that makes him easily the most prolific wide receiver in Patriots history. The franchise's all-time leader in pass receiving yardage (10,352), touchdown receptions (67), touchdowns scored (68), and yards per reception (19.4), Morgan also ranks third in team annals in receptions (534), second in all-purpose yards (11,468), and sixth in points scored (408). One of only two players in NFL history to average more than 20 yards per reception for six straight seasons, Morgan led the league in that category three times, en route to compiling the highest yards-per-reception average of any player with more than 500 career catches. A member of the 1985 AFC champion Patriots, Morgan surpassed 1,000 receiving yards three times, appeared in four Pro Bowls, made Second-Team All-Pro twice, and earned two First-Team All-AFC nominations. The speedy wide-out accomplished this despite playing for a team that predicated most of its offense on its running game.

Born in Easley, South Carolina, on February 17, 1955, Stanley Douglas Morgan attended Easley High School, where he helped his team win a state championship in 1972 with his stellar play on the gridiron. After enrolling at the University of Tennessee, Morgan spent the next four years splitting his time between the running back and wide receiver positions, while also returning punts and kickoffs. Following his graduation, Morgan's offensive versatility and blinding speed prompted the Patriots to select him in the first round of the 1977 NFL Draft, with the 25th overall pick.

Joining cornerback Raymond Clayborn as one of two rookies the Patriots selected in the first round of that year's draft (they took Clayborn with the 16th overall pick), Morgan experienced a moderate amount of success his first year in the league. In addition to making 21 receptions for 443 yards and 3 touchdowns, he averaged 13.8 yards per punt return—a figure that placed him second in the league rankings. Even though the Patriots established an all-time NFL record by rushing for 3,165 yards the following year, Morgan emerged as one of their top offensive threats, making 34 receptions for 820 yards and 5 touchdowns. By averaging a career-high 24.1 yards per reception, he placed second in the league to Wesley Walker of the Jets, who finished just percentage points ahead of him, with a mark of 24.4. Morgan also returned 32 punts for another 335 yards, enabling him to amass more than 1,000 all-purpose yards for the first of five times.

Morgan subsequently began an exceptional three-year run during which he led the NFL in yards per reception each season. After making 44 receptions for 1,002 yards and a league-leading 12 touchdowns in 1979, he caught 45 passes for 991 yards and 6 touchdowns the following year. Morgan then made 44 receptions for 1,029 yards and another 6 touchdowns in 1981, despite missing the first two games of the season with a left knee sprain. In addition to being named to the AFC Pro Bowl roster in both 1979 and 1980, he earned First-Team All-Conference and Second-Team All-NFL honors in the second of those campaigns.

The 1982 player's strike, which shortened the regular season to only nine games, prevented Morgan from surpassing 1,000 all-purpose yards for the fifth straight time. Yet, even though he caught just 28 passes for 584 yards, he managed to join Paul Warfield as the only players in NFL history to average more than 20 yards per reception six consecutive times (Warfield accomplished the feat seven years in a row).

Morgan remained one of the NFL's most dangerous deep threats the next three years, making a total of 135 receptions for more than 2,300 yards and 12 touchdowns from 1983 to 1985, before having the most productive season of his career in 1986. In addition to finishing fifth in the NFL with 10 touchdown receptions, he placed among the league leaders with a career-high 84 receptions and 1,491 receiving yards. Morgan's fabulous performance earned him the third of his four Pro Bowl selections and his second First-Team All-AFC and Second-Team All-Pro nominations.

Limited to only 10 games in 1987 by hamstring problems and another player's strike, Morgan made just 40 receptions for 672 yards and 3 touchdowns. Nevertheless, he made the AFC Pro Bowl squad for the fourth and final time. No longer blessed with the blazing speed that terrorized opposing cornerbacks earlier in his career, Morgan spent his final two years in New England depending more on his guile and experience to make a total of 59 catches for 7 touchdowns and nearly 1,000 yards. Released by the Patriots at the end of 1989, he joined the Indianapolis Colts for one more season, retiring at the conclusion of the 1990 campaign with a career total of 557 receptions, for 10,716 yards and 72 touchdowns. He also carried the ball 21 times for 127 yards, and returned 92 punts for 960 yards and one touchdown.

Some 25 years after he played his last game in New England, Morgan continues to hold numerous franchise pass-receiving records. Extremely proud of his accomplishments, Morgan expressed his satisfaction with his place in Patriots history when he stated, "That means a great deal to me. It's something I am proud of, and I'm in shock that it (his team record for pass-receiving yardage) hasn't been broken yet. I think it's something that I worked hard at, and it paid off for me."

Still, Morgan believes that he could have accomplished considerably more had he played in an offense that relied more heavily on the passing game, noting, "Back when I was playing, we basically relied on our running game and threw when we had to. It wasn't uncommon to go a couple of games and not have a pass thrown to me if our running game was doing well. I just wish we threw the ball a bit more, but I am sure you will hear that from every receiver."

Inducted into the Patriots Hall of Fame in 2007, Morgan received the additional honor of being named to the franchise's 50th Anniversary Team two years later. At Morgan's Patriots Hall of Fame induction ceremony, team owner Robert Kraft took the opportunity to campaign for the former wide receiver's induction into the Pro Football Hall of Fame as well, suggesting, "There are 18 receivers in the Pro Football Hall of Fame, and only one (Paul Warfield) has a higher career average than Stanley's 19.2 yards per catch. He was really a great player and always a fan favorite."

PATRIOT CAREER HIGHLIGHTS

Best Season

Morgan played exceptionally well in 1979, earning Pro Bowl honors for the first time in his career by making 44 receptions for 1,002 yards and a league-leading 12 touchdowns. He also led the NFL in yards per reception for the first of three straight times by averaging 22.8 yards per catch. Morgan had another big year in 1981, when he again made 44 receptions, this time for 1,029 yards and six touchdowns. By averaging 23.4 yards per reception that season, Morgan posted the second-highest mark of his career (he averaged 24.1 yards per catch in 1978). Nevertheless, there can be no doubting that Morgan had his finest all-around season in 1986, when, in addition to finishing fifth in the league with 10 touchdown receptions, he established career highs with 84 catches and 1,491 receiving yards, en route to earning First-Team All-AFC and Second-Team All-NFL honors. Morgan's total of 1,491 yards through the air continues to rank as one of the highest single-season marks ever posted by a Patriots wide-out, trailing only the 1,569 yards Wes Welker amassed in 2011 and the 1,493 yards Randy Moss accumulated in 2007. In addition to leading the AFC in receiving yardage, Morgan finished third in the conference in pass receptions and total yardage. By surpassing 100 receiving yards nine times over the course of the campaign, Morgan finished just one game shy of tying the then-existing NFL record of ten 100-yard games. His exceptional performance prompted the 1776 QB Club to name him the team's Most Valuable Player.

Memorable Moments/Greatest Performances

Morgan had his breakout game for the Patriots on September 18, 1978, when he made three receptions for 125 yards and a touchdown during a 34-27 loss to the Baltimore Colts at Schaefer Stadium. Morgan temporarily gave the Pats a 13-7 lead in the second quarter when he hooked up with quarterback Steve Grogan on a 62-yard scoring play. Morgan had another big day against the Colts later in the year, helping New England defeat Baltimore 35-14 by making five receptions for 170 yards, including a 75-yard TD grab. The speedy wide receiver also returned one punt for 37 yards during the contest.

Morgan again riddled Baltimore's defensive secondary the following year, when, during a 31-26 October 28, 1979, loss to the Colts, he hauled in five passes for 151 yards and two touchdowns, hooking up with Grogan on scoring plays of 56 and 27 yards. Morgan had a similarly productive day against Buffalo the very next week, leading the Patriots to a 26-6 victory over the Bills by making five receptions for 158 yards and a pair of touchdowns, those two coming on pass plays that covered 63 and 34 yards.

An outstanding punt returner his first few years in the league, Morgan scored the only special teams touchdown of his career on November 18, 1979, when he returned a punt 80 yards for a TD during a 50-21 blowout of the Colts. Morgan also scored another touchdown during the contest on a 25-yard pass from Steve Grogan.

Although the Patriots lost to the New York Jets 27-26 on December 9, 1979, Morgan turned in one of the finest all-around performances of his career, making six receptions for 129 yards and two touchdowns, returning three punts for 52 yards, carrying the ball once, and returning a kickoff, en route to amassing a total of 197 all-purpose yards on the day.

Morgan turned in another exceptional effort in defeat, making five catches for 182 yards and a touchdown, and accumulating 219 all-purpose yards during a 30-27 overtime loss to the Miami Dolphins on November 8, 1981. Morgan's 76-yard TD reception in the first quarter of the contest proved to be the longest of his career.

Morgan came up big for the Patriots in the 1982 regular-season finale, helping them advance to the playoffs as a wild-card by making seven receptions for 141 yards during a 30-19 win over the Buffalo Bills.

Although the Baltimore Colts defeated the Patriots 12-7 on October 9, 1983, Morgan made a career-high nine receptions during the contest, accumulating a total of 136 yards through the air in the process.

Morgan scored three touchdowns in one game for the only time in his career on September 21, 1986, when he hooked up with quarterback Tony Eason on pass plays that covered 27, 44, and 30 yards during a 38-31 loss to the Seattle Seahawks. Morgan finished the day with seven receptions for 161 yards. He had another big game three weeks later, when he made seven receptions for 162 yards and a touchdown during a 31-24 home loss to the New York Jets.

However, Morgan experienced the most memorable moment of his exceptional 1986 campaign in the regular-season finale, when he hauled in a 30-yard touchdown pass from Steve Grogan with only 44 seconds remaining in regulation to give the Patriots a 34-27 win over Miami. The victory, which came in the final NFL game ever played at the Orange Bowl, enabled the Patriots to lay claim to the AFC East title. Morgan, who also scored a first-quarter touchdown on a 22-yard pass from Tony Eason, finished the day with eight receptions for 148 yards and two touchdowns.

Nevertheless, Morgan, who made only two receptions for 30 yards on the day, considers the 1985 AFC Championship Game against Miami to be the highlight of his career. Reflecting back on the Patriots' 31-14 victory over the Dolphins, Morgan stated, "I think that game in Miami when we played for the AFC Championship was unbelievable. That was our first time winning down there, and that game carried a lot of importance. You just do not forget something like that."

NOTABLE ACHIEVEMENTS

- Caught more than 50 passes twice, topping 80 receptions once (84 in 1986).
- Surpassed 1,000 receiving yards three times, topping 1,400 yards once (1,491 in 1986).
- Averaged more than 20 yards per reception six straight times (1977–82).
- Scored at least 10 touchdowns twice (1979 & 1986).
- Returned one punt for a touchdown.
- Led NFL in yards-per-reception average three times and touchdown receptions once.
- Finished second in NFL with 1,491 receiving yards in 1986.
- Finished second in NFL with 13.8 yard punt-return average in 1977.
- Finished fourth in NFL with 84 receptions in 1986.
- Holds Patriots career records for: most receiving yardage (10,352); most touchdown receptions (67); most touchdowns scored (68); and highest yards-per-reception average (19.4).
- Ranks among Patriots all-time leaders in: pass receptions (3rd); all-purpose yards (2nd); and points scored (6th).
- 1985 AFC champion.

- Holds NFL record for highest yards-per-reception average (19.2) of any player with more than 500 career receptions.
- One of only two players in NFL history to average more than 20 yards per reception in six straight seasons (1977–82).
- Four-time Pro Bowl selection (1979, 1980, 1986 & 1987).
- Two-time Second-Team All-Pro selection (1980 & 1986).
- Two-time First-Team All-AFC selection (1980 & 1986).
- Pro Football Reference 1980s All-Decade Second Team.
- Named to Patriots' 50th Anniversary Team in 2009.
- Inducted into Patriots Hall of Fame in 2007.

6

Bruce Armstrong

Bruce Armstrong, center (#78).
(Courtesy George A. Kitrinos)

The greatest offensive tackle in Patriots history, Bruce Armstrong spent 14 seasons in New England, appearing in more games during that time than any other player ever to wear a Pats uniform. Starting 212 of a possible 220 non-strike games over the course of his career, Armstrong proved to be a pillar of strength on the Patriots' offensive line, protecting at different times the blind side of quarterbacks Steve Grogan, Tom Ramsey, Tony Eason, Doug Flutie, Marc Wilson, Tom Hodson, Hugh Millen, Scott

Zolak, and Drew Bledsoe. One of only three players in league history to play with the same team in three different decades, Armstrong starred for the Patriots from 1987 to 2000, appearing in six Pro Bowls during that time, while also earning six All-AFC nominations and two Second-Team All-Pro selections. Performing at an extremely high level for virtually his entire career, Armstrong also eventually earned a spot on the Patriots' 50th Anniversary Team and a place in their Hall of Fame. The massive left tackle is also one of only seven players in franchise history to have his number retired.

Born in Miami, Florida, on September 7, 1965, Bruce Charles Armstrong attended Miami Central High School, before enrolling at the University of Louisville, where he began his football career as a tight end. After making a total of 33 receptions his first two years at Louisville, Armstrong moved to left tackle as a junior following the hiring of Howard Schnellenberger as head coach. Although Armstrong initially balked at the idea of switching positions, recalling years later, "I wasn't happy about it to say the least," he ended up excelling at his new spot, anchoring the Cardinals line for the next two seasons, earning a berth in the 1986 Senior Bowl, and being named Louisville's "Most Outstanding Lineman" following his senior season.

Subsequently selected by the Patriots in the first round of the 1987 NFL Draft, with the 23rd overall pick, Armstrong wasted little time in establishing himself as the mainstay of New England's offensive line, earning a starting job as a rookie. In fact, after sitting out the first four games of the 1987 campaign due to a player's strike, Armstrong started the next 84 games at left tackle for the Patriots. Only a career-threatening injury suffered during a loss to Buffalo on November 1, 1992, brought Armstrong's streak to an end, forcing him to miss the final eight games of the season. However, despite tearing the medial collateral ligament and both his anterior and posterior cruciate ligaments in his right knee, Armstrong returned to action the following season to begin another consecutive games played streak that lasted until he finally retired at the conclusion of the 2000 campaign. At one point during that stretch, he displayed his grit and determination by starting the last eight games of the 1999 season with three torn ligaments in his right knee.

Standing 6'4" tall and weighing 295 pounds, Armstrong had good size and strength for an offensive tackle. He also possessed quick feet and excellent technique that enabled him to protect his quarterback from some of the league's top pass-rushers, including Buffalo's Bruce Smith, who, as a division rival, he faced twice a year for 13 straight seasons.

Yet, in spite of the outstanding competition he faced week after week, Armstrong managed to excel, earning First-Team All-AFC and Second-Team All-Pro honors for the first time in 1988, when he helped the Patriots post their fifth consecutive winning record. Even though the Pats proved to be less successful in each of the next five seasons as they searched for a quarterback capable of running their offense, Armstrong continued to be singled out for personal honors, earning his first two Pro Bowl selections and two more All-AFC nominations.

With Drew Bledsoe subsequently assuming the reigns of New England's offense for the remainder of Armstrong's career, the latter continued to receive numerous individual accolades, being named to the Pro Bowl four straight times from 1994 to 1997, earning All-AFC honors three more times, and being awarded Second-Team All-Pro honors for the final time in 1996, when he helped the Patriots advance to the Super Bowl.

A 5-11 record in 2000 prompted the Patriots to revamp their offensive line with younger players the following year, forcing Armstrong to announce his retirement earlier than he originally anticipated. Looking back at the events that transpired during the subsequent offseason, Armstrong recalled, "I always said I wanted to play here, finish my career in one place, and I made no bones about wanting to play another year. But it didn't work out that way."

Therefore, after serving as Drew Bledsoe's security blanket for the previous eight seasons, Armstrong elected to retire at the conclusion of the 2000 campaign. In addition to appearing in more games than any other Patriots player, Armstrong ended his career with a streak of 128 consecutive starts. Upon learning of Armstrong's decision, the Patriots immediately retired his No. 78 and inducted him into their Hall of Fame, waiving the usual five-year waiting period. In addressing the contributions Armstrong made to the Patriots through the years, owner Robert Kraft stated, "Bruce is the greatest left tackle in the history of the franchise, and one of the best players ever to wear a Patriots uniform. His unique accomplishments justify waiving the rule for induction into our Hall of Fame, where he will take his proper place alongside the very best who have played for the Patriots."

CAREER HIGHLIGHTS

Best Season

Armstrong earned Second-Team All-Pro honors twice in his career, doing so for the first time in 1988, and then again in 1996. New England's offense performed much better in the second of those campaigns, scoring 168 more points (418 to 250) and gaining some 1,700 more yards through the air (3,901 to 2,173), en route to finishing the season with the NFL's second-ranked offense. Although quarterback Drew Bledsoe, running back Curtis Martin, and tight end Ben Coates all made significant contributions to the Patriots' potent offense, Armstrong has to receive some of the credit as well since he anchored their offensive line and served as the unit's unquestioned leader. Nevertheless, it could be argued that Armstrong played just as well in 1988, when the Patriots rushed for nearly 700 more yards (2,120 to 1,468), posted a higher rushing average (3.6 to 3.4), and allowed fewer sacks as a team (23 to 30). Many other factors certainly came into play, and it is impossible to know, with any degree of certainty, just how much Armstrong's performance influenced the discrepancy in those numbers. But, with the Patriots winning two more games in 1996 and capturing the AFC championship, I opted to identify that as his finest overall season.

Memorable Moments/Greatest Performances

Armstrong's one-on-one battles with Buffalo's Hall of Fame defensive end Bruce Smith became the stuff of legend, with the two men squaring off against one another twice a year for 13 straight seasons. Still, the most memorable incident of Armstrong's career arguably took place off the field—at least according to teammate Chris Slade, as told by Michael Madden in the January 9, 1997, edition of the *Boston Globe*.

With the Patriots preparing to play the Pittsburgh Steelers in the first round of the playoffs, Armstrong continued his daily ritual of joining fellow co-captains Mike Jones and Willie McGinest in addressing the rest of the team after the coaches left the field for the meeting rooms. However, Slade revealed that Armstrong showed up one day with a baseball bat in his hands in order to drive home the points he wished to make. The Patriots linebacker recalled, "That's the speech I remember most, when Bruce came into a team meeting with a bat in his hands last week, like he was going to beat somebody up."

Armstrong admitted to resorting to such tactics, stating, "I was mad. I was sick and tired of hearing all this stuff about the Steelers." Yet, at the same time, Armstrong suggested, "The bat was only an exclamation point to the words I was saying. But I didn't hit anybody with the bat . . . put it that way."

Still, Slade did not remain totally convinced, saying, "That was pretty scary. Bruce almost hit a few people with the bat. He almost hit Willie (Mc-

Ginest). Yeah, that was the most memorable speech of the year, last week with Bruce and the bat."

NOTABLE ACHIEVEMENTS

- Missed only eight non-strike games entire career, starting 212 out of a possible 220 games, and compiling streaks of 84 and 128 consecutive starts at different points.
- Holds Patriots franchise record for most games played (212).
- 1996 AFC champion.
- Six-time Pro Bowl selection (1990, 1991, & 1994–97).
- Two-time Second-Team All-Pro selection (1988 & 1996).
- Four-time First-Team All-AFC selection (1988, 1991, 1994 & 1996).
- Two-time Second-Team All-AFC selection (1989 & 1995).
- Named to Patriots' 50th Anniversary Team in 2009.
- Inducted into Patriots Hall of Fame in 2001.
- Number 78 retired by Patriots.

7

Mike Haynes

One of two Patriot players named to the NFL's 75th Anniversary Team in 1994 (John Hannah was the other), Mike Haynes spent seven seasons in New England before moving on to Los Angeles, where he continued his Hall of Fame career as a member of the Raiders. An exceptional cornerback known for his tenacious man-to-man coverage, Haynes played for the Patriots from 1976 to 1982, recording during that time a total of 28 interceptions that places him sixth in franchise history. Excelling on special teams as well, Haynes returned two punts for touchdowns as a rookie, becoming in the process the first Patriots player ever to score in that manner. Haynes' outstanding all-around play earned him six trips to the Pro Bowl, six All-AFC nominations, and six All-Pro selections in his seven years in New England, prompting the Patriots to eventually induct him into their Hall of Fame and retire his number 40.

Born in Denison, Texas, on July 1, 1953, Michael James Haynes grew up in Los Angeles, California, where he attended John Marshall High School. While starring at cornerback for his high school football team, Haynes also participated in track and field, setting a school long-jump record that still stands by leaping 23'5" in his final regular season track meet. Recruited by several colleges following his graduation from John Marshall, Haynes elected to enroll at Arizona State University. While playing cornerback and returning punts at ASU, Haynes earned All-WAC (Western Athletic Conference) honors three times and All-America honors in his junior and senior years. In discussing his star defensive back, ASU head coach Frank Kush once described him as a "luxury," stating, "We'd put Mike on the opponent's top receiver, one-on-one, with no help, short or deep. That's a hell of a responsibility, but Mike handled it beautifully. Leaving Mike by himself would enable us to give free safety help to the other corner, or even utilize the safety blitz. It was a great four years, at least from the standpoint of our secondary."

Subsequently selected by the Patriots with the fifth overall pick of the 1976 NFL Draft, Haynes became the first defensive back to have his name called so early on draft day since the St. Louis Cardinals selected Jerry Stovall with the second overall pick in 1963. Yet, in spite of his tremendous natural ability, Haynes found himself struggling during the early stages of his rookie campaign, recalling years later the impact that head coach Chuck Fairbanks made on him: "He (Fairbanks) took me under his wing as a rookie. I didn't have the greatest start, but I finished pretty strong, mainly because of the conversations I had with him. He helped me understand the pros, the learning curve. He told me you don't just show up and be great from day one. You have to work hard to be great. He challenged me to do it. I did."

Responding to the challenge of his head coach, Haynes ended up having a sensational rookie campaign, finishing third in the NFL with 8 interceptions, placing second in the league with 608 punt-return yards and an average of 13.5 yards per punt return, and returning two punts for touchdowns, en route to earning First-Team All-AFC honors, Second-Team All-NFL honors, and the first of five consecutive trips to the Pro Bowl. The Associated Press also named Haynes its NFL Defensive Rookie of the Year.

Although Haynes surrendered some of his punt-return duties in 1977, he had another outstanding year on defense, earning First-Team All-AFC and Second-Team All-NFL honors for the second straight time by recording 5 interceptions and 2 fumble recoveries. Fast becoming the league's premier shut-down corner, the 6'2", 192-pound Haynes used his speed, quickness, and range to discourage opposing quarterbacks from throwing to his area. Coach Fairbanks noted at one point during the 1977 season, "Mike hasn't seen a ball come his way in over three weeks." Meanwhile, a member of Fairbanks' coaching staff remarked, "If Mike has a problem of any kind, it is that he may go for a while, even a couple of games, without ever seeing the ball in his area. His biggest problem may be to keep from getting too relaxed."

In discussing the technique he used to blanket opposing wide receivers, Haynes explained, "The receiver tells you where the ball is. If the defensive back looks back and the ball's not there, he's beaten."

Haynes continued to excel at cornerback for the Patriots from 1978 to 1980, earning Pro Bowl, First-Team All-Conference, and Second-Team All-NFL honors all three years. Performing particularly well in 1978, he ranked among the league leaders in interceptions (6) and interception return yards

(123). However, injuries and contract squabbles cut into Haynes' playing time significantly in two of the next three seasons, ultimately bringing his time in New England to an end. After sitting out the first three games of 1980 due to a contract dispute, Haynes appeared in only 8 games the following season, failing to earn a trip to the Pro Bowl for the first time in his career. He returned to top form in 1982, though, being named to the AFC's Pro Bowl roster and earning All-Conference and All-NFL honors for the sixth time. Unfortunately, the 1982 campaign proved to be Haynes' last in New England. Choosing to sit out the first 11 games of the 1983 season while waiting for his contract demands to be met, Haynes ended up playing out his option with the Patriots. His contract was subsequently awarded to the Los Angeles Raiders in a settlement that sent the star cornerback and a mid-round draft pick to the Raiders for a first round draft pick in 1984 and a second round pick in 1985. In addition to intercepting 28 passes during his time in New England, Haynes returned 111 punts for a total of 1,159 yards, averaging in the process 10.4 yards per return. He also averaged 14 yards per interception return.

After leaving the Patriots, Haynes moved seamlessly into the Raiders' secondary, appearing in their final five regular-season contests, before intercepting a pass and recording 2 pass breakups and a tackle in their Super Bowl victory over the Washington Redskins. He spent six more years in Los Angeles, appearing in three more Pro Bowls and earning First-Team All-Pro honors for the only two times in his career. During his time with the Raiders, Haynes combined with Lester Hayes to form one of the greatest cornerback tandems in NFL history. He retired at the conclusion of the 1989 campaign having intercepted another 18 passes as a member of the Raiders, giving him a total of 46 picks over the course of his career. Haynes also amassed 688 interception return yards and scored five touchdowns, three of which came on interception returns, with the other two coming on punt returns.

In addition to earning him a spot on the NFL's 75th Anniversary Team and a place in the Pro Football Hall of Fame, Haynes' total body of work prompted the NFL to name him to its 1980s All-Decade Team. The Patriots also named him to their 50th Anniversary Team in 2009, 10 years after the *Sporting News* placed him 93rd on its list of the 100 Greatest Players in NFL History.

Following his retirement, Haynes spent seven years at Callaway Golf, a global leader in the development and manufacturing of golf equipment, before returning to the NFL in 2002. Since assuming his role with the league office, Haynes has led the Player Development Department, which creates and manages programs to help players transition into and out of the NFL. While serving in that capacity in 2008, Haynes discovered that he had prostate cancer, prompting him to later become a spokesman for the Know Your Stats About Prostate Cancer Campaign, which focuses on encouraging men to talk with their doctors about getting tested for this deadly disease.

PATRIOT CAREER HIGHLIGHTS

Best Season

Haynes played exceptionally well for the Patriots in 1978, recording 6 interceptions, which he returned for 123 yards and one touchdown. However, he made his greatest overall impact two years earlier, earning AP NFL Defensive Rookie of the Year and consensus First-Team All-AFC honors by making a career-high 8 interceptions, recovering 3 fumbles, returning 2 punts for touchdowns, and finishing second in the league with 608 punt-return yards and an average of 13.5 yards per punt return. In assessing Haynes' value to the Patriots on defense alone that year, it must be considered that the 3-11 Pats allowed their opponents a total of 358 points over the course of the 1975 campaign, intercepting just 13 passcs as a team in the process. But, with Haynes and fellow rookie defensive back Tim Fox helping to solidify a porous New England secondary that one reporter referred to as the "true Adventure Land in American entertainment," the Patriots surrendered only 236 points to their opposition in 1976, en route to compiling an exceptional 11-3 record.

Memorable Moments/Greatest Performances

After experiencing the usual growing pains of most NFL rookies early in 1976, Haynes performed brilliantly during the season's second half, at one point intercepting 7 passes over a four-game stretch. The string began on November 7, when he recorded an interception during a 20-10 victory over the Buffalo Bills. The very next week, Haynes helped lead the Patriots to a 21-14 win over the Baltimore Colts by intercepting another 2 passes, which he returned for 42 yards. Haynes continued his streak by recording a career-high 3 interceptions during a 38-24 victory over the Jets on November 21, making such a strong impression on New York quarterback Joe Namath that the signal-caller said following the contest, "That kid is a helluva player. He has great range. I didn't think I made any bad throws, and I was reading the coverages pretty well. He just went out there and got the ball." Haynes concluded his extraordinary run by picking off another pass during a 38-14 win over the Broncos on November 28.

Haynes' performances in the November 7 game against Buffalo and the November 28 contest against Denver were even more impressive when his contributions to the Patriots on special teams are taken into account. During the 20-10 win over the Bills, Haynes made history by becoming the first Patriots player to return a punt for a touchdown, going 89 yards for a score that put his team out in front 13-0 late in the second quarter. Fielding a bouncing Marv Bateman punt on his own 11-yard line, Haynes demonstrated his tremendous speed by taking off for the left sideline and going untouched the rest of the way after receiving a key block from Tim Fox. He finished the game with four punt returns, for a total of 156 yards. Although Haynes amassed fewer total yards against the Broncos three weeks later, returning three punts for 99 yards, he returned one of those for a 62-yard touchdown.

Haynes had another big day on October 9, 1977, when he helped the Patriots shut out the Seahawks 31-0 by recording two of New England's four interceptions against Seattle quarterback Steve Myer. Nearly two months later, on December 4, Haynes intercepted another two passes during a 16-10 victory over the Atlanta Falcons.

Haynes played an outstanding all-around game against the Jets on November 19, 1978, intercepting Richard Todd twice and returning one punt for 35 yards during a hard-fought 19-17 Patriots victory. The very next week, he recorded the first touchdown interception of his career, going 36 yards for a score after picking off a Bill Troup pass during a 35-14 win over the Colts.

Haynes scored his last touchdown as a member of the Patriots on October 5, 1980, when he raced 65 yards following a blocked field goal attempt, in helping the Pats defeat the Jets 21-11.

NOTABLE ACHIEVEMENTS

- Intercepted at least 5 passes three times.
- Returned one interception for a touchdown.
- Finished third in NFL with 8 interceptions in 1976.
- First Patriots player to return a punt for a touchdown.
- Returned 2 punts for touchdowns.
- Led AFC with 608 punt return yards in 1976.

- Finished second in NFL with 608 punt return yards and 13.5 yards-per-punt return average in 1976.
- Ranks sixth all-time on Patriots with 28 career interceptions.
- Six-time Pro Bowl selection (1976, 1977, 1978, 1979, 1980 & 1982).
- Six-time All-AFC selection (1976, 1977, 1978, 1979, 1980 & 1982).
- Six-time Second-Team All-Pro selection (1976, 1977, 1978, 1979, 1980 & 1982).
- 1976 AP NFL Defensive Rookie of the Year.
- 1976 UPI AFC Rookie of the Year.
- NFL 1980s All-Decade Team.
- Named to Patriots' 50th Anniversary Team in 2009.
- Inducted into Patriots Hall of Fame in 1994.
- Number 40 retired by Patriots.
- Number 93 on the *Sporting News'* 1999 list of 100 Greatest Players in NFL History.
- Named to NFL's 75th Anniversary Team in 1994.
- Elected to Pro Football Hall of Fame in 1997.

8

Houston Antwine

(Courtesy sportsofboston.com)

Easily the best player yet to be inducted into the Patriots Hall of Fame, Houston Antwine spent 11 of his 12 professional seasons in Boston, establishing himself during that time as one of the AFL's premier defensive linemen. Excelling against both the pass and the run from his right tackle position, Antwine used his tremendous strength and exceptional quickness to dominate opposing offensive linemen. A six-time All-AFL selection, Antwine earned First-Team All-Pro honors once and Second-Team honors five other times. He also appeared in six consecutive Pro Bowls, en route to earning spots on the All-Time All-AFL Team and the Patriots' 50th Anniversary Team. That the Patriots have yet to retire Antwine's number 65 or induct him into their Hall of Fame remains something of a mystery.

Born in Louise, Mississippi, on April 11, 1939, Houston J. Antwine grew up in Memphis, Tennessee, where he attended Manassas High School. After enrolling at Southern Illinois University, Antwine established himself as a multi-sport star for the Salukis, excelling as a defensive tackle on the football field, while also becoming a National Association of Intercollegiate Athletics (NAIA) wrestling champion. Following his graduation from Southern Illinois, Antwine elected to pursue a career in professional football when both the NFL's Detroit Lions and the AFL's Houston Oilers selected him in the 1961 draft for their respective leagues. After opting to sign with the Oilers, who claimed him in the eighth round with the 64th overall pick, Antwine soon found himself headed for Boston when the Patriots acquired him for a third-round selection in the 1962 draft.

The deal proved to be a steal for the Patriots, for whom Antwine made his professional debut later in the year. After spending most of his rookie campaign playing on the left side of Boston's defensive line, the six-foot, 270-pound Antwine subsequently moved over to right tackle, where he found a permanent home. Playing between left tackle Jim Lee Hunt and right end Larry Eisenhauer, Antwine emerged as Boston's defensive catalyst, controlling the line of scrimmage with his strength, quickness, and outstanding technique, which his experience as a wrestler in college helped him develop.

Commenting on the impact Antwine made on the Patriots' defense, longtime teammate Gino Cappelletti stated, "It didn't take long for him to establish his identity. He was so quick and durable. He never missed a game. I can't recall him ever missing a practice. He was all-out all the time. He plugged a lot of holes for us."

After helping the Patriots compile a record of 9-4-1 in each of his first two seasons in Boston, Antwine began a dominant stretch in 1963 that saw him earn All-Pro honors in five of the next six seasons and a spot in the Pro Bowl in each of those years. Antwine perhaps played his best ball for Boston's 1963 AFL Eastern Division championship team, earning unanimous First-Team All-AFL honors for the only time in his career.

The most complete player along the Patriots' defensive front, Antwine played both the run and the pass extremely well, performing very much like a man among boys during his time in Boston. Antwine's great strength and balance made him virtually impossible to move out of the middle, making him a superb run-stuffer. Meanwhile, his quickness and athleticism made him an outstanding pass-rusher as well, enabling him to lead the Patriots in quarterback sacks three straight years at one point. In fact, he compiled an "unofficial" total of 39 sacks over the course of his career, placing him in the team's all-time top 10 in that category. Antwine's tremendous all-around ability forced opposing teams to double-team him on virtually every play, opening up the pass-rushing lanes for fellow tackle Jim Lee Hunt, defensive end Larry Eisenhauer, and linebackers Nick Buoniconti and Tom Addison, who the Patriots often used to blitz opposing quarterbacks.

Pro Football Hall of Famer Billy Shaw, who, as a guard for the Buffalo Bills, frequently had the unenviable task of going head-to-head against Antwine, identified his former opponent as one of the AFL's best pass-rushers, making particular note of his athleticism and quickness afoot.

After being named to the AFL East All-Star squad six straight times from 1963 to 1968, Antwine failed to be so honored in 1969. However, he earned his fourth consecutive Second-Team All-Pro selection by the Associated Press. With Larry Eisenhauer announcing his retirement at the conclusion of that 1969 campaign, the Patriots shifted Antwine over to right defensive end, where he did a creditable job for a Boston team that finished just 2-12 in 1970. Injuries subsequently forced Antwine to miss all but three games in 1971, which turned out to be his last year with the Patriots. He spent his final NFL season with the Philadelphia Eagles, starting 9 of the team's 14 games at his familiar right tackle position, before choosing to call it quits at the end of the year. Antwine appeared in a total of 156 games over the course of his career, starting 139 out of a possible 140 contests in his first 10 years with the Patriots.

Since Antwine's retirement, 13 members of the All-Time All-AFL team have been inducted into the Pro Football Hall of Fame. One of those players was Buck Buchanan, who starred at defensive tackle for the Kansas City Chiefs from 1963 to 1975. Yet, ironically, even though Antwine has yet to have a bust of him configured for Canton, he finished ahead of Buchanan in the voting for a spot on the AFL's All-Time First Team; Buchanan had to settle for Second-Team honors.

Antwine lived another 39 years following his retirement, passing away from heart failure on December 26, 2011, at the age of 72. Following his passing, Patriots owner Robert Kraft said in a statement released by the team, "For those of us who grew up watching the Boston Patriots, this is really a sad day. In the 1960s, the defensive tackle tandem of 'Twine and Jim Lee Hunt was as good as any in the league and helped propel the Patriots to the franchise's first division championship in 1963."

Boston Herald columnist Ron Borges acknowledged Antwine's passing by writing a piece in which he stated, "Houston Antwine was the kind of football player you don't forget if you ever saw him, but he's the kind few remember today because he did his playing before *ESPN* highlight shows existed. If they had, 'Twine would have been a staple because he was everything you wanted in a defensive tackle—Warren Sapp before there was a Warren Sapp, but without the need for volume control."

PATRIOT CAREER HIGHLIGHTS

Best Season

As previously mentioned, Antwine appeared in the AFL All-Star Game six straight times, from 1963 to 1968, being named First-Team All-Pro by at least one major news wire service in each of the final three campaigns. However, he earned unanimous First-Team All-AFL honors for the only time in his career in 1963, when he helped the Patriots capture the AFL Eastern Division title.

Memorable Moments/Greatest Performances

Antwine performed brilliantly during a 26-10 Patriots win over the New York Jets at Boston College Alumni Stadium on September 27, 1964, being presented with the game ball at the conclusion of the contest for leading a Boston defense that surrendered just 46 yards on the ground to New York, recorded 4 sacks, and intercepted Jet quarterbacks a total of six times.

Antwine earned AFL Defensive Player of the Week honors on September 8, 1968, by sacking Buffalo quarterback Dan Darragh three times during the Patriots' 16-7 victory over the Bills in the regular-season opener. Antwine had another huge game later in the year, amassing a career-high 10 tackles during a 33-14 win over the Cincinnati Bengals on December 1.

Antwine, though, experienced perhaps his most memorable moment on December 12, 1965, when he recorded the only interception of his career during a 28-20 win over the Broncos in Denver. The massive defensive lineman subsequently returned the ball 2 yards before being brought down by a number of Broncos.

NOTABLE ACHIEVEMENTS

- Led Patriots in sacks three straight seasons (1967, 1968 & 1969).
- 1963 AFL Eastern Division champion.
- Six-time AFL Pro Bowl selection (1963, 1964, 1965, 1966, 1967 & 1968).
- 1963 First-Team All-AFL selection.
- Five-time Second-Team All-AFL selection (1964, 1966, 1967, 1968 & 1969).
- Member of All-Time All-AFL Team.
- AFL Hall of Fame All-1960s First Team.
- Pro Football Reference AFL 1960s All-Decade First Team.
- Named to Patriots' 50th Anniversary Team in 2009.

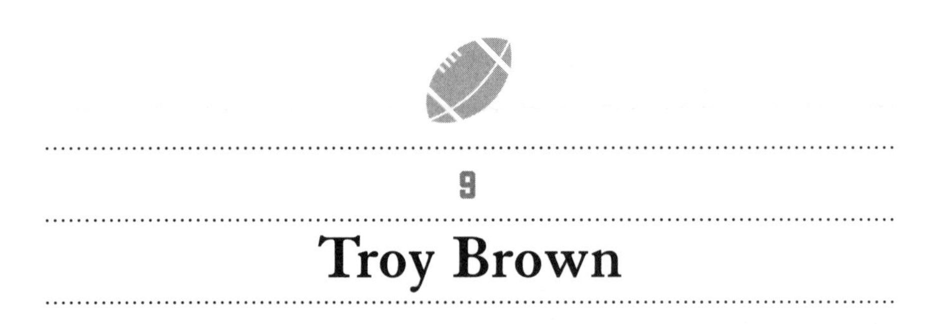

9

Troy Brown

(Courtesy Cris Yarborough)

One of the most versatile and beloved players in Patriots history, Troy Brown spent his entire 15-year NFL career in New England, contributing to the success of the team in all three phases of the game—offense, defense, and special teams. A member of Patriot squads that won five AFC Championships and three Super Bowls, the 5'10", 196-pound Brown, who the Pats selected in the eighth round of the 1993 NFL Draft, proved to be a huge overachiever, retiring as the franchise's all-time leader in pass receptions, punt returns, and punt-return yardage, while also becoming, in 2001, the first Patriots player to record 100 receptions in a season. The ultimate team player, Brown did whatever the Patriots asked of him, even playing cornerback one year due to a rash of injuries the team experienced at the position. Extremely durable as well, Brown played in a total of 192 games before retiring at the conclusion of the 2007 campaign, placing him behind only Tom Brady, Bruce Armstrong, and Julius Adams in team annals. Meanwhile, his 15 years in New England ties him with Adams for the third-longest tenure in a Patriots uniform, with only Brady and Steve Grogan having spent more years with the club. Brown's versatility, longevity, and vast contributions to the Patriots through the years eventually earned him a spot on their 50th Anniversary Team and a place in their Hall of Fame.

Born in Barnwell, South Carolina, on July 2, 1971, Troy Fitzgerald Brown attended Hilda High School in nearby Blackville, where he lettered in football and track and field. After leading his high school football team to a state championship in 1988, Brown enrolled at Marshall University. While at Marshall, Brown excelled as a wide receiver and special teams player, leading all of Division I-AA football in both kickoff and punt return average in 1991, en route to posting a career kickoff return average of 29.69 yards that remains an NCAA record.

Selected by New England with the 198th overall pick of the 1993 NFL Draft following his graduation from Marshall, Brown saw his professional career get off to an inauspicious beginning when the Patriots cut him just prior to the start of the regular season. However, they re-signed him a little over one month later, after which Brown spent the remainder of the year playing on special teams, amassing a total of 489 all-purpose yards returning punts and kickoffs. After serving the Pats almost exclusively as a punt-returner in the nine games in which he appeared the following year, Brown began to garner more significant playing time in 1995. In addition to accumulating 672 yards on 31 kickoff returns, he made 14 receptions for 159 yards, while playing behind starting wide receivers Vincent Brisby and Will Moore. Although Brown continued to make his greatest contributions to the Patriots on special teams in 1996, amassing a total of 634 yards for the AFC champions as a kickoff-returner, he increased his offensive output to 21 receptions and 222 receiving yards.

Able to focus more extensively on developing his pass-receiving skills after having his special teams duties assigned to Dave Meggett prior to the start of the 1997 campaign, Brown assumed a much more prominent role in the Patriots' offense, making 41 receptions, for 607 yards and six touchdowns, despite serving the team primarily as a third receiver. Reassigned to special teams the following year, Brown received less playing time on offense, limiting him to just 23 catches, 346 receiving yards, and one touchdown. Yet, even though he assumed a similar role in 1999, Brown managed to amass a total of 1,147 all-purpose yards, gaining 676 of those on special teams and another 471 on 36 pass receptions.

Brown finally became a full-time member of the Patriots' starting offense in 2000, a season in which he caught 83 passes, for 944 yards and four touchdowns. He also gained more than 500 yards and scored a touchdown on special teams, giving him a total of 1,509 all-purpose yards and five touchdowns. Brown emerged as New England's primary offensive weapon the following year, teaming up with Tom Brady to lead the Pats to their first Super Bowl Championship. In addition to returning two punts for touchdowns, amassing 426 yards on special teams, and averaging a league-leading 14.2 yards per punt return, Brown made 101 receptions, for 1,199 yards and five touchdowns, en route to earning First-Team All-AFC and Pro Bowl honors for the only time in his career. He continued his outstanding play during the playoffs, leading the Patriots with 18 postseason receptions and returning a punt for a touchdown against Pittsburgh in the AFC Championship Game.

Brown had another big year in 2002, surpassing 1,000 all-purpose yards for the fourth straight time by accumulating 175 yards returning punts, while also making 97 receptions for 890 yards and three touchdowns. Limited by injuries to just 12 games in 2003, Brown caught only 40 passes, for 472 yards and four touchdowns, before taking on an even more diverse role the following year, when he spent much of the season serving as the Pats' nickel back after injuries ravaged the team's defensive secondary. In addition to making 17 receptions for 184 yards and one touchdown on offense, Brown returned 12 punts for 83 yards and finished second on the team with three interceptions.

Released by the Patriots for salary cap reasons on March 1, 2005, Brown re-signed with the team nearly three months later, after which he assumed a backup role the remainder of his career, totaling 82 receptions, 850 receiving yards, and six touchdowns from 2005 to 2006. He subsequently appeared in just one game in 2007, before officially announcing his retirement just prior to the start of the ensuing campaign. Brown ended his career with 557 receptions, 6,366 receiving yards, and 31 touchdown catches. He also carried the ball 29 times for 178 yards, returned three punts for touchdowns, and gained another 4,487 yards on special teams, giving him a total of 11,053 all-purpose yards that places him third in franchise history. In addition to returning more punts (252) for more yards (2,625) than any other player in Patriots history, Brown ranks among the team's all-time leaders in pass receptions, receiving yardage, and touchdown receptions. The Patriots qualified for the playoffs in 10 of his 15 years with the club, winning eight division titles, five conference championships, and three Super Bowls.

Elected to the Patriots Hall of Fame on June 4, 2012, Brown drew praise from Bill Belichick, who stated upon learning of the news, "I can't think of anybody more deserving to go in than him; special player. Came in very unheralded, worked his way up on the roster offensively, returned kicks, ended up playing for us defensively. He won championships, played at a very high level, and played his best football in big games."

Belichick continued, "Troy was a great leader. He worked as hard as anybody, unselfishly; always did what we asked him to do from a team standpoint, whether it was block, catch passes, return kicks, cover kicks, cover receivers. He truly was a good player in all three phases of the game, an outstanding player offensively and in the kicking game. Always did it for the good of the team and he was a big reason why we won a lot of games. You can never really replace a guy like that. He's just special."

Belichick concluded, "Troy Brown is the ultimate team player and one of the greatest competitors I have ever had the privilege of coaching. Offense, defense, special teams—if there was a job to do, Troy embraced it and did it at a championship level. No matter the situation or conditions, Troy raised the bar of excellence and helped create a winning tradition we strive to uphold. The bigger the game, the more Troy stepped up. There is no more deserving player of any accolade that comes his way than Troy Brown."

When asked what comes to mind when he thinks of Brown's career, Vince Wilfork suggested, "Leadership. You're talking about a leader on and off the field. He'd give you the shirt off his back. He's a helluva person, not just a football player. He's a great, great man and a helluva father . . . .You hear people talk all the time about what it means to be a Patriot. He's a walking Patriot. Every example of what this organization stands for, that's Troy Brown."

Meanwhile, in summing up Brown's career, Patriots chairman and CEO Robert Kraft stated:

> To me, Troy was the consummate Patriot who always put team goals ahead of personal ones. His height and speed made him a proverbial underdog in a league that always featured taller and faster players. But,

his heart and perseverance made him a champion and a fan favorite. The Patriots record books will always show that Troy was one of the greatest receivers and punt returners in franchise history, but Patriots fans know that he was so much more than that. His selfless contributions to the success of the team on offense, defense and special teams made him unique as a player and helped deliver three Super Bowl titles. For 15 years, Troy personified what it meant to be a Patriot, both on and off the field. With his induction into the Patriots Hall of Fame, his legacy will be preserved for generations to come.

CAREER HIGHLIGHTS

Best Season

Brown had his three most productive seasons for the Patriots in 2000, 2001, and 2002, making more than 80 receptions and gaining well in excess of 1,000 all-purpose yards in each of those years. In addition to catching 83 passes for 944 yards and four touchdowns in the first of those campaigns, Brown gained a career-high 504 yards on punt returns, accumulating in the process 1,509 all-purpose yards. Two years later, he made 97 receptions for 890 yards and three touchdowns, en route to amassing 1,079 all-purpose yards. However, Brown posted the best overall numbers of his career in 2001, when he earned his lone Pro Bowl selection by making 101 receptions for 1,199 yards and five touchdowns, carrying the ball 11 times for 91 yards, and returning 29 punts for 413 yards and two touchdowns. Brown's 101 receptions, which placed him fifth in the NFL rankings, established a new single-season franchise record (since broken). Meanwhile, his 14.2 yard punt return average and two punt returns for touchdowns both led the league.

Memorable Moments/Greatest Performances

Brown scored the first touchdown of his career on special teams, racing 75 yards after recovering a fumble during a 31-28 victory over the New York Jets on December 10, 1995.

Brown had his breakout game as a wide receiver on September 21, 1997, making six receptions for 124 yards and one touchdown during a 31-3 pasting of the Chicago Bears. Brown scored his TD on a 52-yard hookup with quarterback Drew Bledsoe in the second quarter. Although the Patriots lost their matchup with the Jets four weeks later 24-19, Brown had another big day, scoring a touchdown and making five receptions for 125 yards, including a season-long 67-yard catch-and-run.

After the Patriots started out the 2000 season 0-4, Brown helped them earn their first victory of the year in Week 5 by scoring two first-quarter touchdowns during a 28-19 win over the Denver Broncos. After connecting with Drew Bledsoe on TD passes that covered 11 and 44 yards, Brown went on to finish the game with five receptions for 108 yards. Brown helped the Pats improve their record to 4-9 later in the year, when he made a season-high 12 catches, for 119 yards and one touchdown, during a 30-24 victory over the Kansas City Chiefs on December 4, 2000.

The Patriots got off to a similarly slow start in 2001, winning just one of their first four games. However, Brown helped the eventual Super Bowl champions right themselves in Week 5, leading them to a 29-26 overtime win over the San Diego Chargers by making 11 receptions for 117 yards and returning one punt for 40 yards. Particularly effective during the final few minutes of regulation, Brown allowed the Patriots to begin their game-tying touchdown drive in excellent field position by returning a Darren Bennett punt to near midfield. He then made three receptions for 31 yards, before Tom Brady hit Jermaine Wiggins with a three-yard TD pass that tied the score at 26-26 with less than a minute left in the fourth quarter. Brown also played a pivotal role in the Patriots' 38-17 win over Indianapolis the following week, making eight receptions for 120 yards, and hauling in a 60-yard TD pass from fellow wide receiver David Patten on a reverse play.

Brown established a franchise record by making 16 receptions during a 41-38 overtime win over the Kansas City Chiefs on September 22, 2002, finishing the game with 176 yards and one touchdown.

Brown experienced one of his most memorable moments on October 19, 2003, when he teamed up with Tom Brady on an 82-yard TD pass play with 5:57 remaining in overtime to give the Patriots a 19-13 victory over the Miami Dolphins.

Brown returned four punts for touchdowns over the course of his career, with his first such score coming during a 21-16 loss to the Tampa Bay Buccaneers in the opening game of the 2000 campaign. Brown's 66-yard return midway through the second quarter of that contest gave the Patriots their first touchdown of the year. Brown scored in similar fashion on December 9, 2001, when he returned a Chris Gardocki punt 85 yards during a 27-16 victory over the Cleveland Browns. He returned another punt for a TD just four weeks later, scoring from 68 yards out during a 38-6 victory over the Carolina Panthers in the regular-season finale.

However, Brown saved his most memorable return for the 2001 AFC Championship Game against Pittsburgh, when he gave the Patriots an early lead by returning a Josh Miller punt 55 yards for the game's first score. In one of his finest all-around performances, Brown helped lead New England to a 24-17 victory by making eight receptions for 121 yards, returning three punts for 80 yards, and assisting on the Pats' final touchdown by scooping up a loose ball following a blocked field goal attempt by Steelers' place-kicker Kris Brown and making a lateral pass to teammate Antwan Harris, who completed the 49-yard scoring play.

Brown followed up his exceptional performance in the AFC Championship Game with another strong effort against the St. Louis Rams in Super Bowl XXXVI, making six receptions for 89 yards, including a key 23-yard grab on the game-winning drive.

Brown again came up big in Super Bowl XXXVIII, helping the Patriots defeat Carolina, 32-29, by making eight receptions for 76 yards, returning four punts for 40 yards, and gaining 43 yards on three pass receptions during New England's game-winning drive that began with just 1:08 remaining in regulation.

Brown experienced one final moment of glory in the 2006 divisional playoffs, when he helped the Patriots overcome a 21-13 fourth-quarter deficit to the favored San Diego Chargers by forcing a key fumble with just under five minutes remaining in the contest. Following a Marlon McCree interception that appeared to seal the game for San Diego, Brown stripped the ball from McCree, allowing Reche Caldwell to recover the fumble and return possession to the Patriots, who subsequently tied the score with a touchdown and two-point conversion, before winning the game on a Stephen Gostkowski field goal with just over one minute left on the clock.

NOTABLE ACHIEVEMENTS

- Caught more than 80 passes three times, topping 100 receptions once (101 in 2001).
- Surpassed 1,000 receiving yards once (1,199 in 2001).
- Accumulated more than 1,000 all-purpose yards four times.
- Returned three punts for touchdowns.
- Led NFL with 14.2 punt-return average and two punt-return touchdowns in 2001.
- Finished fifth in NFL with 101 receptions in 2001.

- Holds Patriots career records for most punt returns (252) and most punt-return yards (2,625).
- Ranks among Patriots all-time leaders in: pass receptions (2nd); receiving yardage (3rd); all-purpose yards (3rd); and touchdown receptions (9th).
- Five-time AFC champion (1996, 2001, 2003, 2004 & 2007).
- Three-time Super Bowl champion (XXXVI, XXXVIII & XXXIX).
- 2001 Pro Bowl selection.
- 2001 First-Team All-AFC selection.
- 1998 Ed Block Courage Award winner.
- Member of Patriots' 2000s All-Decade Team.
- Named to Patriots' 50th Anniversary Team in 2009.
- Inducted into Patriots Hall of Fame in 2012.

10

Nick Buoniconti

Nick Buoniconti (51) and Tom Addison (53) at the 1964 AFL All-Star Game
(Courtesy Tales from the American Football League)

Although he is perhaps remembered more for his time with the Miami Dolphins, Nick Buoniconti spent the first half of his career in Boston, anchoring the Patriots' defense for seven seasons from his middle linebacker position, before moving on to Miami, where he helped lead the Dolphins to consecutive NFL championships in 1972 and 1973. Starting all but one game for the Patriots in his first six years with them, the man once considered by NFL scouts as "too small" to succeed at the professional level proved to be a tower of strength in the middle, calling the team's defensive signals, while also doing an exceptional job of dropping into pass coverage and defending against the run. Eventually named to the AFL's All-Time Team, primarily on the strength of his performance during his time in Boston, Buoniconti earned First-Team All-Pro honors four straight times as a member of the Patriots. He also appeared in five consecutive AFL All-Star Games before leaving for Miami, earning in the process a place in the Patriots' Hall of Fame and a spot on their 50th Anniversary Team.

Born in Springfield, Massachusetts, on December 15, 1940, Nicholas Anthony Buoniconti attended local Cathedral High School before enrolling at Notre Dame University, where he spent his college career playing defensive tackle. After earning Second-Team All-America honors as a senior while serving as co-captain of the *Fighting Irish* in 1961, Buoniconti went undrafted by the NFL, whose scouts considered his 5'11", 220-pound frame too small to make him a legitimate pro prospect. Yet, even though his own coach at Notre Dame had reservations about Buoniconti's ability to succeed at the next level, several other coaches later noted that he "played bigger than his size."

Finally selected by the Boston Patriots in the 13th round of the 1962 AFL Draft, with the 102nd overall pick, Buoniconti entered the infant league with a huge chip on his shoulder. After being shifted to middle linebacker, he made an immediate impact on the Patriots, helping them compile the same 9-4-1 record they posted the previous season, even though they scored almost 70 fewer points on offense. Buoniconti's strong performance prompted the Patriots to name him their rookie of the year, and the UPI to accord him Second-Team All-AFL honors. The following season, Buoniconti led a defense that finished second in the league in points allowed. Boston also surrendered fewer total yards to the opposition than any other team in the league, helping Buoniconti earn a spot on the AFL-East All-Star squad for the first of five consecutive times and Second-Team All-AFL honors once again.

Recognized as the AFL's best middle linebacker by his third year in the league, Buoniconti began in 1964 a string of four straight seasons in which he received consensus First-Team All-Pro honors, even though the Patriots' defense slipped to the bottom half of the league rankings by the end of the period. An excellent run-defender, Buoniconti perhaps played even better against the pass, accumulating a total of 16 interceptions over the course of that four-year stretch, including a career-high 5 picks in 1964. His total of 24 interceptions as a member of the Patriots continues to place him among the franchise's all-time leaders. Buoniconti also did an outstanding job of rushing the passer, amassing a total of 18 quarterback sacks during his time in Boston. Absolutely relentless in his pursuit of opposing quarterbacks and running backs, Buoniconti drew praise from Chiefs Hall of Fame signal-caller Len Dawson, who said of his adversary, "If you are lucky enough to knock him down, you have to lay on him or he'll get right back into the play."

In discussing the intensity with which he approached each play, Buoniconti explained, "Every play is like life or death. I can't think of anything except the play that is taking place at the moment."

In spite of Buoniconti's aggressive on-field mentality, he remained an extremely cerebral player, serving as the Patriots' quarterback on defense his entire time in Boston. Quite intelligent off the field as well, Buoniconti earned his law degree while playing for the Patriots by taking night classes at Suffolk University.

After being selected to appear in the Pro Bowl in each of the five previous seasons, Buoniconti failed to earn All-Star honors in 1968 when an injury sidelined him for six games. Nevertheless, he finished third on the Patriots with 3 interceptions, en route to earning Second-Team All-AFL honors from UPI.

Subsequently dealt to the Dolphins at the conclusion of the 1968 campaign, Buoniconti spent his final seven seasons spearheading Miami's "No Name Defense." Serving as the veteran presence on a young Miami team that entered the AFL just three seasons earlier, Buoniconti quickly established himself as the club's foremost leader, calling out all the defensive signals, imparting to his younger teammates his vast knowledge of the intricacies of the sport, and teaching them how to win. Before long, the Dolphins became one of the NFL's most successful franchises, improving their record in each of the next four seasons until finally posting the only undefeated mark in league history in 1972, when they finished a perfect 17-0, winning their first of two straight Super Bowls.

Buoniconti remained one of the NFL's most respected players during his time in Miami, earning two more All-Pro selections and three more Pro Bowl nominations. He had his best year for the Dolphins in 1973, when he won the team's Most Valuable Player Award for one of three times by making a then-franchise record 162 tackles, 91 of which were unassisted. Age and injuries finally began to catch up to Buoniconti in 1976, forcing the 36-year-old veteran to announce his retirement at season's end, after he started just 4 games over the course of the campaign. He ended his career with 32 interceptions, an "unofficial" total of 24 quarterback sacks, eight

Pro Bowl selections, five First-Team All-Pro nominations, and four Second-Team selections.

Following his playing career, Buoniconti became a practicing attorney for a short period of time, before serving as president of the US Tobacco Company during the late 1970s and early 1980s. In that position, he proved to be a leading critic of studies that showed that smokeless tobacco caused various types of cancer. Buoniconti subsequently became the public face of the group that founded the Miami Project to Cure Paralysis after his son Marc suffered a paralyzing spinal cord injury while making a tackle for The Citadel in 1985. He also spent several years serving as co-host of the HBO series *Inside the NFL*, finally relinquishing his position in 2001—the same year the Pro Football Hall of Fame inducted him into its ranks.

PATRIOT CAREER HIGHLIGHTS

Best Season

It could be argued that Buoniconti played his best ball for the Patriots in 1964, when he earned the first of his four straight First-Team All-AFL selections by leading a defense that finished second in the league in points allowed (297), and that also placed fourth in the circuit in total yardage surrendered to the opposition. The middle linebacker established career highs with 5 interceptions and 75 return yards over the course of the campaign, helping the Patriots compile an exceptional 10-3-1 record in the process. Nevertheless, the feeling here is that Buoniconti had his finest all-around season in 1966. Although the Patriots won two fewer games (8-4-2) and finished towards the middle of the league rankings in points (3rd) and total yards allowed (5th), they actually surrendered 14 fewer points (287) to their opponents than they did two years earlier. Meanwhile, Buoniconti, who intercepted 4 passes, which he returned for 43 yards, garnered more votes for the AFL All-Star Game than any other player in the league in 1966.

Memorable Moments/Greatest Performances

Buoniconti made a key play in Week 3 of the 1963 season, securing a 20-14 Patriots victory over the Raiders by ending a last-minute Oakland drive with an interception of quarterback Tom Flores. The pick, which was Buoniconti's second of the game, prevented the Patriots from blowing a 20-0 fourth-quarter lead.

Later that same year, Buoniconti led a ferocious Patriots defense to a 26-8 mauling of the Buffalo Bills in the AFL Eastern Division Championship Game. Boston's swarming defense allowed Buffalo's star running back Cookie Gilchrist a total of only 7 yards on 8 rushing attempts, preventing him on three separate occasions from gaining a first down when he needed just one yard to move the chains. Buoniconti hit Gilchrist so hard on one of those attempts that he lifted the running back off the ground.

Although the Patriots posted just four victories in 1968, they notched two of those wins against the Buffalo Bills, with Buoniconti turning in one of his finest performances in the second contest. The Patriots evened their record at 3-3 with a 23-6 win over the Bills at Fenway Park on October 20, with Buoniconti leading the way by intercepting three Dan Darragh passes.

NOTABLE ACHIEVEMENTS

- Tied for eighth all-time on Patriots with 24 career interceptions.
- 1963 AFL Eastern Division champion.
- Five-time AFL Pro Bowl selection (1963, 1964, 1965, 1966 & 1967).
- Four-time First-Team All-AFL selection (1964, 1965, 1966 & 1967).
- 1963 Second-Team All-AFL selection.
- Member of All-Time All-AFL Team.
- AFL Hall of Fame All-1960s First Team.
- Pro Football Reference AFL 1960s All-Decade First Team.
- Named to Patriots' 50th Anniversary Team in 2009.
- Inducted into Patriots Hall of Fame in 1992.
- Elected to Pro Football Hall of Fame in 2001.

11

Bob Dee

Bob Dee (89) and Jim Lee Hunt (79)
(Courtesy Tales from the American Football League)

A New Englander through and through, Bob Dee grew up in Braintree, Massachusetts, and played his college ball at the College of the Holy Cross, located in Worcester, Massachusetts. One of the first players signed by the Patriots after they joined the newly-formed AFL in 1960, Dee went on to establish himself as one of the league's true ironmen, starting every game for the Pats over the course of the next eight seasons, before electing to announce his retirement at the conclusion of the 1967 campaign. An outstanding defensive end, Dee earned four Second-Team All-AFL selections and appeared in four AFL All-Star Games during his time in Boston, en route to earning a spot on the Pro Football Reference All-1960s First Team and a place in the Patriots Hall of Fame.

Born in Quincy, Massachusetts, on May 18, 1933, Robert Henry Dee grew up in nearby Braintree, where he attended high school before enrolling at the College of the Holy Cross. A three-sport star in college, Dee waited to hear his name called until the 19th round of the 1955 NFL Draft, when the Washington Redskins finally selected him with the 220th overall pick. The young defensive end saw very little action over the course of the next three seasons, failing to make a single appearance in 1956, and serving almost exclusively as a backup in both 1957 and 1958. Unhappy with his situation in Washington, Dee chose to leave professional football in 1959 to return to Holy Cross, where he spent the next year coaching the linemen at his alma mater.

Dee's future plans changed dramatically shortly thereafter when the Boston Patriots of the newly formed American Football League offered him a chance to return to the professional ranks in 1960. After earning a starting job on the defensive line during the preseason, Dee went on to serve as one of the Patriots' defensive captains in their inaugural season. Although the Patriots struggled somewhat in their first year in the new league, compiling a record of just 5-9, they soon developed into one of the circuit's stronger clubs, with their exceptional defensive line proving to be their greatest strength. Dee, who led the unit from his spot at left end, played alongside left tackle Jim Lee Hunt, right tackle Houston Antwine, and right end Larry Eisenhauer, giving the Patriots the AFL's most imposing defensive front. While Hunt and Antwine provided pressure up the middle, Dee and Eisenhauer helped dominate opposing lines from their posts on the outside.

Dee, considered to be somewhat undersized at 6'3½" and 248 pounds, stressed a finesse game, preferring to use his quickness and outstanding moves to overcome blockers, rather than employing brute force. In fact, he possessed such outstanding foot speed that the Patriots often dropped him into pass coverage, allowing their linebackers to rush the opposing quarterback instead.

Dee earned Second-Team All-AFL honors in each of his first three seasons, before being accorded the same honor for the final time in 1964, when he helped lead the Patriots to an exceptional mark of 10-3-1 that nevertheless failed to earn them a playoff berth. He also appeared in the AFL All-Star Game in 1961 and in each season from 1963 to 1965. During that time, Dee demonstrated his tremendous durability, continuing to build on his reputation as one of the sport's true ironmen by starting 112 consecutive games for the Patriots. An extremely superstitious player as well, Dee insisted on wearing the same helmet throughout his career, donning it for virtually all of the 112 games he played.

Citing a business opportunity he considered "too good to resist," Dee announced his retirement at only 34 years of age after the Patriots finished just 3-10-1 in 1967. He left the game having accumulated an "unofficial" total of 33 quarterback sacks over the course of his career. In addition to his four Second-Team All-AFL selections and four All-Star Game nominations, Dee eventually earned a spot on the Patriots' All-1960s Team.

Unfortunately, Dee lived only another 11 years after he retired, passing away on April 18, 1979, after suffering a heart attack while on a business trip. He was one month shy of his 45th birthday. The Patriots later retired his number 89 and inducted him into their Hall of Fame, doing so on August 18, 1993.

PATRIOT CAREER HIGHLIGHTS

Best Season

Although Dee earned Second-Team All-Pro honors four times over the course of his career, the 1961 campaign would have to be considered his finest. In addition to making All-Pro and appearing in the Pro Bowl in the same season for one of only two times (he also accomplished the feat in 1964), Dee led the AFL with 5 fumble recoveries and helped the Patriots raise their record from 5-9 the previous season to 9-4-1 by improving their defense to the point that it placed third in the league rankings (it finished fifth in 1960). Furthermore, Dee's leadership helped rookies Larry Eisenhauer and Houston Antwine rapidly develop into forces along the defensive front.

Memorable Moments/Greatest Performances

Dee attained a level of immortality on July 30, 1960, when he scored the first touchdown in AFL history. With the Patriots facing the Buffalo Bills in the league's first exhibition game, Dee dove onto a second-quarter fumble by Bills quarterback Tommy O'Connell in the end zone, giving his team a 7-0 lead. The Patriots went on to win the contest 28-7.

Dee played exceptionally well during a 34-17 Patriots win over the Houston Oilers on November 29, 1964, being presented with a game ball at the conclusion of the contest for applying constant pressure to Oiler quarterbacks George Blanda and Don Trull. In addition to leading a Boston defense that surrendered only 44 yards on the ground to Houston, Dee helped the Patriots register 7 sacks and 4 interceptions.

Dee made a huge impact during Boston's 26-8 Eastern Division Playoff Game win over the Buffalo Bills on December 28, 1963. Playing at snow-covered War Memorial Stadium in Buffalo, Dee improved his traction by wearing one sneaker and one football shoe with spikes. Dee's increased maneuverability enabled him to intercept 2 passes, with his second pick early in the fourth quarter leading to a Gino Cappelletti field goal that gave the Patriots an insurmountable lead that all but clinched a spot in the AFL title game for the Patriots.

NOTABLE ACHIEVEMENTS

- Scored first touchdown in AFL history.
- Started 112 consecutive games.
- Led AFL with 5 fumble recoveries in 1961.
- 1963 AFL Eastern Division champion.
- Four-time AFL Pro Bowl selection (1961, 1963, 1964 & 1965).
- Four-time Second-Team All-AFL selection (1960, 1961, 1962 & 1964).
- Pro Football Reference AFL 1960s All-Decade First Team.
- Number 89 retired by Patriots.
- Inducted into Patriots Hall of Fame in 1993.

12

Drew Bledsoe

(Courtesy George A. Kitrinos)

Widely recognized as the greatest quarterback in Patriots history prior to the arrival of Tom Brady, Drew Bledsoe spent eight years guiding the Patriots' offense before giving way to Tom Terrific in 2001. Blessed with a powerful throwing arm and tremendous natural ability, Bledsoe established himself as the face of the Patriots franchise from 1993 to 2000, after being selected by them with the first overall pick of the 1993 NFL Draft. During that time, Bledsoe led the Pats to four playoff appearances, two division titles, and one trip to the Super Bowl, setting numerous team records along the way. In addition to establishing new career passing records for most attempts (4,518), completions (2,544), and yards (29,657) by a Patriots quarterback, Bledsoe set a still-standing single-season franchise record by attempting 691 passes in 1994. Unfortunately for Bledsoe, his failure to guide New England to a Super Bowl championship has made him a mere afterthought in the minds of most Patriots fans, who have since had the good fortune to spend the past 14 years watching arguably the finest "big-game" quarterback of this generation lead their team to 12 AFC East titles and four NFL championships. Nevertheless, Bledsoe accomplished enough during his time in New England to eventually gain induction into the Patriots Hall of Fame and earn a lofty spot in these rankings.

Born in Ellensburg, Washington, on February 14, 1972, Drew McQueen Bledsoe attended Walla Walla High School, where he lettered in football, basketball, and track, competing in the discus and javelin throws in the latter sport. After being named a First-Team All-State selection in football by the *Tacoma News Tribune*, Bledsoe enrolled at Washington State University. He spent the next three years starring at quarterback for the Cougars, setting several school records during that time. Named the Pac-10 Offensive Player of the Year for leading his team to a 9-3 record as a junior, Bledsoe elected to forego his final year of collegiate eligibility and enter the NFL Draft. With the Patriots having concluded the previous campaign with a league-worst 2-14 record, they held the rights to the first overall pick of the 1993 Draft, which they used to select Bledsoe.

Bledsoe made an immediate impact in New England, going 5-7 in his 12 starts, to help the Patriots improve their record to 5-11. Although he completed just 50 percent of his passes, the Washington native had a solid rookie season, passing for 2,494 yards and 15 touchdowns, throwing 15 interceptions, and posting a quarterback rating of 65.0. Despite tossing a league-leading 27 interceptions the following year, Bledsoe emerged as one of the AFC's top quarterbacks in his sophomore campaign of 1994. In addition to setting a new single-season NFL record by attempting 691 passes, he became just the second NFL quarterback to complete as many as 400 passes in a season, joining Warren Moon on an extremely exclusive list. Connecting on 57.9 percent of his pass attempts, Bledsoe also finished first in the league with 4,555 passing yards, placed fourth with 25 TD passes, and raised his quarterback rating to 73.6, en route to earning Second-Team All-AFC honors and his first Pro Bowl selection. His strong performance helped lead the Patriots to a 10-6 record, enabling them to advance to the playoffs for the first time in eight years.

Bledsoe's production fell off considerably in 1995, contributing to the Patriots' poor 6-10 record. In addition to completing just 50.8 percent of his passes, the third-year quarterback amassed 1,000 fewer yards through the air (3,507) than he did the previous season, tossed only 13 touchdown passes, and posted a quarterback rating of just 63.7. However, Bledsoe rebounded the following year to lead the Pats to their second Super Bowl appearance. In addition to leading all NFL quarterbacks with 623 pass attempts and 373 completions, Bledsoe placed among the league leaders with 4,086 passing yards, 27 touchdown passes, a 59.9 completion percentage, and a quarterback rating of 83.7. His outstanding play earned him Pro Bowl and Second-Team All-AFC honors for the second time each.

The arrival of Terry Glenn in New England contributed greatly to the success Bledsoe and the Patriots experienced in 1996. The rookie wide receiver made 90 receptions for 1,132 yards, giving the Pats a legitimate deep threat for the first time in Bledsoe's young career. Nevertheless, Bledsoe deserves most of the credit for the team's turnaround, maturing into one of the league's top quarterbacks and a true team leader over the course of the campaign. Blessed with good size and a strong throwing arm, the 6'5", 238-pound Bledsoe possessed all the physical tools needed to succeed at the pro level from the time he first entered the league. However, he began to display a greater sense of awareness and an increasing knowledge of opposing defenses in 1996, making him a far more effective quarterback.

After leading the Patriots past Pittsburgh and Jacksonville in the AFC playoffs, Bledsoe came up short against Brett Favre and the Packers in Super Bowl XXXI, throwing four interceptions during a 35-21 loss to Green Bay. He rebounded once again the following year, though, leading the Pats to their second straight AFC East title by finishing among the league's leading quarterbacks with 3,706 passing yards, 28 touchdown passes, a 60.2 completion percentage, and a career-high 87.7 passer rating, en route to earning Pro Bowl honors for the third time.

The free agent departure of star running back Curtis Martin at the conclusion of the 1997 campaign subsequently forced Bledsoe to shoulder more of the team's offensive burden, causing him to regress somewhat the following year. Nevertheless, Bledsoe continued to post solid numbers, finishing the season with 3,633 passing yards, 20 touchdown passes, 14 interceptions, a 54.7 completion percentage, and a quarterback rating of 80.9. Bledsoe's job became even more difficult in 1999, when the Patriots began rebuilding their aging offensive line. With a number of younger, less-experienced players being assigned the task of protecting him, the somewhat immobile Bledsoe suffered the indignity of being sacked a total of 100 times between 1999 and 2000. Still, he remained one of the AFC's more productive quarterbacks, passing for 3,985 yards and 19 touchdowns in the first of those campaigns, before passing for 3,291 yards and 17 touchdowns in the second.

Despite signing a then-record 10-year, $103 million contract with the Patriots in March 2001, Bledsoe started just two more games for them at quarterback. Injured during the second game of the season when New York Jets linebacker Mo Lewis delivered a vicious hit to him, shearing a blood vessel in his chest, Bledsoe spent the next several games on the sidelines watching second-year QB Tom Brady assume control of the team's offense. Unable to regain his starting job once healthy due to the success of Brady, who led the Patriots to victories in 11 of their next 14 games, Bledsoe remained a spectator during New England's 16-13 overtime win against Oakland in the first round of the playoffs. However, he suddenly found himself pressed into action when Brady suffered an injury during the early stages of the Conference Championship Game against Pittsburgh. Taking the field for the first time in four months, Bledsoe delivered an 11-yard scoring pass to David Patten late in the second quarter, giving the Patriots their only offensive touchdown of a game they eventually won by a score of 24-17.

After Brady subsequently led the Patriots to a 20-17 victory over the St. Louis Rams in Super Bowl XXXVI, Bledsoe asked to be traded to another team. Wishing to grant the veteran quarterback's request since he had remained supportive of Brady and the Patriots throughout their Super Bowl run, the Pats dealt Bledsoe to the Buffalo Bills, who had finished the previous campaign just 3-13 with veterans Alex Van Pelt and Rob Johnson splitting time at quarterback.

The change in scenery did wonders for Bledsoe, who led the Bills to an 8-8 record in 2002 by having one of his finest statistical seasons. In addition to posting a career-high 61.5 completion percentage, Bledsoe placed among the league leaders with 4,359 passing yards, 24 touchdown passes, and a passer rating of 86.0, en route to earning the last of his four Pro Bowl selections. He remained in Buffalo two more years, experiencing a moderate amount of success, before being released by the Bills following the 2004 campaign in order to allow second-year quarterback J.P. Losman to assume control of the team's offense.

Bledsoe subsequently signed a three-year, $23 million deal with the Dallas Cowboys, where he reunited with Bill Parcells, who had served as the Patriots' head coach his first four years in New England. Bledsoe played well for the Cowboys in 2005, passing for 3,639 yards and 23 touchdowns, and leading a team that finished just 6-10 the previous season to a record of 9-7. However, with Bledsoe struggling somewhat during the early stages of the ensuing campaign, the Cowboys replaced him with Tony Romo, once again relegating the veteran QB to backup duties. Released by the Cowboys at season's end, the 34-year-old Bledsoe faced the prospect of spending the remainder of his career coming off the bench. Instead, he chose to retire, making his decision official on April 11, 2007. Upon his retirement, Bledsoe ranked fifth all-time among NFL quarterbacks in pass attempts (6,717) and pass completions (3,839). He also ranked seventh in passing yards (44,611) and 13th in touchdown passes (251).

Subsequently criticized by some, including sportswriter Don Banks, who suggested that his rather impressive career totals "reveal more about his longevity than about his excellence," Bledsoe nevertheless ranked 30th on *Football Nation*'s July 2012 listing of the NFL's greatest quarterbacks of the post-merger era.

Following his retirement, Bledsoe and his close friend Chris Figgins founded the Doubleback Winery, a vineyard in Walla Walla, Washington, that continues to produce fine wine for satisfied customers throughout the nation. Bledsoe also later became the offensive coordinator/quarterbacks coach at Summit High School in Bend, Oregon.

PATRIOT CAREER HIGHLIGHTS

Best Season

Bledsoe compiled the most prolific passing numbers of his Patriots career in 1994, when he established a new NFL record (since broken) by attempting 691 passes, led the league with 400 completions and 4,555 passing yards, and threw 25 touchdown passes. However, he also led all NFL quarterbacks with 27 interceptions and posted a rather mediocre passer rating of 73.6. Bledsoe actually performed better in both 1996 and 1997, when he earned his second and third Pro Bowl selections. In addition to leading the NFL in pass attempts (623) and pass completions (373) in the first of those campaigns, Bledsoe ranked among the league leaders with 4,086 passing yards, 27 touchdown passes, a 59.9 completion percentage, and a quarterback rating of 83.7. He also threw only 15 interceptions. Bledsoe again threw 15 interceptions and placed near the top of the league rankings in each of the other categories in 1997, when he passed for 3,706 yards, compiled a 60.2 completion percentage, and established career highs with 28 touchdown passes and a quarterback rating of 87.7. It's an extremely close call, but we'll opt for 1996 since Bledsoe led the Patriots to the AFC Championship and a berth in the Super Bowl that year.

Memorable Moments/Greatest Performances

In addition to coming off the bench to lead the Patriots to victory in the 2001 AFC Championship Game, Bledsoe turned in a number of other memorable performances during his time in New England. He had the first truly big game of his career in the 1993 regular-season finale, completing 27 of 43 passes, for 329 yards and 4 touchdowns, during a 33-27 overtime win over the Miami Dolphins. The rookie quarterback's 36-yard TD pass to Michael Timpson in OT gave the Patriots their fifth victory of the season.

Although the Patriots ended up losing their 1994 season opener to Miami by a score of 39-35, Bledsoe had another huge game, completing 32 of 51 passes, for 421 yards and 4 touchdowns. After the Pats opened the scoring in the first quarter with a one-yard run by Kevin Turner, Bledsoe accounted for their other four touchdowns, hooking up with Michael Timpson on a five-yard scoring play, Ray Crittenden from 23 yards out, and twice with Ben Coates, once from 16 yards out, and, again, from 63 yards out.

Bledsoe followed that up with another solid effort, this time passing for 380 yards and 3 touchdowns during a 38-35 loss to the Buffalo Bills. In addition to completing a 21-yard TD pass to Michael Timpson, Bledsoe again tossed a pair of touchdown passes to Ben Coates, connecting with his tight end from 18 and 5 yards out.

Later that same year, Bledsoe helped the Patriots completely turn around their season when he led them to a memorable comeback win over the Minnesota Vikings on November 13, 1994. Having won just three of their first nine games, the Pats appeared to be on the verge of falling to 3-7 when they trailed Minnesota 20-3 at halftime. However, after switching to a no-huddle offense, they scored 17 second-half points to tie the score at 20-20, before winning the game in overtime when Bledsoe threw a 14-yard TD pass to Kevin Turner. Bledsoe finished the game with 45 pass completions in 70 attempts, for 426 yards and 3 touchdowns. His 45 completions and 70 attempts both established new single-game NFL records. The Patriots subsequently won their six remaining games as well, enabling them to advance to the playoffs as a wild card with a record of 10-6.

Bledsoe had a number of outstanding games during New England's successful run to the 1996 AFC Championship, with the first of those coming on October 6, when he passed for 310 yards and 4 touchdowns during a 46-38 win over the Baltimore Ravens. Three weeks later, Bledsoe completed 32 of 45 passes, for 373 yards and one touchdown, in leading the Patriots to a hard-fought 28-25 home win over the Buffalo Bills. The very next week, during a 42-23 trouncing of the Miami Dolphins on November 3, Bledsoe completed 30 of 41 passes, for 419 yards and 3 touchdowns. One of his TD passes—an 84-yarder to Ben Coates—proved to be the second-longest of his career. Bledsoe continued his success against San Diego the following week, leading the Patriots to a 45-7 victory over the Chargers by tossing another 4 touchdown passes—one each to Terry Glenn (8 yards), Keith Byars (19 yards), Sam Gash (7 yards), and Shawn Jefferson (11 yards).

Bledsoe had his biggest game of the 1997 campaign in the regular-season opener, once again torching the San Diego secondary, this time for 340 yards and 4 touchdowns, during a 41-7 Patriots win.

Bledsoe displayed his toughness in 1998 when, despite playing with a broken finger, he helped save the Patriots' season by leading them to late fourth-quarter comebacks in consecutive weeks against division rivals Miami and Buffalo. In the first of those contests, played against Miami on November 23, Bledsoe completed a 25-yard touchdown pass to Shawn Jefferson with only 34 seconds remaining in regulation, to give the Pats a 26-23 victory. The very next week, he completed a one-yard TD pass to Ben Coates as time expired, giving the Patriots a 25-21 win over the Bills.

Even though opposing defenses put a considerable amount of pressure on Bledsoe throughout the 1999 campaign, forcing him to endure a career-high 55 sacks, he still managed to turn in a number of notable performances. After the Patriots fell behind the Indianapolis Colts and second-year quarterback Peyton Manning 28-7 at halftime in the second game of the season, Bledsoe led them on a furious second-half comeback that resulted in a 31-28 victory. He finished the game with 299 yards passing and 4 touchdown passes. During a 19-7 victory over Cleveland on October 3, Bledsoe passed for 393 yards and one touchdown, hooking up with Terry Glenn on a 54-yard scoring play at the start of the fourth quarter. Four weeks later, Bledsoe led the Patriots to a lopsided 27-3 win over the Arizona Cardinals by passing for 276 yards and 4 touchdowns. In addition to throwing TD passes of 3 and 36 yards to Lamont Warren and Terry Glenn, respectively, Bledsoe connected twice with Shawn Jefferson, once from 64 yards out, and, again, from 35 yards out.

Bledsoe had his last big day for the Patriots on October 1, 2000, when he passed for 271 yards and 4 touchdowns during a 28-19 win over the Broncos in Denver.

NOTABLE ACHIEVEMENTS

- Passed for more than 3,000 yards seven times, topping 4,000 yards twice (1994 & 1996).
- First Patriots quarterback to pass for more than 4,000 yards in a season.
- Surpassed 20 touchdown passes four times.
- Completed more than 60 percent of passes twice.
- Led NFL quarterbacks in: passing yardage once; pass completions twice; and pass attempts three times.
- Ranks among Patriots all-time leaders in: passing yardage (2nd); pass completions (2nd); pass attempts (2nd); touchdown passes (3rd); completion percentage (3rd); and quarterback rating (3rd).
- Two-time AFC champion (1996 & 2001).
- Super Bowl XXXVI champion.
- Three-time Pro Bowl selection (1994, 1996 & 1997).
- Two-time Second-Team All-AFC selection (1994 & 1996).
- Member of Patriots' 1990s All-Decade Team.
- Inducted into Patriots Hall of Fame in 2011.

13

Wes Welker

(Courtesy Aaron Frutman of DGA Productions)

Considered by most pro scouts to be too small and slow to succeed at the NFL level, Wes Welker signed as a free agent with San Diego after no team selected him in the 2004 NFL Draft following his graduation from Texas Tech University. However, after being cut by the Chargers and joining the Miami Dolphins, with whom he spent the next three seasons primarily returning kickoffs and punts, Welker went on to establish himself as arguably the league's top slot receiver as a member of the New England

Patriots. Playing for the Pats from 2007 to 2012, Welker caught more than 100 passes and surpassed 1,000 receiving yards five times each, leading the league in pass receptions on three separate occasions. Along the way, he set franchise records for most career pass receptions (672), most catches in a season (123), and most pass receiving yards in a season (1,569). The first receiver in NFL history to catch as many as 100 passes five times, Welker also ranks among the Patriots all-time leaders in pass receiving yardage, all-purpose yards, and touchdown receptions. Welker contributed significantly to two AFC championship teams during his time in New England, earning in the process five Pro Bowl nominations and four All-Pro selections. The diminutive receiver's outstanding play also earned him a spot on the Patriots' 2000s All-Decade Team.

Born in Oklahoma City, Oklahoma, on May 1, 1981, Wesley Welker began his football career at Heritage Hall High School, where he helped lead his team to the 2A State Football championship as a junior by excelling on offense, defense, and special teams. Displaying a tremendous amount of versatility, Welker not only starred for Heritage Hall at running back and defensive back, but he also shone as a punt returner and placekicker, once converting a 58-yard field goal attempt. After being named All-State Player of the Year by the *Daily Oklahoman* and Oklahoma State Player of the Year by *USA Today*, Welker enrolled at Texas Tech University. While playing for the Red Raiders the next four years, Welker made 259 receptions for 3,019 yards and 21 touchdowns, rushed for another 456 yards and two touchdowns, and tied an NCAA record by returning eight punts for touchdowns, earning in the process the 2003 Mosi Tatupu Award, presented annually to the best special teams player in college football.

Yet, in spite of Welker's outstanding play at the collegiate level, his 5'9", 190-pound frame and lack of superior running speed scared off most pro scouts, causing all 32 teams to bypass him in the 2004 NFL Draft. Welker subsequently signed with the San Diego Chargers as a free agent, but remained on their roster for just one game before being released after the regular-season opener when they claimed safety Clinton Hart off waivers. Signed by Miami following his release by the Chargers, Welker spent his rookie campaign returning punts and kickoffs for the Dolphins, finishing second in the NFL with 1,415 kickoff return yards and 464 punt return yards, while also placing fifth in the league with 1,879 all-purpose yards.

Welker's role in Miami expanded somewhat in 2005, as, in addition to returning kickoffs and punts, he established himself as the Dolphins' third wide receiver, joining starters Chris Chambers and Marty Booker on the field in passing situations. Performing well over the course of his sophomore campaign, Welker finished the year with 29 receptions for 434 yards, 390 punt return yards, and 1,379 kickoff return yards, amassing in the process a total of 2,208 all-purpose yards that placed him third in the league rankings. Welker assumed an even more prominent role in Miami's offense the following year, accumulating 687 yards on a team-leading 67 pass receptions, while gaining another 1,442 yards on special teams.

Perhaps recalling the 71-yard punt return Welker recorded against them during a 29-28 loss to the Dolphins three years earlier, the Patriots worked out a trade with Miami prior to the 2007 campaign that netted them Welker, in exchange for their second and seventh-round picks in the 2007 NFL Draft. Welker left Miami holding franchise records for total kickoff returns, most kickoff return yards, and total punt returns. Meanwhile, only Gale Sayers accumulated more all-purpose yards than Welker did over the course of his first three NFL seasons.

Upon his arrival in New England, Welker developed a unique rapport with Tom Brady, rapidly ingratiating himself to his new quarterback with his soft hands, precise route-running ability, and tremendous quickness. Although the combination of Brady and Randy Moss garnered most of the headlines in the local newspapers as the Patriots moved inexorably towards compiling a perfect 16-0 regular-season record, Welker ended up leading the league with 112 receptions, while also amassing 1,175 yards and eight touchdowns through the air. Continuing to return punts as well, Welker gained another 425 yards on special teams, giving him a total of 1,634 all-purpose yards, en route to earning Second-Team All-Pro honors for the first of two straight times.

Standing just 5'9" tall and possessing only marginal straight-ahead running speed, Welker compensated for his physical shortcomings by relying heavily on his intelligence, exceptional "feel" for the game, and superior quickness, which enabled him to get in and out of his cuts before most defensive backs had an opportunity to react accordingly. Meanwhile, Welker's soft hands and ability to detect the "soft spots" in opposing defenses made him Brady's favorite target in third-down situations, also helping him to establish himself as the league's premier slot receiver.

Despite the loss of Brady for virtually all of the 2008 campaign, Welker continued to post impressive numbers with backup quarterback Matt Cassel, finishing the season with a team-leading 111 receptions and 1,165 receiving yards. Welker's 111 catches made him the first player in Patriots history to surpass 100 receptions in back-to-back years. Welker followed that up in 2009 by leading the league with a career-high 123 receptions, for 1,348 yards and four touchdowns, earning in the process First-Team

All-Pro honors for the first time and his second of five consecutive Pro Bowl selections. Yet, Welker also experienced a considerable amount of adversity over the course of the campaign, missing two games with a knee injury and suffering a torn MCL and ACL in his left knee in the regular-season finale that forced him to sit out New England's loss to Baltimore in the opening round of the playoffs.

After rehabilitating his knee during the subsequent offseason, Welker ended up missing just one game in 2010, finishing the year with 86 receptions for 848 yards and seven touchdowns. Returning to top form in the ensuing campaign, Welker helped the Patriots compile a conference-best 13-3 record during the regular season by leading the league with 122 receptions, scoring nine touchdowns, and amassing a career-high 1,569 receiving yards that established a new franchise record, surpassing the mark of 1,493 yards that Randy Moss posted four years earlier. For his outstanding performance, Welker received Pro Bowl and First-Team All-Pro honors.

Welker had another big year in 2012, earning the last of his five straight Pro Bowl selections by finishing tied for second in the NFL with 118 receptions. He also scored six touchdowns and finished eighth in the league with 1,354 receiving yards. However, with Welker and the Patriots unable to come to terms on a new contract when he became a free agent at season's end, the 31-year-old receiver signed a two-year, $12 million deal with the Denver Broncos on March 13, 2013. Welker left New England having caught 672 passes, for 7,459 yards and 37 touchdowns. In addition to setting franchise records for most career receptions, most catches in a season, and most pass receiving yards in a season, Welker ranks second in team annals in career pass receiving yardage, fourth in all-purpose yards, and eighth in touchdown receptions. He also holds team marks for most receptions in a single game, most receiving yards in a single game, and longest reception.

Although Welker has been somewhat less successful since leaving New England, due in large part to a string of concussions, he has proven to be one of Peyton Manning's favorite targets over the course of the past two seasons. Despite missing three games in 2013 as a result of head trauma, Welker concluded the campaign with 73 receptions, for 778 yards and a career-high 10 touchdowns. After suffering his third concussion in 10 months during the 2014 preseason, Welker found himself suspended by the NFL for the start of the regular season for violating the league's drug policy by testing positive for amphetamines. He ended up appearing in Denver's final 14 games, making only 49 receptions, for just 464 yards and two touchdowns.

With Welker becoming a free agent again at the end of 2014, it remains to be seen if he will re-sign with Denver or pursue other options. Welker will enter the 2015 campaign with career totals of 890 receptions, 9,822 receiving yards, and 51 touchdowns. He has gained another 6,699 yards on special teams and 151 yards on the ground, giving him a total of 16,672 all-purpose yards over the course of his 11 years in the league.

PATRIOT CAREER HIGHLIGHTS

Best Season

Welker performed brilliantly in five of his six seasons in New England, accumulating well in excess of 100 receptions and 1,000 receiving yards in each of those years. Nevertheless, the 2007, 2009, and 2011 campaigns would have to be considered his three finest, since he led the NFL in receptions each year and helped the Patriots advance to the Super Bowl twice. In addition to making 112 receptions for 1,175 yards and eight touchdowns in the first of those campaigns, Welker gained another 425 yards on special teams, en route to earning Second-Team All-Pro honors for the first of two straight times. He compiled even better numbers two years later, when he made a career-high 123 receptions, for 1,348 yards and four touchdowns, while amassing another 383 yards on special teams. Welker's exceptional all-around performance enabled him to make First-Team All-Pro for the first time in his career. However, Welker made his greatest overall impact in 2011, when he helped the Patriots capture the AFC title for the second time in four years by making 122 receptions, for nine touchdowns and a franchise-best 1,569 receiving yards. In addition to earning Pro Bowl honors for the fourth straight time, Welker earned the second of his two First-Team All-Pro selections.

Memorable Moments/Greatest Performances

Welker had his first big game for the Patriots on October 14, 2007, making 11 receptions for 124 yards and two touchdowns during a 48-27 road win over the Dallas Cowboys. He followed that up the very next week by catching nine passes for 138 yards and another two touchdowns, in helping the Patriots defeat Miami 49-28. However, Welker had his most productive day of the year against Philadelphia on November 25, making 13 receptions for 149 yards during a hard-fought 31-28 victory over the Eagles. Although the Patriots subsequently lost their Super Bowl XLII matchup with the New

York Giants 17-14, Welker turned in another solid performance, tying a Super Bowl record by making 11 receptions.

Welker had a pair of huge games in 2008, with the first of those coming against Miami on November 23, when he made eight receptions for 120 yards, including a 64-yard catch-and-run that represented the longest pass play of his NFL career, to that point. Welker's effort helped the Patriots record a 48-28 victory over their AFC East rivals. Welker made 12 catches for 134 yards during a 24-21 win over the Seattle Seahawks two weeks later, becoming in the process the first Patriots player to surpass 100 receptions in consecutive seasons.

Welker waited until Week Six of the 2009 campaign to turn in his first notable performance of the year, making 10 receptions for 150 yards and two touchdowns during a 59-0 dismantling of the Tennessee Titans. Four weeks later, during New England's 35-34 loss to the Colts in Indianapolis, Welker returned a punt 69 yards, recording in the process his longest such return as a member of the Patriots. He finished the game with 117 punt-return yards and another 94 yards on nine pass receptions, giving him a total of 211 all-purpose yards on the day.

Welker, though, had his two biggest pass-receiving games of the 2009 campaign on November 22 and December 6, making 15 receptions for 192 yards during the Patriots' 31-14 victory over the Jets on the first of those days, before catching 10 passes for 167 yards during New England's 22-21 loss to Miami two weeks later.

Welker put his name in the record books on September 12, 2011, when he helped the Patriots record a 38-24 victory over Miami in the regular-season opener by catching a 99-yard touchdown pass from Tom Brady. Welker's TD catch-and-run, which tied the NFL record for the longest play from scrimmage, represented the 12th such play in league history. He finished the day with eight receptions, for 160 yards and two touchdowns.

Although the Patriots lost their matchup with the Buffalo Bills two weeks later 34-31, Welker turned in the most prolific pass-receiving performance of his career, making 16 receptions, for 217 yards and two touchdowns. He also carried the ball once for 19 yards, giving him 236 total yards of offense on the day. Welker's 16 catches tied Troy Brown's single-game franchise record, while his 217 pass-receiving yards broke Terry Glenn's previous franchise mark of 214 yards, which the latter set in 1999. Welker continued his exceptional run the following week, making nine receptions for 158 yards and one touchdown during the Patriots' 31-19 victory over Oakland on October 2.

Welker had another big day on November 27, 2011, when he made eight receptions for 115 yards and two touchdowns during New England's 38-20 win over Philadelphia. Four weeks later, during the Patriots' 27-24 victory over Miami, Welker established a new franchise record by making 12 receptions for 138 yards, surpassing in the process Randy Moss's 2007 season mark of 1,493 receiving yards.

Before electing to leave New England via free agency at the conclusion of the 2012 campaign, Welker performed extremely well for the Patriots in that year's postseason. After making eight receptions for 131 yards, in helping the Pats defeat Houston 41-28 in their divisional playoff matchup, Welker ended his time in New England by catching eight passes for 117 yards and one touchdown during their 28-13 loss to Baltimore in the AFC Championship Game.

NOTABLE ACHIEVEMENTS

- Caught more than 100 passes five times, topping 120 receptions twice.
- Surpassed 1,000 receiving yards five times, topping 1,300 yards three times and 1,500 yards once (1,569 in 2011).
- Surpassed 1,500 all-purpose yards four times.
- Led NFL in pass receptions three times.
- Finished second in NFL in pass receptions twice and receiving yardage twice.
- Finished third in NFL with 12.5-yard punt-return average in 2009.
- Holds Patriots career record for most pass receptions (672).
- Ranks among Patriots all-time leaders in: pass receiving yardage (2nd); all-purpose yards (4th); and touchdown receptions (8th).
- Holds Patriots single-season records for most pass receptions (123 in 2009) and most pass receiving yardage (1,569 in 2011).
- Holds Patriots single-game records for most pass receptions (16) and most pass receiving yardage (217), both vs. Buffalo on 9/25/11.
- First receiver in NFL history to surpass 100 receptions five times.
- Two-time AFC champion (2007 & 2011).
- Five-time Pro Bowl selection (2008, 2009, 2010, 2011 & 2012).
- Two-time First-Team All-Pro selection (2009 & 2011).
- Two-time Second-Team All-Pro selection (2007 & 2008).
- Two-time Ed Block Courage Award winner (2007 & 2010).
- Member of Patriots' 2000s All-Decade Team.

14

Jim Lee Hunt

In hot pursuit of Jack Kemp.
(Courtesy Tales from the American Football League)

An original Patriot who spent his entire career in Boston, Jim Lee Hunt holds the distinction of being one of only 20 men who played all 10 AFL seasons. An exceptional pass-rusher who did a solid job against the run as well, Hunt starred at defensive tackle for the Patriots for 11 seasons, earning Pro Bowl and All-Pro honors four times each. Spending most of his time playing between left end Bob Dee and right tackle Houston Antwine, Hunt helped give the Patriots the AFL's most formidable defensive front, building a reputation along the way as arguably the league's fastest lineman. Hunt's exceptional play ended up earning him a place in the Patriots Hall of Fame and spots on the Pro Football Reference All-1960s Second Team and the Patriots' All-1960s Team.

Born in Atlanta, Texas, on October 5, 1938, James Lee Hunt attended Houston's Booker T. Washington High School, after which he enrolled at Prairie View A&M University, a historically black school located in Prairie View, Texas. Selected by the St. Louis Cardinals in the 16th round of the 1960 NFL Draft, with the 181st overall pick, Hunt instead chose to sign with the AFL's Boston Patriots prior to the new league's inaugural season.

After appearing in only six games as a rookie, Hunt became the Patriots' starting right tackle on defense in his second season, earning Pro Bowl and Second-Team All-AFL honors for his outstanding all-around play. He shifted over to the left side of Boston's defensive line the following year, spending the remainder of his career at left tackle, although the Patriots occasionally used him as a defensive end as well.

Despite performing extremely well for the Patriots from 1962 to 1965, Hunt often found himself being overshadowed by fellow linemates Bob Dee, Houston Antwine, and Larry Eisenhauer, preventing him from earning either Pro Bowl or All-AFL honors in any of those four seasons. However, Hunt stepped out of the shadows in 1966, when he led the Patriots with a career-high 9 quarterback sacks. His dominating performance earned him his second of four trips to the Pro Bowl and the first of three consecutive Second-Team All-AFL nominations. Hunt followed that up by being named the "best pass-rushing tackle in the AFL" by AFL scouts in 1967.

A ferocious pass-rusher, the 5'11", 255-pound Hunt gradually developed a reputation during his time in Boston as arguably the AFL's fastest lineman on either side of the ball. He helped foster that notion early in his career when he returned an interception 78 yards for a touchdown, outrunning in the process a pair of Houston Oiler running backs. Blessed with tremendous physical strength as well, Hunt recovered a fumble on another occasion and returned it 11 yards, leaving behind him a trail of fallen bodies. In addressing his former teammate's rare combination of speed and power during Hunt's 1993 induction into the Patriots Hall of Fame, Larry Eisenhauer said, "Jim Lee Hunt was called 'Earthquake' because the ground trembled when he rushed the passer. He was the fastest defensive lineman in Patriots history."

Hunt continued to man the left tackle spot for the Patriots until the end of the 1970 campaign, remaining with them after the two leagues merged that year. He announced his retirement at season's end, concluding his career with an "unofficial" total of 29 quarterback sacks and an AFL record 8 fumble recoveries. Hunt appeared in a total of 146 games in his 11 years with the Patriots, playing in their final 141 games with him as a member of the team.

Hunt lived just five more years following his retirement, passing away at only 37 years of age on November 22, 1975, after suffering a heart attack. The Patriots later named an award for their best lineman in his honor, with John Hannah proving to be the first recipient in 1981. They also eventually retired Hunt's number 79 and inducted him into their Hall of Fame in 1993, along with Steve Nelson, Babe Parilli, and former linemate Bob Dee, who also died from a heart attack several years earlier.

CAREER HIGHLIGHTS

Best Season

Hunt had his two best seasons for the Patriots in 1966 and 1967, earning Second-Team All-Pro and Pro Bowl honors in each of those campaigns. His team-high 9 sacks in 1966 represented a personal best, helping the Patriots finish third in the league in points allowed (283), en route to posting a record of 8-4-2. Yet, even though the Pats allowed the opposition some 100 more points (389) the following year, compiling in the process a dismal mark of 3-10-1, Hunt's stellar play prompted AFL scouts to name him the league's best pass-rushing tackle. All things considered, Hunt played his best ball for the Patriots in 1967.

Memorable Moments/Greatest Performances

The AFL's all-time leader in fumble recoveries, Hunt scored the second and last touchdown of his career during a 17-10 loss to Denver at Fenway Park on November 6, 1966, when he fell on a loose ball in the end zone.

Although he failed to cross the opponents' goal line on the play, Hunt travelled much farther in the 1968 regular season finale, returning a Don Trull fumble 51 yards during a 45-17 loss to the Oilers at the Houston Astrodome on December 15, 1968.

Hunt recorded the only safety of his career during a 44-16 loss to the Buffalo Bills on December 9, 1967, when he tackled Bills quarterback Jack Kemp in the end zone.

However, Hunt experienced the greatest moment of his career on November 1, 1963, when he capped off a 45-3 pasting of the Houston Oilers by intercepting a fourth-quarter George Blanda pass and rumbling 78 yards to a touchdown that closed out the scoring. In the process, Hunt outran Houston running backs Billy Cannon and Charlie Tolar, who found themselves unable to catch up to the 255-pound defensive lineman. The play proved to be the highlight of a dominating performance by the Patriots defense during which they allowed Houston only 19 yards rushing, recorded 5 quarterback sacks, and intercepted 6 passes, with cornerback Bob Suci returning another pick 98 yards for a score.

NOTABLE ACHIEVEMENTS

- One of only 20 men to play all 10 AFL seasons.
- Led AFL with 4 fumble recoveries and 51 fumble return yards in 1968.
- Holds AFL record for most career fumble recoveries (8).
- 1963 AFL Eastern Division champion.
- Named "Best Pass-Rushing Tackle in AFL" by AFL scouts in 1967.
- Four-time AFL Pro Bowl selection (1961, 1966, 1967 & 1969).
- Four-time Second-Team All-AFL selection (1961, 1966, 1967 & 1968).
- Pro Football Reference AFL 1960s All-Decade Second Team.
- Number 79 retired by Patriots.
- Inducted into Patriots Hall of Fame in 1993.

15

Larry Eisenhauer

(Courtesy Mainline Autographs)

The final member of the Patriots' outstanding defensive line of the 1960s to earn a place in our rankings, Larry Eisenhauer rushed the quarterback as well as any AFL defensive end during the first decade of the league's existence. Playing the game with tremendous intensity, Eisenhauer employed his patented "bull rush" to wreak havoc on opposing offenses, earning in the process three consecutive First-Team All-Pro selections, a total of four All-AFL nominations, and four trips to the Pro Bowl. Yet, perhaps the most noted feature of Eisenhauer's legacy is the unpredictability of his nature that prompted his teammates to nickname him "Wildman."

Born in Hicksville, New York, on February 22, 1940, Lawrence Conway Eisenhauer attended Chaminade High School in nearby Mineola, before enrolling at Boston College, where he proved to be a standout defensive lineman. After being selected by the Patriots in the sixth round of the 1961 AFL Draft, with the 42nd overall pick, Eisenhauer became one of the many Boston-area athletes to sign with the city's local professional football team.

Eisenhauer adapted to the pro game quickly, earning a starting job as a rookie, en route to being named Second-Team All-AFL by the *New York Daily News*. He developed into a star in his second season, earning the first of three straight First-Team All-AFL selections. Manning the right defensive end position along the Patriots' defensive front, Eisenhauer teamed up with right tackle Houston Antwine to apply tremendous pressure to opposing quarterbacks from the blind side. While Antwine used his quickness, strength, and girth to occupy multiple blockers on the inside, the 6'5", 250-pound Eisenhauer employed a ferocious pass rush from the outside that had opposing QB's constantly looking over their shoulders.

Still, even as Eisenhauer rose to the ranks of the AFL's elite, he became best known to his teammates as "Wildman" because of his unpredictable antics, which included running out onto Kansas City's snow-covered Municipal Stadium field clad in only his helmet and athletic supporter, and hitting his head on metal locker doors or ramming his forearms through locker room walls as a means of motivating himself. Teammate Tom Neville stated in the *1969 Patriots Media Guide*, "I've never seen anyone get so keyed up before a game." Eisenhauer also had a softer side, though, frequently hosting defensive linemates Houston Antwine and Jim Lee Hunt on his fishing boat as a way of relaxing between games.

After failing to represent the East in the All-Star Game for the first time in four years in 1965, Eisenhauer earned Pro Bowl and Second-Team All-Pro honors in 1966. He appeared headed for another Pro Bowl appearance the following season, before a knee injury sidelined him for the final five games. Not yet fully recovered by the start of the ensuing campaign, Eisenhauer missed almost half of the 1968 season as well. Although he returned to the Patriots full time in 1969, Eisenhauer never quite regained his earlier form, failing to show the burst at the line of scrimmage that previously made him one of the league's most feared pass-rushers. He subsequently elected to announce his retirement, ending his nine-year career at only 30 years of age. In addition to his multiple Pro Bowl appearances and All-AFL selections, Eisenhauer eventually earned a spot on the Pro Football Reference AFL 1960s All-Decade Second Team. Although he has not yet been inducted into the Patriots Hall of Fame or had his number retired by the team, Eisenhauer may one day have those honors bestowed upon him as well.

CAREER HIGHLIGHTS

Best Season

Eisenhauer appeared in the AFL All-Star Game and was named First-Team All-Pro three straight times, from 1962 to 1964. However, he earned unanimous First-Team All-AFL honors for the only time in 1963, when every major news wire service selected him to its squad (he almost duplicated that feat in 1964, but UPI named him to its Second Team). Eisenhauer's exceptional performance helped the Patriots advance to the AFL Championship Game for the only time in the 10-year history of the league, making 1963 the finest season of his career.

Memorable Moments/Greatest Performances

Eisenhauer turned in one of his finest all-around performances on December 4, 1966, when he led an overwhelming Patriots defense that held the archrival Buffalo Bills to just 3 points and 40 yards rushing during a key 14-3 Boston victory that gave the Patriots sole possession of first place in the AFL East with only two games left to play. Although the Pats failed to register a sack in the game, they applied constant pressure to Buffalo quarterbacks Jack Kemp and Daryle Lamonica throughout the contest, with Eisenhauer spearheading their pass rush. The game's pivotal play occurred early in the third quarter, when, with the Patriots leading by a score of 7-3, Eisenhauer delivered a hit to Kemp that knocked the Bills' starting QB out of the contest. The Patriots increased their lead to 14-3 shortly thereafter. Meanwhile, after Lamonica replaced Kemp behind center for Buffalo, the Bills failed to get past midfield in the second half until the final three minutes.

Eisenhauer turned in another memorable effort against the Bills less than one year later, on September 24, 1967, when, after using his helmet to put a hole in Buffalo's locker room wall prior to the contest, he earned AFL Lineman of the Week honors by leading the Patriots to a 23-0 victory. Providing a fierce pass rush to Bills quarterback Tom Flores throughout the game, Eisenhauer helped force the Buffalo signal-caller to throw a career-high 5 interceptions.

Yet, the game Eisenhauer recalls most took place on December 28, 1963, when the Patriots faced the Bills in a one-game playoff to determine the Eastern Division champion. Playing on a field frozen solid by the icy temperatures that filled the Buffalo air that day, the Patriots romped to a 26-8 victory over their bitter rivals, earning in the process a berth in the AFL title game. The contest's most intriguing play occurred when Eisenhauer lived up to his "Wildman" reputation by sinking his teeth into the left ankle of Bills star running back Cookie Gilchrist underneath a pile of players. Reflecting back on the incident, Eisenhauer explained, "I wanted to see if he was frozen. He wasn't, and he screamed, and then he got real mad. He jumped up and tried to kick me in the face. But he missed, slipped on the ice, and fell right on his head. It was a very memorable play in my career."

NOTABLE ACHIEVEMENTS

- 1963 AFL Eastern Division champion.
- Four-time AFL Pro Bowl selection (1962, 1963, 1964 & 1966).
- Three-time First-Team All-AFL selection (1962, 1963 & 1964).
- 1966 Second-Team All-AFL selection.
- Pro Football Reference AFL 1960s All-Decade Second Team.

16

Sam Cunningham

(Courtesy Pristine Auctions)

The Patriots' all-time leading rusher with 5,453 yards to his credit, Sam Cunningham spent his entire nine-year career in New England, helping the Pats advance to the playoffs three times between 1973 and 1982. An outstanding blocker and powerful runner who excelled in short-yardage situations, Cunningham led the Patriots in rushing in six of his first seven seasons, gaining more than 800 yards on the ground three times, including 1977, when he became just the second player in franchise history to surpass the magical 1,000-yard mark in a season. Named to the Patriots' 50th Anniversary Team in 2009 and inducted into their Hall of Fame one year later, Cunningham also ranks among the team's all-time leaders in rushing touchdowns, total touchdowns scored, and total points scored. Yet, as much as Cunningham contributed to the success of the Patriots during his time in New England, he is remembered equally for a pair of brilliant performances he turned in while playing his college ball at USC.

Born in Santa Barbara, California, on August 15, 1950, Samuel Lewis Cunningham Jr. attended Santa Barbara High School, after which he accepted a scholarship offer from the University of Southern California. Playing both running back and fullback in college, Cunningham acquired the nickname Sam "Bam" Cunningham for his ability to dive over piles of players into the opponent's end zone. Part of USC's "all-black" backfield (the first in NCAA Division I history) that also included quarterback Jimmy Jones and halfback Clarence Davis, the 6'3", 226-pound Cunningham made a memorable debut for the Trojans as a sophomore, rushing for 135 yards and 2 touchdowns against an all-white University of Alabama team that USC defeated by a score of 42-21 in Birmingham, on September 12, 1970. Legend has it that Cunningham's performance played a huge role in convincing the University of Alabama and its fans to allow legendary head coach Bear Bryant to subsequently recruit African-American players. Jerry Claiborne, a former assistant under Bryant, later said, "Sam Cunningham did more to integrate Alabama in 60 minutes than Martin Luther King did in 20 years."

In spite of Cunningham's exceptional effort against the Crimson Tide, the Trojans used him sparingly over the course of his first two seasons—mostly in short-yardage situations. However, with Clarence Davis having moved on to the pros by 1972, Cunningham became a much more integral part of the USC offense as a senior, enabling him to earn All-America honors. The powerful fullback turned in the most memorable performance of his college career in front of a national television audience at the 1973 Rose Bowl, leading USC to a 42-17 victory over Ohio State by scoring a Rose Bowl record 4 touchdowns. Cunningham's effort, which helped the Trojans capture the national championship, earned him Rose Bowl Player of the Game honors.

Subsequently selected by the Patriots in the first round of the 1973 NFL Draft, with the 11th overall pick, Cunningham played well in his 10 starts as a rookie, rushing for 516 yards and 4 touchdowns, while also making 15 receptions for another 144 yards and one touchdown. Despite being limited by injuries to just 10 games the following year, Cunningham dramatically increased his production, rushing for 811 yards and 9 touchdowns, catching 22 passes for 214 yards and 2 touchdowns, and finishing third in the NFL with a rushing average of 4.9 yards per carry, en route to earning Second-Team All-AFC honors for the first of two times. Seemingly on the precipice of stardom, Cunningham regressed somewhat in 1975, gaining only 666 yards on the ground and another 253 through the air, scoring 8 touchdowns, and fumbling the ball a league-leading 12 times for a Patriots team that finished the season just 3-11. However, the big fullback rebounded the following year, amassing 1,123 yards from scrimmage, averaging 4.8 yards per carry, and cutting his fumble total down to just 5, in helping the Patriots improve their record to 11-3.

Having established himself as New England's primary offensive weapon, Cunningham took another step forward in 1977, rushing for a career-high 1,015 yards that made him the first Patriots player in a decade to reach the 1,000-yard plateau. He also made 42 receptions for another 370 yards, amassing in the process a total of 1,385 yards from scrimmage that placed him seventh in the league rankings.

Considered to be one of the NFL's elite running backs following his exceptional 1977 campaign, Cunningham held a reputation second to none in terms of his physicality and willingness to take on opposing tacklers. Patriots' linebacker Steve Nelson revealed that he dreaded facing Cunningham in practice, stating, "When Sam hit you, it just stung."

Cunningham also embraced the blocking responsibilities of a fullback, saying, "I really, really enjoyed trying to dominate a linebacker or a defensive lineman."

Cunningham followed up his outstanding 1977 season with another solid year in 1978, earning Second-Team All-AFC honors and his lone Pro Bowl selection by accumulating more than 1,000 yards from scrimmage for the third straight time and scoring 8 touchdowns. His 768 yards rushing helped the Patriots amass a total of 3,165 yards on the ground that remains the NFL single-season record.

Unfortunately the 1978 campaign proved to be Cunningham's last big year. After rushing for just 563 yards and scoring 5 touchdowns in 1979, he missed all of 1980 due to injury. Cunningham subsequently assumed a part-time role after he returned to the team the following year, before announcing his retirement after appearing in only six games in 1982. In addition to ending his career with a franchise-record 5,443 yards rushing, Cunningham scored 43 touchdowns on the ground—the second most in team history. He also made a total of 210 receptions, for another 1,905 yards and 6 touchdowns.

Cunningham, who returned to his California roots following his retirement, ultimately received the honor of being inducted into the Patriots Hall of Fame in 2010. Upon learning of his election, Cunningham stated, "It's humbling, it's exciting, it's otherworldly. I just played as hard as I could and tried to complement my teammates."

CAREER HIGHLIGHTS

Best Season

Cunningham played very well for the Patriots in 1974, gaining 811 yards on the ground and another 214 in the air, placing among the NFL leaders with 11 touchdowns and a rushing average of 4.9 yards per attempt, and fumbling the ball just twice—the fewest times in his career. He also performed well in 1976 and 1978, accumulating 1,123 yards from scrimmage and averaging 4.8 yards per carry in the first of those campaigns, before amassing a total of 1,065 yards and scoring 8 touchdowns, en route to earning Pro Bowl honors for the only time in his career in 1978. Nevertheless, Cunningham had his finest all-around season in 1977, when, despite scoring only 5 touchdowns and fumbling the ball 10 times, he established career highs with 1,015 yards rushing, 42 pass receptions, 370 receiving yards, and 1,385 yards from scrimmage.

Memorable Moments/Greatest Performances

Cunningham had his breakout game for the Patriots on October 20, 1974, carrying the ball 11 times for 125 yards and 3 touchdowns during a 30-28 loss to the Bills in Buffalo. After scoring the game's first points in the opening quarter on a career-long 75-yard scamper that represented the NFL's longest run from scrimmage all year, Cunningham helped the Pats close the gap to 20-14 with a 12-yard, second-quarter TD run. He later scored the only points of the third quarter by going in from one yard out, to once again put the Patriots behind by only six points, this time 27-21. Cunningham followed that up with another extremely impressive performance the very next week, gaining 129 yards on 22 carries, while also making 5 receptions for 40 yards, in leading the Patriots to a 17-14 win over the Minnesota Vikings. Although the Pats subsequently lost their November 17 matchup with the Jets 21-16, Cunningham had another big day, carrying the ball 21 times for 113 yards, and making 2 receptions for another 17 yards.

Cunningham turned in another exceptional effort in a losing cause in 1975, gaining 100 yards on the ground and scoring 3 touchdowns during a 45-31 loss to the Bills.

Although injuries limited Cunningham to just 11 games in 1976, he performed at an extremely high level much of the time, having his first big day on September 19, when he carried the ball 21 times for 106 yards during a 30-14 win over the Miami Dolphins. Two weeks later, Cunningham helped the Patriots hand the Raiders their only loss of the season by rushing for 101 yards and making 5 catches for a career-high 94 receiving yards during a 48-17 rout of Oakland. Cunningham had another huge game in Week 7, leading the Pats to a 26-22 road win over the Bills by rushing for 118 yards and one touchdown, and making 3 receptions for another 43 yards.

Cunningham turned in his finest performance of the 1977 campaign on October 16, making 5 receptions for 41 yards and rushing for a career-high 141 yards during a 24-20 win over the San Diego Chargers.

Cunningham had one more big game left in him before injuries began to compromise his performance, carrying the ball 14 times for 93 yards during a 17-10 loss to the eventual NFC champion Dallas Cowboys on December 3, 1978. Cunningham scored the Patriots' only touchdown of the contest with a 52-yard, first-quarter run.

NOTABLE ACHIEVEMENTS

- Rushed for more than 1,000 yards once (1,015 in 1977).
- Scored more than 10 touchdowns once (11 in 1974).
- Surpassed 40 receptions once (42 in 1977).
- Averaged better than 4.5 yards per carry twice.
- Registered NFL's longest run from scrimmage in 1974 (75 yards).
- Finished third in NFL with 9 rushing touchdowns and 4.9-yard rushing average in 1974.
- Holds Patriots career record for most yards rushing (5,453).
- Ranks among Patriots all-time leaders in: rushing touchdowns (2nd); total touchdowns scored (5th); and total points scored (9th).
- 1978 Pro Bowl selection.
- Two-time Second-Team All-AFC selection (1974 & 1978).
- Named to Patriots' 50th Anniversary Team in 2009.
- Inducted into Patriots Hall of Fame in 2010.

17

Steve Nelson

(Courtesy Mainline Autographs)

The heart and soul of the Patriots defense for more than a decade, Steve Nelson spent his entire 14-year career in New England, establishing himself during that time as the team's inspirational leader and one of the AFC's top linebackers. An inside backer who possessed outstanding range and exhibited tremendous passion on the playing field, Nelson recorded well in excess of 100 tackles nine times for the Patriots, leading them in that category on eight separate occasions, en route to amassing a patriotic total of 1,776 stops over the course of his career that places him first in franchise history. Along the way, Nelson earned Pro Bowl honors three times, All-AFC honors five times, a spot on the Patriots' 50th Anniversary Team, and a place in their Hall of Fame.

Born in Farmington, Minnesota, on April 26, 1951, Steven Lee Nelson was exposed to football at an early age while growing up some 50 miles north in Anoka. With Nelson's dad, Stan, spending 26 years coaching at Anoka High, the state's largest secondary school, the younger Nelson caught the football bug early in life, stating years later, "Ever since I can remember, I had the dream. My dad was a coach, and, being around him and football players all the time, I wanted to be one of them."

After starring in baseball, football, and basketball at Anoka High School, Nelson found himself being pursued by Ev Kjelbertsen, who recruited for North Dakota State in the Twin Cities. Commenting on the impression Nelson made on him the first time he saw him play, Kjelbertsen said, "He had quickness. He had hitting ability. He was a good student. And he wanted to play football. What more could you ask?"

In spite of Kjelbertsen's efforts, Nelson enrolled at tiny Augsburg, where he had an opportunity to play for his uncle Edor. However, by the end of his freshman year, Nelson realized that he had undervalued himself, after which he transferred to North Dakota State.

Nelson spent his first season at his new school playing defensive end under head coach Ron Erhardt. But, after Erhardt departed for New England to help Chuck Fairbanks resuscitate the Patriots, Kjelbertsen shifted Nelson to linebacker to take full advantage of his quickness, instincts, and aptitude for the game. Recalling his reasoning at the time, Kjelbertsen later said, "If he's at end, he's only on one side of the formation. But, at linebacker, he's got more of the field to cover, and he can play against both the run and the pass."

The experiment proved to be a stroke of genius, with Nelson subsequently earning Second-Team All-America honors twice and being named Bison MVP in both 1972 and 1973. Meanwhile, with Erhardt singing the praises of Nelson in New England, the Patriots ended up selecting him in the second round of the 1974 NFL Draft, with the 34th overall pick. Explaining the team's decision years later, head coach Chuck Fairbanks recollected, "All the reports had high praise for Steve. He was very smart, a natural. He played faster and better than his overall speed would have indicated. Every move he made was in a positive direction—he always went right for the ball, and he had a way of evading blockers. He was also a great tackler."

Fitting right in with the Patriots' newly installed 3-4 defense, Nelson earned a starting job as a rookie, joining New England's youthful core of linebackers that also included Sam Hunt, Steve Zabel, and George Webster. Recalling the youngest of his fellow linebackers, Zabel said, "Nellie was like a Ted Johnson and Tedy Bruschi rolled into one. He was quick and agile, and strong enough to take on the guards and others who'd come after him. He always played the strong side, and most teams in those days were right-handed and would run to the right."

After a solid rookie campaign, the 6'2", 230-pound Nelson emerged as the Patriots' defensive MVP in 1975, leading the team with 157 tackles. He subsequently missed the final four games of the 1976 regular season, before returning the following year to make 4 ½ sacks and a team-leading 134 tackles, en route to being named the Patriots' "Unsung Hero." Nelson repeated as New England's leading tackler in 1978, recording 115 tackles and 4 fumble recoveries, while also making a career-high 5 interceptions. His strong all-around performance earned him Second-Team All-AFC honors for the first of four times.

Despite missing almost two full games in 1979 with a concussion, Nelson eclipsed the century-mark in tackles for the third straight time, amassing a total of 123 stops over the course of the campaign. He followed that up in 1980 by making a team-leading 186 tackles, en route to earning his first Pro Bowl selection and Second-Team All-AFC honors for the third straight time. Meanwhile, *Pro Football Weekly* and the *Sporting News* both accorded him First-Team All-Pro honors.

Injuries cut into Nelson's playing time significantly in two of the next three seasons, limiting to some degree his production on the defensive side of the ball. However, a return to full health in 1984 enabled him to make a career-high (and Patriots record) 207 tackles, earning him in the process his second Pro Bowl nomination, his lone First-Team All-AFC selection, and Second-Team All-Pro honors from the Newspaper Enterprise Association.

Recognized as the unquestioned leader of the New England defense by the mid-1980s, Nelson served as the elder statesman of an outstanding quartet of linebackers that also included Andre Tippett, Don Blackmon, and Larry McGrew. In assessing the qualities possessed by Nelson that made him such a key contributor to the success of the unit, former Patriots coach Chuck Fairbanks stated, "He knew his role, what job he had to do, and what he could depend on others to do. And, beyond his performance, he was totally unselfish and dedicated to the team."

Fairbanks continued, "Another thing about Steve was his work ethic and his preparation. He was always studying opponents and finding ways to give himself an edge. You never had to tell him what you wanted more than once. We used to give him a couple of different defensive signals to call on the field, depending on what the other team did. For us, it was like having another coach in the game."

Quarterback Steve Grogan also praised Nelson, saying, "He was one of the toughest players I knew, and he had a great knack of putting himself into position to make plays."

Center Bill Lenkaitis added, "Nellie ran a 5.1 (40-yard dash) and O.J. (Simpson) was a 4.2, but Nellie always got to the corner first."

Nelson followed up his exceptional 1984 season with another productive year, helping the Patriots capture their first AFC championship in 1985 by earning Second-Team All-AFC honors for the final time and the last of his three Pro Bowl selections. However, after being plagued by injuries in each of the next two seasons, Nelson elected to announce his retirement at the conclusion of the 1987 campaign. In addition to making 1,776 tackles over the course of his career, Nelson intercepted 17 passes and recovered 16 fumbles.

Following his retirement, Nelson briefly served as an assistant under Patriots head coach Rod Rust, losing his job after one year when the Patriots posted a horrendous 1-15 record in 1990. Admitting the failures of the coaching staff, Nelson later said, "We all got fired, and we all deserved it."

Nelson subsequently went into business with former teammate Bill Lenkaitis, opening a restaurant called *Doc & Nellie's* in Stoughton, Massachusetts. However, he eventually decided to return to football, accepting a job as head football coach and athletic director at Curry College. Serving from 1998 to 2006, Nelson turned the school into a perennial powerhouse, losing a total of just four games over one four-year period. In discussing the philosophy he attempted to instill in the young men who played under him, Nelson noted, "The first thing you have to recognize about playing on a team is that the team comes first. Once you understand and accept that, you really start enjoying what team sports are all about. When you're part of an effectively functioning team, you appreciate everyone else more. And as you become a better teammate that translates into you becoming a better person."

After leaving his post at Curry College, Nelson reentered the business world, assuming a position as a business development executive for Lighthouse Computer Services, Inc., a Lincoln, Rhode Island-based technology company. He also remains active with the Patriots, regularly appearing on the team's All Access television show, WEEI radio, and New England Cable

News. The Patriots, who inducted Nelson into their Hall of Fame in 1993, later retired his number 57 as well, making him one of only seven players to be so honored.

CAREER HIGHLIGHTS

Best Season

Nelson earned team MVP honors twice as a member of the Patriots, doing so in both 1975 and 1980. In 1975, just his second year in the league, Nelson recorded a team-leading 157 tackles. He again led the team in tackles five years later, making 186 stops, en route to earning the first Pro Bowl selection of his career. Nelson also performed extremely well in 1977 and 1978, making 134 tackles and 4 ½ sacks in the first of those campaigns, before recording 115 tackles, 4 fumble recoveries, and a career-high 5 interceptions the following year. Nevertheless, there is little doubt that Nelson had the finest season of his career in 1984, when he earned his only First-Team All-AFC selection by recording a Patriots record 207 tackles (71 solos and 136 assists).

Memorable Moments/Greatest Performances

Nelson made a key play in New England's 27-21 win over San Diego on September 23, 1979, helping the Patriots preserve their 6-point victory by intercepting a Dan Fouts pass at the goal line with just 1:30 remaining in the game.

Nelson turned in a pair of epic performances in 1982, one in victory and one in defeat. After making a career-high 22 tackles during a 31-7 loss to the Jets on September 19, Nelson recorded 6 tackles, 10 assists, and 3 quarterback pressures during a 29-21 win over the Houston Oilers two weeks later.

Nelson displayed tremendous courage in helping the Patriots defeat the Jets 26-14 in the wild-card round of the 1985 playoffs, continuing to play after dislocating his shoulder in the second quarter. He finished the game with 7 tackles and a fumble recovery.

Nelson played one of his finest all-around games the following year, leading the Patriots to a 30-21 win over the Colts in Indianapolis by making a team-leading 10 tackles and recording two interceptions for the only time in his career. The two picks came against Colts quarterback Jack Trudeau.

NOTABLE ACHIEVEMENTS

- Surpassed 100 tackles nine times, topping 200-mark once (207 in 1984).
- Led Patriots in tackles eight times.
- Holds Patriots single-season record with 207 tackles in 1984.
- Intercepted 5 passes in 1978.
- Ranks first all-time on Patriots with 1,776 tackles.
- 1985 AFC champion.
- Two-time Patriots' MVP (1975 & 1980).
- Three-time Pro Bowl selection (1980, 1984 & 1985).
- 1980 First-Team All-Pro selection (*Pro Football Weekly* and the *Sporting News*).
- 1984 Second-Team All-Pro selection (Newspaper Enterprise Association).
- 1984 First-Team All-AFC selection (UPI).
- Four-time Second-Team All-AFC selection (1978, 1979, 1980 & 1985).
- Named to Patriots' 50th Anniversary Team in 2009.
- Number 57 retired by Patriots.
- Inducted into Patriots Hall of Fame in 1993.

18

Richard Seymour

(Courtesy Keith Allison)

Excelling as both a 4-3 defensive tackle and a 3-4 defensive end during his time in New England, Richard Seymour played every position along the defensive line at one point or another for the Patriots. An outstanding pass-rusher and superb run-stuffer, the 6'6", 310-pound Seymour gained general recognition over the course of his eight seasons with the Pats as one of the NFL's most dominant defensive linemen, earning four All-Pro selections, four All-AFC nominations, and five consecutive trips to the Pro Bowl as a member of the team. Later named to the Pro Football Hall of Fame 2000s All-Decade First Team, Seymour helped the Patriots win four AFC championships and three Super Bowls, en route to earning a spot on their 50th Anniversary Team in 2009. After leaving New England at the conclusion of the 2008 campaign, Seymour spent his final four seasons with the Oakland Raiders, garnering one more All-Pro selection and two more Pro Bowl nominations.

Born in Gadsden, South Carolina, on October 6, 1979, Richard Vershaun Seymour attended Lower Richland High School in nearby Hopkins, where he won First-Team All-Region honors and served as captain of his team as a senior. After enrolling at the University of Georgia, Seymour spent the next four years playing on a Bulldogs defensive line that featured at different times four future first-round draft picks: Seymour, Marcus Stroud of the Jacksonville Jaguars and Buffalo Bills, Charles Grant of the New Orleans Saints, and Johnathan Sullivan, also of the Saints. Seymour, who proved to be easily the best of the four as a pro, garnered First-Team All-American honors as a senior, prompting the Patriots to select him with the sixth overall pick of the 2001 NFL Draft.

Spending most of his first NFL season playing right defensive end in New England's 4-3 defense, Seymour had a solid rookie campaign, helping the Patriots win their first Super Bowl and making *Pro Football Weekly's* All-Rookie Team by recording 3 sacks and 44 tackles in the 13 games in which he appeared. Seymour continued his strong play in 2002, earning First-Team All-AFC honors for the first time and the first of five straight Pro Bowl selections by registering 5 ½ sacks and 56 tackles, intercepting a pass, and contributing on special teams by blocking field goals in back-to-back November games against Oakland and Minnesota.

With the Patriots switching to a 3-4 defensive scheme in 2003, Seymour manned virtually every position along their defensive line, although he continued to spend the vast majority of his time at right defensive end. Named a defensive co-captain for the first time in his career prior to the start of the season, Seymour responded by making 8 sacks and 57 tackles for a Patriots team that won its second Super Bowl in three years. His outstanding play earned him First-Team All-Pro honors for the first of three consecutive times.

Playing right defensive end almost exclusively for the Patriots in subsequent seasons, Seymour remained one of the NFL's most formidable linemen, averaging 5 sacks and 42 tackles from 2004 to 2006, despite missing four games in 2005 due to a left knee injury he suffered while playing fullback in a goal line situation against the San Diego Chargers in Week

4. He also found his performance compromised somewhat the following year by a left elbow injury he sustained in Week 7. Nevertheless, Seymour continued his streaks of four consecutive All-Pro selections and five straight Pro Bowl nominations, becoming in the process just the fifth player in Patriots history to appear in the Pro Bowl that many times in succession (John Hannah, Mike Haynes, Andre Tippett, and Ben Coates were the others).

As Seymour further established himself as one of the NFL's premier defensive linemen, he also developed a reputation as one of the league's fiercest competitors. Frequently displaying a short fuse and a mean temperament on the playing field, Seymour prompted former teammate and current NBC analyst Rodney Harrison to say on one occasion, "Let me tell you about Richard. He's a quiet guy off the field, really laid-back. But, when he gets on the field, he wants to rip your head off."

In one of the more notable displays of Seymour's bad temper and aggressive style of play, the massive defensive lineman stepped on the head of Indianapolis Colts offensive tackle Tarik Glenn during a November 5, 2006 game. Although Seymour, who claimed that Glenn provoked him by diving for his knees, later apologized for his actions, the NFL levied a $7,500 fine against him as a result. And, after he joined the Raiders later in his career, Seymour drew another pair of fines—once for pulling the hair of Denver tackle Ryan Clady, and once for slapping Pittsburgh quarterback Ben Roethlisberger with an open hand through the face mask.

In discussing Seymour just a few days before the Roethlisberger incident, former Oakland defensive coordinator John Marshall stated, "He's a professional who takes care of business. But, as you watch film of Richard, he's not a very nice man on the football field."

After undergoing offseason surgery to repair an injured left knee that had hampered his performance in each of the previous two campaigns, Seymour spent the first half of 2007 on the Physically Unable to Perform List. Finally activated on October 27, Seymour appeared in New England's final nine games, recording just 1 ½ sacks and 23 tackles. Healthy again in 2008, Seymour made 52 tackles and tied his career high with 8 sacks, although he failed to garner All-Pro or Pro Bowl honors for the second straight year.

With Seymour approaching free agency and the Patriots seeking to reduce their payroll in order to accommodate other impending free agents such as Tom Brady, Vince Wilfork, and Logan Mankins, New England elected to trade the star defensive end to the Oakland Raiders just prior to the start of the 2009 campaign for a first-round pick in the 2011 NFL Draft. Claiming he had been "blindsided" by the trade, Seymour initially refused to report to the Raiders. However, after a few days of soul-searching, he changed his mind, eventually coming to view the sudden turn in events as a new challenge in his life.

In assessing his former teammate's state of mind at that particular time, Rodney Harrison suggested, "He was hurt because that was the team that drafted him. But there's a point where this thing is a business, and he learned the business of football. A lot of times our experiences shape and form us."

Harrison added, "It made him a better person. It made him see things more clearly. He's in a place now where he has the respect he deserves. He feels like he's making an impact in the locker room, and he's the leader of that team."

Seymour did indeed establish himself as a leader in Oakland, averaging 5 sacks and 41 tackles his first three years on the West Coast, before choosing to announce his retirement at the conclusion of the 2012 campaign after appearing in only eight games for the Raiders due to injury. Seymour ended his career with 57 ½ sacks and nearly 500 tackles (324 solos). During his time in New England, he recorded 39 sacks and 357 tackles. He also intercepted two passes.

While Seymour thrived in Oakland, the Patriots never fully recovered from his loss. After placing in the league's top 10 in total defense in each of Seymour's final three years with them, the Patriots gradually slipped to 25th by 2010 and 31st by 2011. Analyzing the impact that Seymour's departure made in New England, former teammate and current ESPN analyst Tedy Bruschi noted, "Since Richard left, there hasn't been that kind of presence on the defensive line. He got that pocket pushed, and that's what they've missed."

Rodney Harrison responded incredulously when asked if the Patriots missed Seymour, saying, "Are you crazy? I don't care if you bring Albert Haynesworth in. Superman might be able to replace him, but you can't replace Richard Seymour."

When asked during a conference call if the Patriots had ever adequately replaced Seymour, head coach Bill Belichick admitted that he may have made a mistake by trading away the star defensive end, suggesting, "I don't think, with top-level players, you ever get the same guy. You construct other parts of your team. Even if you find a guy to play that position, they play it a bit differently."

Although Seymour came to enjoy his time in Oakland, he continued to harbor ill feelings towards Belichick and the Patriots the remainder of his career, expressing no interest in returning to the team after Vince Wilfork tore his Achilles in September 2013. Contacted by the *Boston Herald* about a possible return to New England as a replacement for Wilfork, Seymour, then a free agent, said, "No way."

Seymour later told the *Herald*'s Ron Borges, "I know I could have helped. No doubt about that. I know what I bring to the table. They wish it was that easy to replace me, but it's not."

Seymour added, "You can't just have great coaching and no talent. You have to have both. Bill (Belichick) is an extremely smart coach. Extremely . . . but he thinks it's his schemes all the time. He had players like 'Hot Rod' (Rodney Harrison), myself, Ty (Law), Willie (McGinest), (Tedy) Bruschi, and (Mike) Vrabel in that system to make it look good."

PATRIOT CAREER HIGHLIGHTS

Best Season

Even though Seymour failed to earn All-Pro or Pro Bowl honors in 2008, he had one of his finest seasons, making 52 tackles, tying his career high with 8 sacks, and leading the Patriots with 17 quarterback hits. He also played extremely well in 2004, helping to anchor the league's second-ranked defense in terms of points allowed by recording 5 sacks and 39 tackles. However, Seymour had the finest all-around season of his career in 2003, when he earned unanimous First-Team All-Pro honors by establishing career highs with 8 sacks, 57 tackles, and 10 pass deflections. His exceptional play helped the Patriots finish first in the NFL with only 238 points allowed—the second-lowest total surrendered by any Patriots team since the league expanded its regular season schedule to 16 games in 1978.

Memorable Moments/Greatest Performances

Seymour intercepted two passes over the course of his career, with his first pick coming against former Patriots teammate Drew Bledsoe during a 27-17 victory over the Buffalo Bills on December 8, 2002. Seymour grabbed a Bledsoe pass that had been tipped by Anthony Pleasant and returned it six yards to the Buffalo nine yard line. The Patriots converted the turnover into seven points a couple of plays later when Tom Brady delivered a strike to Donald Hayes in the end zone. The touchdown gave New England a commanding 17-0 first-quarter lead that the Bills found themselves unable to overcome. Seymour also registered a sack and four tackles during the contest. He recorded his only other interception on December 17, 2006, picking off a David Carr pass during a 40-7 blowout of the Houston Texans.

Seymour also recovered six fumbles during his time in New England, one of which he returned for his only career touchdown during a 31-17 win over the Bills on October 3, 2004. With the Pats holding a 24-17 lead over Buffalo late in the fourth quarter, Seymour scooped up a Drew Bledsoe fumble at his own 32 yard line and put an end to any hopes the Bills had of tying the score by rumbling 68 yards for the game-clinching touchdown. Seymour also sacked Bledsoe once and recorded five tackles during the game.

Seymour earned AFC Special Teams Player of the Week honors twice in 2003, doing so for the first time on October 19, when he helped preserve a 13-13 tie with Miami by blocking Olindo Mare's potential game-winning 35-yard field goal with two minutes remaining in regulation. The Patriots subsequently won the game 19-13 when Tom Brady connected with Troy Brown on an 82-yard TD pass with 5:57 left in OT. Seymour was accorded the same honor following New England's 17-14 divisional playoff victory over the Tennessee Titans. In addition to blocking a 31-yard field goal attempt by Gary Anderson late in the first half, Seymour made seven tackles (5 solo) during the contest.

Seymour turned in several dominant performances during his time in New England, with one of those coming against Pittsburgh on October 31, 2004, when he recorded a career-high 16 tackles (8 solo) during a 34-20 loss to the Steelers. Seymour played two of his best games in back-to-back weeks early in 2005, registering a team-leading 14 tackles during a 27-17 loss to Carolina on September 18, before recording nine tackles, sacking Ben Roethlisberger twice, and knocking down a pass during a 23-20 victory over Pittsburgh on September 25.

Seymour turned in another brilliant all-around effort on October 26, 2008, when he helped lead the Patriots to a 23-16 win over the St. Louis Rams by registering eight tackles, four quarterback hits, and one sack. Five of his eight tackles came on plays that resulted in a loss or no gain.

NOTABLE ACHIEVEMENTS

- Surpassed 50 tackles three times.
- Led Patriots in sacks twice.
- Scored one defensive touchdown during career.
- Four-time AFC champion (2001, 2003, 2004 & 2007).
- Three-time Super Bowl champion (XXXVI, XXXVIII & XXXIX).

- Five-time Pro Bowl selection (2002, 2003, 2004, 2005 & 2006).
- Three-time First-Team All-Pro selection (2003, 2004 & 2005).
- 2006 Second-Team All-Pro selection.
- Four-time First-Team All-AFC selection (2002, 2003, 2004 & 2005).
- Member of Pro Football Hall of Fame 2000s All-Decade First Team.
- Member of Pro Football Reference 2000s All-Decade Second Team.
- Member of Patriots' 2000s All-Decade Team.
- Named to Patriots' 50th Anniversary Team in 2009.

19

Ty Law

(Courtesy George A. Kitrinos)

A three-time Super Bowl champion who excelled for the Patriots at cornerback for 10 seasons, Ty Law established himself as one of the greatest defensive backs in franchise history during his time in New England. Playing his position with tremendous physicality and supreme confidence, Law tied Raymond Clayborn's team record for most career interceptions (36), en route to earning four Pro Bowl selections, two First-Team All-Pro nominations, and two First-Team All-AFC selections.

The first Patriots player to lead the NFL in interceptions, Law also holds franchise records for most career interception return yards (583) and most interceptions returned for touchdowns (6). The physical nature of Law's game also made him a solid player against the run, enabling him to surpass 70 tackles on five separate occasions. Law's all-around excellence eventually earned him spots on the NFL 2000s All-Decade Team and the Patriots' 50th Anniversary Team, as well as a place in the Patriots Hall of Fame.

Born in Aliquippa, Pennsylvania, on February 10, 1974, Tajuan E. Law attended Beaver County's Aliquippa High School, where he starred in football, basketball, and track. In addition to playing cornerback, safety, wide receiver, and running back on the gridiron, Law excelled on the basketball court, earning team MVP honors as a senior. Following his graduation from Aliquippa, Law enrolled at the University of Michigan, where he spent the next three years lettering in football, garnering First-Team All-American honors as a senior and unanimous All-Big Ten Conference honors in each of his last two seasons.

Subsequently selected by the Patriots in the first round of the 1995 NFL Draft, with the 23rd overall pick, Law spent much of his rookie season sharing time at right cornerback with Maurice Hurst, before earning the starting job during the latter stages of the campaign. Playing well in his first NFL season, Law intercepted three passes and made 47 tackles. After being shifted to left cornerback the following year, Law found a permanent home, spending his remaining time in New England at that post. Despite missing three games due to injury in 1996, Law recorded 62 tackles (56 solo) and finished second on the team with three interceptions, one of which he returned 38 yards for his first career touchdown.

Law had another very solid year in 1997, intercepting three passes and recording a career-high 77 tackles (69 solo), in helping the defending AFC champions capture their second consecutive division title. Although the Patriots failed to repeat as AFC East champs in 1998, Law had arguably his finest all-around season, making a league-leading nine interceptions, which he returned for 133 yards and one touchdown, while also registering 70 tackles (60 solo). His exceptional performance earned him a spot in the Pro Bowl and unanimous First-Team All-NFL honors.

After playing well despite missing a significant amount of time due to injuries in each of the next two seasons, Law earned his second Pro Bowl nomination in 2001. En route to helping the Patriots advance to the Super Bowl, he made 69 tackles (59 solo) and recorded three interceptions, which he returned for a total of 91 yards and two touchdowns. Law then helped lead the Pats to a 20-17 victory over St. Louis in Super Bowl XXXVI by intercepting a Kurt Warner pass and returning it 47 yards for the game's first touchdown.

Law also made the AFC Pro Bowl roster in each of the next two seasons, performing particularly well in 2003, when he earned First-Team All-Pro honors by making 73 tackles (60 solo) and intercepting six passes, one of which he returned 65 yards for a touchdown. Proving once again to be an outstanding big-game player, Law intercepted Peyton Manning three times during New England's 24-14 win over Indianapolis in the 2003 AFC Championship Game.

As Law gradually evolved into one of the NFL's elite cornerbacks, he also developed a reputation as one of the league's most physical defensive backs. Known for the manner in which he tended to manhandle some of the game's top wide receivers, Law is considered to be largely responsible for the NFL's decision to enforce the five-yard illegal contact rule on defenders following the conclusion of the 2003 campaign.

Perhaps the most notable example of Law's physical style of play could be found in the way he abused Marvin Harrison during that 2003 AFC title game against the Colts. Informed by master psychologist Bill Belichick earlier in the week that the Patriots head coach did not plan to allow him to cover Harrison, Law took the slight as a personal affront. Ignoring Belichick's original edict, Law lined up opposite Harrison at the beginning of the contest. After subsequently being told by Belichick that he could cover Harrison, but that they would revert to the head coach's original plan if he gave up any plays, Law ended up limiting the star wideout to just three catches, for 19 yards, while intercepting Peyton Manning three times.

Possessing tremendous self-confidence, Law discussed with ESPNBoston.com the attitude he brought with him to the playing field:

> It's all about swagger when you're playing defensive back. If you get beat as a defensive back early, you have to expect for them to come at you often. To the best of your ability, you want to nip that in the bud and show swagger right off the rip. Let's say they did get you, just make sure they don't get you again the next time. Do whatever is in your power to say "You know what, you're going to stay off of me. I'm going to make you throw the ball over there." And then the guy over there says "Hey, you aren't going to throw at me, you better throw it at him."

Commenting on the braggadocio Law often displayed to others, Patriots owner Robert Kraft said, “How good was Ty Law? The best. And if you don’t believe it, just ask him.”

Kraft then related a story about Law’s failed attempt to receive a new contract offer from the Patriots at the conclusion of the 2004 campaign. Not yet having received an offer to remain with the team, Law approached Kraft in the locker room after a game and began screaming at him, “You guys are out of your mind! Don’t you know who I am! I’m Ty (expletive) Law! Ty (expletive) Law!”

After a foot injury forced Law to miss the final nine regular-season games and all three of the Patriots’ postseason contests in 2004, New England elected to release him due to salary cap concerns. The 10-year veteran signed with the rival New York Jets shortly thereafter, earning the last of his five Pro Bowl selections in 2005 by leading the NFL with 10 interceptions, recording 62 tackles, and scoring the last of his seven career touchdowns. With the Jets also experiencing difficulties getting under the salary cap at season’s end, they, too, released Law, who moved on to Kansas City, where he spent the next two years recording a total of six interceptions and 112 tackles. Law returned to the Jets in 2008, suffering through an injury-marred campaign, before spending the last of his 15 NFL seasons serving as a backup in Denver. Released by the Broncos at the conclusion of the 2009 campaign, Law announced his retirement, ending his career with 53 interceptions, 828 interception return yards, seven touchdowns, and 838 tackles (707 solo). In addition to recording a franchise-best 36 interceptions and 583 interception-return yards during his time in New England, Law made 635 tackles (539 solo).

Even though Law spent his final five seasons playing for other teams, he remained a Patriot at heart, stating after his nomination to the team’s Hall of Fame in 2014:

> Coming back full circle now and being considered one of the Patriots’ all-time greats is very humbling to me. I left and I played on different teams, but my heart was always with the Patriots regardless of where I was. It’s an amazing feeling. I’m never one to be too lost on words, but I am right now. It’s still fresh, it’s new. . . . I feel like I’ve already been accepted just by being nominated and by being one of the finalists. It’s a great feeling, but it’s all about the journey to this moment right now.

The Patriots inducted Law into their Hall of Fame later in 2014, making him the 20th player to be so honored.

PATRIOT CAREER HIGHLIGHTS

Best Season

Law played extremely well in 1997, when he intercepted three passes and recorded a career-high 77 tackles (69 solo). He also had a big year in 2003, helping the Patriots advance to the Super Bowl for the first of two straight times by making six interceptions, defending against 23 passes, and registering 73 tackles (60 solo), earning in the process Pro Bowl honors and the second of his two First-Team All-Pro selections. Law's stellar play helped New England's defense lead the NFL in four key categories: fewest points allowed per game (14.9), fewest passing touchdowns surrendered (11), most interceptions (29), and lowest opponents' passer rating (56.2). Nevertheless, the 1998 campaign would have to be considered Law's finest in New England. En route to earning Pro Bowl and First-Team All-Pro honors for the first time in his career, Law led the league with nine interceptions, which he returned for 133 yards and one touchdown, recorded 70 tackles (60 solo), and recovered a fumble.

Memorable Moments/Greatest Performances

Law scored the first of his six career touchdowns as a member of the Patriots on December 8, 1996, when he intercepted a Glenn Foley pass and returned it 38 yards for a TD during a 34-10 win over the Jets. Although the Pats lost their next game to the Dallas Cowboys by a score of 12-6, Law once again made his presence felt, picking off two Troy Aikman passes.

Law had another huge day on September 13, 1998, intercepting Peyton Manning twice and scoring his second career touchdown when he returned one of those picks 59 yards for a TD during a convincing 29-6 victory over the Colts.

Law again crossed the opponent's goal line on October 17, 1999, when he intercepted a Damon Huard pass and returned it 27 yards for a touchdown during a 31-30 loss to the Miami Dolphins.

A constant thorn in the side of Peyton Manning, Law registered his second pick-six against the legendary quarterback on September 30, 2001, when he returned an interception 23 yards for a score during a lopsided 44-13 win over the Colts.

Law scored his second touchdown of the 2001 campaign in the regular-season finale, returning an interception 46 yards for a TD, in helping the Patriots defeat Carolina 38-6.

Law scored his final touchdown as a member of the Patriots on October 5, 2003, when he intercepted a Steve McNair pass late in the fourth quarter and returned it 65 yards for a TD that clinched a 38-30 win over the Tennessee Titans. Law also played a huge role in New England's 12-0 shutout of the Dallas Cowboys six weeks later, picking off two Quincy Carter passes, which he returned for a total of 47 yards.

Yet, Law will always be remembered most for two games in particular. Facing the St. Louis Rams and their powerful offense in Super Bowl XXXVI, Law scored the game's first touchdown with just under nine minutes remaining in the second quarter when he intercepted a Kurt Warner pass and returned it 47 yards for a score. Law also made eight tackles during the contest, which the Patriots went on to win in the closing moments 20-17. Law also came up big against Peyton Manning and the Colts in the 2003 AFC Championship Game, picking off Manning three times during New England's 24-14 victory.

NOTABLE ACHIEVEMENTS

- Recorded at least 6 interceptions twice.
- Returned 6 interceptions for touchdowns.
- Surpassed 70 tackles five times.
- Led NFL with 9 interceptions in 1998.
- Led NFL with 2 interceptions returned for touchdowns in 2001.
- Tied for first all-time on Patriots with 36 career interceptions (Raymond Clayborn).
- Holds Patriots career record for most interception return yards (583).
- Four-time AFC champion (1996, 2001, 2003 & 2004).
- Three-time Super Bowl champion (XXXVI, XXXVIII & XXXIX).
- 1998 Pro Bowl Co-MVP.
- Four-time Pro Bowl selection (1998, 2001, 2002 & 2003).
- Two-time First-Team All-Pro selection (1998 & 2003).
- Two-time First-Team All-AFC selection (1998 & 2003).
- Two-time NFL Alumni Defensive Back of the Year (1998 & 2003).
- NFL 2000s All-Decade Team.
- Member of Patriots' 1990s All-Decade Team.
- Member of Patriots' 2000s All-Decade Team.
- Named to Patriots' 50th Anniversary Team in 2009.
- Inducted into Patriots Hall of Fame in 2014.

20

Ben Coates

(Courtesy George A. Kitrinos)

The favorite receiver of Drew Bledsoe during their time together in New England, Ben Coates spent nine years playing tight end for the Patriots, establishing himself as the greatest player ever to man the position for the Pats. A tough and dependable receiver with good speed and soft hands, Coates led the team in touchdown receptions six straight times between 1993 and 1998, while also finishing first on the club in total receptions in five of those years. Named to the Patriots' 50th Anniversary

Team in 2009 after being inducted into their Hall of Fame one year earlier, Coates ranks among the franchise's all-time leaders in every major pass-receiving category, with his 490 receptions as a member of the team placing him fourth in team annals. A five-time Pro Bowl selection and three-time All-Pro nominee, Coates set a new single-season record for NFL tight ends (since broken) by making 96 catches in 1994. A solid blocker as well, Coates earned a spot on the Pro Football Hall of Fame's All-1990s Second Team with his outstanding all-around play. Some 15 years after he played his last game, Coates continues to rank among the top 10 tight ends in NFL history in career receptions, yards, and touchdowns.

Born in Greenwood, South Carolina, on August 16, 1969, Ben Terence Coates Jr. attended local Greenwood High School, where he didn't begin playing football until his senior year. Following his graduation, Coates' relative lack of experience on the gridiron prompted only three colleges to offer him an athletic scholarship—Savannah State, Johnson C. Smith, and Livingstone. After choosing Livingstone, a small, historically black school in Salisbury, North Carolina, Coates established himself as a multi-sport star, excelling in particular on the football field, where he broke nearly all of the college's meaningful receiving records. Still, since Coates did so against lesser competition, for a non-notable school, pro scouts paid him little attention, causing him to last until the fifth round of the 1991 NFL Draft, when the Patriots selected him with the 124th overall pick. Looking back years later at the unheralded manner in which he entered the NFL, Coates recalled, "I remember a couple of *Boston Globe* writers asking, 'Why did they draft this guy? . . . Where's this guy from?' I'm pretty sure they're not writing that anymore."

Coates' first two NFL seasons proved to be quite uneventful, with the tight end starting only four games and making a total of just 30 receptions for a Patriots team that finished a combined 8-24 under head coach Dick MacPherson. However, everything changed for Coates and the Patriots in his third season after the team selected Drew Bledsoe with the first overall pick of the 1993 NFL Draft and made Bill Parcells their new head coach. Parcells, who tended to rely heavily on his tight ends as part of his team's passing game, gradually turned over the starting duties to the 6'4", 245-pound Coates, who thrived in New England's new offensive scheme. With Bledsoe often looking to him when he needed a key completion, Coates led the team with 53 receptions, for 659 yards and 8 touchdowns. Coates improved upon those numbers significantly in 1994, when he scored another 7 touchdowns and placed near the top of the league rankings with 96 receptions and 1,174 receiving yards, en route to earning his first of five consecutive Pro Bowl selections, and First-Team All-Pro honors for the first of two straight times.

Coates later gave much of the credit for his success to Parcells and Bledsoe, saying first of his somewhat overbearing coach, "If you do your job and do it on a consistent basis, you'll have no problem with Parcells. But, if you're an emotional roller coaster, he'll be on you. I've seen him ride guys and they drop their head and go into a shell, and, when you look up the next time, the guy's been traded or cut."

Coates had even better things to say about his quarterback, suggesting, "There was just something with Drew when we first met. There was a bond there. I'd talk to his grandmother and his father, Matt. . . . In a clutch situation, Drew went to me even though everyone in the stadium knew what was going to happen. He knew wherever he threw it, I was going to be there, and I was going to hang on."

Coates compiled huge numbers again in 1995, making 84 receptions for 915 yards and 6 touchdowns, en route to earning his second straight First-Team All-Pro selection. He followed that up with three more outstanding seasons, surpassing 60 receptions each year from 1996 to 1998. After earning Second-Team All-Conference honors for New England's 1996 AFC Championship team by making 62 receptions for 682 yards and a career-high 9 touchdowns, Coates totaled 133 catches, for 1,405 yards and 14 touchdowns the next two years, earning his lone Second-Team All-Pro selection in 1998.

Coates spent one more year in New England, making just 32 receptions for 370 yards and 2 touchdowns in 1999, before being released by the Patriots at season's end. He subsequently joined the Baltimore Ravens, with whom he spent his final season serving primarily as a backup, before also being released by them at the end of 2000. However, during his time in Baltimore, Coates earned the Super Bowl ring that previously eluded him during his time in New England, serving as a member of the Ravens team that dismantled the New York Giants in Super Bowl XXXV.

Choosing to announce his retirement after being released by Baltimore, Coates ended his career with 499 receptions, 5,555 receiving yards, and 50 touchdowns. He compiled virtually all of those numbers as a member of the Patriots, who inducted him into their Hall of Fame in 2008. At the time of his retirement, Coates ranked fourth all-time in pass receptions among NFL tight ends, trailing only Ozzie Newsome, Shannon Sharpe, and Kellen Winslow.

Following his retirement, Coates returned to Livingstone College, where he briefly served as head football coach, before accepting a position to coach in NFL Europe. Coates also spent one year serving as an assistant under Bill Parcells in Dallas, where he coached the team's tight ends. After leaving Dallas, he joined the Cleveland Browns' coaching staff, where he spent the 2005 campaign serving in the same capacity under former Patriots' defensive coordinator Romeo Crennel. Following the release of Crennel and his coaching staff at the end of 2008, Coates became the offensive coordinator at Central State University—a position he continues to hold.

PATRIOT CAREER HIGHLIGHTS

Best Season

Coates performed extremely well for the 1996 AFC champion Patriots, making 62 receptions for 682 yards and a career-high 9 touchdowns. He also had a big year in 1995, when he hauled in 84 passes for 915 yards and 6 touchdowns. Nevertheless, there is little doubt that Coates had his finest season in 1994, when, in addition to scoring 7 touchdowns, he established career highs with 96 receptions and 1,174 receiving yards. His 96 catches set a new NFL record for tight ends that stood until Tony Gonzalez made 102 receptions for the Kansas City Chiefs in 2004.

Memorable Moments/Greatest Performances

After seeing very little action over the course of his first two seasons, Coates had his breakout game for the Patriots on October 31, 1993, making six receptions for 108 yards during a 9-6 loss to the Indianapolis Colts. He had his most memorable game of the year, though, in the regular-season finale, helping the Patriots defeat division rival Miami 33-27 in overtime by making six receptions for 95 yards and two touchdowns.

Even though the Patriots lost their opening game of the 1994 campaign to Miami 39-35, Coates gave an early indication of what lay ahead by making eight receptions for 161 yards and two touchdowns. His 63-yard hookup with Drew Bledsoe early in the third quarter, which gave New England a short-lived 21-10 lead, proved to be the second-longest TD reception of his career. Coates was at it again the very next week, making nine catches for 124 yards and another two touchdowns during a 38-35 loss to the Buffalo Bills. Coates continued his exceptional month of September against Cincinnati the following week, making eight receptions for 108 yards, in helping the Patriots win their first game of the year 31-28. Coates had another big game against Oakland on October 9, making nine receptions for 123 yards during a 21-17 loss to the Raiders. He turned in another outstanding effort against Indianapolis on November 27, making a career-high 12 receptions for 119 yards during a hard-fought 12-10 victory over the Colts.

Coates had his biggest game of the 1995 campaign on November 26, when he helped the Patriots defeat Buffalo 35-25 by making three touchdown receptions for the only time in his career. The big tight end hooked up with Drew Bledsoe on scoring plays that covered 6, 4, and 15 yards.

Coates had a huge game against Miami on November 3, 1996, making five receptions for 135 yards and two touchdowns during a 42-23 romp over the Dolphins. Coates, who put the Patriots ahead to stay with his two second-half touchdowns, connected with Drew Bledsoe on a career-long 84-yard scoring strike early in the fourth quarter that gave the Pats a 28-17 lead. However, Coates made his biggest play of the year in the regular-season finale, enabling the Patriots to edge out Buffalo for the AFC East title by catching a short pass from Bledsoe and bulling his way through a number of Giants defenders for a 13-yard score late in the fourth quarter of a 23-22 New England victory.

Coates made another clutch reception on November 29, 1998, hauling in a one-yard TD pass from Bledsoe as time expired, to give the Patriots a 25-21 win over the Bills. Coates finished the day with 10 catches for 70 yards.

Coates again displayed his penchant for making big plays on September 19, 1999, when he helped the Patriots come all the way back from a 28-7 halftime deficit to Peyton Manning and the Colts by making two fourth-quarter touchdown receptions. His second TD, which came with just over eight minutes remaining in regulation, tied the score at 28-28. Adam Vinatieri subsequently won the game for the Patriots by kicking a 26-yard field goal with only one minute and 30 seconds left on the clock.

NOTABLE ACHIEVEMENTS

- Caught more than 50 passes six straight times, surpassing 80 receptions twice and 90 receptions once (96 in 1994).
- Topped 1,000 receiving yards once (1,174 in 1994).
- Finished fourth in NFL with 96 receptions in 1994.
- Ranks among Patriots all-time leaders in: pass receptions (4th); receiving yardage (5th); touchdown receptions (tied-3rd); touchdowns scored (tied-3rd); and points scored (tied-8th).
- 1996 AFC champion.

- Five-time Pro Bowl selection (1994, 1995, 1996, 1997 & 1998).
- Two-time First-Team All-Pro selection (1994 & 1995).
- 1998 Second-Team All-Pro selection.
- Two-time First-Team All-AFC selection (1994 & 1995).
- 1996 Second-Team All-AFC selection.
- Pro Football Hall of Fame All-1990s Second Team.
- Named to Patriots' 50th Anniversary Team in 2009.
- Inducted into Patriots Hall of Fame in 2008.

21

Kevin Faulk

(Courtesy Scott Slingsby)

The Patriots' all-time leader in all-purpose yards, Kevin Faulk contributed to the Pats in many different ways over the course of his 13-year NFL career, which he spent entirely in New England. Whether running with the ball, catching passes out of the backfield, or returning kickoffs and punts, Faulk did an excellent job for the Patriots, amassing a franchise-record 12,349 all-purpose yards between 1999 and 2011. Serving the Patriots primarily as a return man and third-down specialist in several of those campaigns, Faulk accumulated as many as 100 carries in only two of his 13 seasons. Yet, he still managed to gain more than 3,600 yards on the ground over the course of his career, while also gaining another 3,701 yards through the air. Meanwhile, Faulk's 4,098 kickoff return yards represent the most in team history, by a fairly wide margin. Faulk's offensive versatility enabled him to surpass 1,000 all-purpose yards seven times, making him a significant contributor to five AFC championship teams and three Super Bowl champions during his time in New England.

Born in Lafayette, Louisiana, on June 5, 1976, Kevin Troy Faulk attended Carencro High School in nearby Carencro, where he twice earned State Most Valuable Player honors (Class 5A) by rushing for a total of 4,877 yards, compiling a total of 7,612 all-purpose yards, and scoring 89 touchdowns. After also being awarded All-American honors by *USA Today* and *Parade* magazine, Faulk elected to enroll at Louisiana State University, where he spent the next four years starring at running back. Voted to the College Football All-American Team by the Associated Press in 1996, Faulk turned in the most memorable performance of his collegiate career on September 7 of that year when he helped LSU overcome a 20-point halftime deficit to the Houston Cougars by rushing for a school record 246 yards and returning four punts for another 106 yards, in a game the Tigers ended up winning by a score of 35-34.

Having concluded his career at LSU as one of the SEC's all-time leaders in rushing yards (4,557), all-purpose yards (6,833), and touchdowns (53), Faulk entered the 1999 NFL Draft, where the Patriots selected him in the second round, with the 46th overall pick. Hampered by ankle injuries throughout much of his rookie campaign, Faulk started only two games, spending most of his time returning kickoffs and serving as a backup to Terry Allen. Nevertheless, he played well in his first NFL season, amassing a total of 1,358 all-purpose yards, 943 of which came on kickoff returns.

Although Faulk continued to return kickoffs in 2000, his role in the New England offense expanded somewhat. Sharing playing time with rookie running back J.R. Redmond, Faulk rushed for a team-leading 570 yards, made 51 receptions for another 465 yards, and scored five touchdowns. He also gained another 874 yards on special teams, giving him a total of 1,909 all-purpose yards that placed him eighth in the league rankings.

The acquisition of Antowain Smith relegated Faulk to backup duties in each of the next two seasons. Yet, he continued to contribute to the Patriots as a reserve running back and return specialist, accumulating 1,047 all-purpose yards and scoring three touchdowns for the 2001 Super

Bowl champions, before amassing 1,440 all-purpose yards and scoring a career-high seven touchdowns the following year.

With Smith battling injuries for much of 2003, Faulk started eight games in the Patriots' backfield, establishing career-highs with 178 carries and 638 yards rushing. He also made 48 receptions for 440 yards and gained another 273 yards on special teams, giving him a total of 1,351 all-purpose yards.

Plagued by injuries himself in each of the next two seasons, Faulk proved to be much less of a factor in both 2004 and 2005. Appearing in a total of only 19 games over the course of those two seasons, he spent most of his time serving as a backup to Corey Dillon, accumulating fewer than 1,000 total yards from scrimmage. Healthy again in 2006, Faulk compiled 1,173 all-purpose yards, gaining the vast majority of those while playing on special teams.

With the departure of Dillon following the conclusion of the 2006 campaign, Faulk spent the next two years splitting time at running back with Laurence Maroney. After Faulk accumulated 648 yards from scrimmage for New England's undefeated 2007 squad, the NFL levied a one-game suspension against him for violating its substance abuse policy by using marijuana while attending a Lil Wayne concert in Louisiana in February 2008. Following his return, though, Faulk went on to have one of his finest seasons, rushing for 507 yards, gaining another 486 yards on 58 pass receptions, and scoring six touchdowns.

Faulk had one more solid season for the Patriots, gaining 335 yards on the ground and another 301 yards through the air in 2009, before a torn ACL suffered in the second game of the ensuing campaign essentially ended his career. Placed on injured reserve for the remainder of 2010, Faulk attempted a comeback the following year. However, he appeared in only seven games and accumulated just 91 yards from scrimmage, forcing him to the realization that the time had come to retire. Yet, even though Faulk barely saw the playing field in his final NFL season, he continued to contribute to the Patriots in other ways, spending most of the campaign tutoring rookie running backs Stevan Ridley and Shane Vereen, who later said that "working with Kevin Faulk has really opened my eyes. His work ethic is on a whole other level. Learning how hard he works has helped me a lot."

Choosing to announce his retirement at a special ceremony held at the Hall at Patriot Place, Faulk made his decision official on October 9, 2012. He ended his career with a total of 3,607 yards rushing, 431 receptions for another 3,701 yards, 33 touchdowns, and a rushing average of 4.2 yards per carry that ranks as the third-highest in Patriots history. In addition to holding franchise records for most all-purpose and kickoff return yards, Faulk's 431 receptions are the most ever recorded by a Patriots running back. He also ranks among the team's all-time leaders in rushing yards and punt return yards.

One of only six players to rush more for more than 3,000 yards and gain over 3,000 yards receiving during the first decade of the 21st century (Tiki Barber, Marshall Faulk, Michael Pittman, LaDanian Tomlinson, and Brian Westbrook were the others), Faulk earned spots on the Patriots' 2000s All-Decade Team and 50th Anniversary Team with the tremendous all-around contributions he made to the organization through the years. In acknowledging those contributions, Patriots chairman and CEO Robert Kraft said at Faulk's retirement ceremony, "Kevin Faulk helped define the way an entire generation of Patriots fans have come to view and appreciate our brand of football. He worked so hard to get better every year. He was always one of the first to arrive in the building and among the last to leave. His work ethic, enthusiasm for the game and clutch performances, especially on third down, earned him the respect of his coaches, teammates and fans alike. He retires a Patriot whose career will always be celebrated for helping deliver three Super Bowl Championships to New England."

CAREER HIGHLIGHTS

Best Season

Faulk had one of his finest seasons for the Patriots in 2003, when he rushed for a career-best 638 yards, made 48 receptions for another 440 yards, and gained 1,351 all-purpose yards. He also performed extremely well the previous year, when he accumulated 1,440 all-purpose yards, finished second in the NFL with a 27.9-yard kickoff return average, and scored a career-high seven touchdowns, two of which came on kickoff returns. By recording multiple touchdowns in three different categories—rushing, receiving, and kick returns—Faulk established himself as the only NFL player to accomplish the feat during the 2002 campaign. Faulk had another very productive year in 2008, when he gained 507 yards on just 83 rushing attempts, averaging in the process a career-high 6.1 yards per carry. He also scored six touchdowns, gained 1,161 all-purpose yards, and established career highs with 58 pass receptions and 486 receiving yards. Nevertheless, Faulk made his greatest overall impact in just his second NFL season, concluding the 2000 campaign with 570 yards rushing, 51 receptions for another 465 yards, five touchdowns, and a career-best 1,909 all-purpose yards.

Memorable Moments/Greatest Performances

Faulk scored his first career touchdown during a 24-23 win over the Denver Broncos on October 24, 1999, opening the game's scoring with a 15-yard TD run on the Patriots' second possession. In an outstanding all-around effort, Faulk gained a total of 238 yards on the day—24 on the ground, 4 through the air, 140 on six kickoff returns, and another 70 on four punt returns.

Three weeks later, during a 24-17 loss to the Jets on November 15, Faulk recorded the longest kickoff return of his career, going 95 yards before finally being brought down by New York's Anthony Pleasant at the Jets eight-yard line. He also scored a touchdown later in the game, hooking up with Drew Bledsoe on a 13-yard TD pass play.

The very next week, during a 27-17 loss to the Miami Dolphins, Faulk burst off left guard for 43 yards, recording in the process the longest run from scrimmage of his career.

Although the Patriots lost their December 24, 2000, matchup with the Dolphins 27-24, Faulk made the longest touchdown reception of his career, hauling in a 52-yard TD pass from Drew Bledsoe.

Faulk played one of his finest all-around games on November 23, 2003, when he helped lead the Patriots to a 23-20 overtime win over the Houston Texans by carrying the ball 23 times for 80 yards, and gaining another 108 yards on eight pass receptions.

Faulk also returned two kickoffs for touchdowns during his career, recording both those TDs in 2002. He accomplished the feat for the first time on November 17, bringing the Patriots to within seven points of Oakland late in the fourth quarter by returning a Sebastian Janikowski kickoff 86 yards for the final score in a game the Raiders won, 27-20. Faulk duplicated his earlier effort five weeks later, returning a John Hall kickoff 87 yards for a touchdown during a 30-17 loss to the Jets on December 22.

NOTABLE ACHIEVEMENTS

- Surpassed 50 receptions twice.
- Topped 400 receiving yards three times.
- Averaged more than five yards per carry four times.
- Surpassed 1,000 yards from scrimmage twice.
- Topped 1,000 all-purpose yards seven times.
- Returned two kickoffs for touchdowns.

- Led NFL with two kickoff-return touchdowns in 2002.
- Finished second in NFL with average of 27.9 yards per kickoff return in 2002.
- Holds Patriots career records for: most all-purpose yards (12,349); most kickoff return yards (4,098); and most pass receptions by a running back (431).
- Ranks among Patriots all-time leaders in: rushing yards (5th); rushing average (tied-2nd); pass receptions (5th); and punt return yards (6th).
- Five-time AFC champion (2001, 2003, 2004, 2007 & 2011).
- Three-time Super Bowl champion (XXXVI, XXXVIII & XXXIX).
- Member of Patriots' 2000s All-Decade Team.
- Named to Patriots' 50th Anniversary Team in 2009.

22

Tom Addison

Tom Addison with other Patriot players at the 1963 AFL All-Star Game (Courtesy Tales of the American Football League)

An original Patriot, Tom Addison spent eight years in Boston, serving as team captain throughout most of that period. Manning the left outside linebacker position his entire time in Boston, Addison appeared in every game for the Patriots from 1961 to 1966, missing a total of only six contests his entire career. One of the first Patriot players to earn All-AFL honors, Addison played in four Pro Bowls and received five All-Pro nominations over the course of his eight-year career, which ended prematurely as the result of a knee injury he sustained late in 1967. Yet, even though Addison retired from the game at only 31 years of age, he accomplished enough during his time in Boston to be awarded a spot on the Patriots' first all-decade team by a fan ballot in 1971.

Born in Lancaster, South Carolina, on April 12, 1936, Thomas Marion Addison went to Lancaster High School, after which he attended the University of South Carolina on an athletic scholarship. A star offensive tackle in college, Addison spurned both the Baltimore Colts, who selected him in the 12th round of the 1958 NFL Draft with the 141st overall pick, and the Canadian Football League's Ottawa Rough Riders, who also drafted him, choosing instead to begin his professional career with the Boston Patriots in 1960.

Shifted to linebacker by the Patriots upon his arrival in Boston, the 6'2", 230-pound Addison adapted quickly to the change in positions, earning a starting job early in his rookie season, and rapidly developing into one of the Patriots' team leaders. An excellent run-defender and capable pass-rusher, Addison made All-Pro in the AFL's inaugural season, although he failed to make an All-Star appearance since the infant league did not formally introduce an All-Star Game until the ensuing campaign. After being named team captain prior to the start of the 1961 season, Addison began an exceptional four-year run during which he made the AFL All-Star Team and earned All-Pro honors each year. Particularly effective from 1961 to 1963, Addison intercepted a total of 13 passes over that three-year stretch, displaying his tremendous versatility by doing an outstanding job of dropping into pass coverage.

A key member of Boston's 1963 AFL Eastern Division Championship team, Addison most certainly benefitted from playing behind arguably the league's most formidable defensive line. Nevertheless, he proved to be a rugged and aggressive defender who excelled in every aspect of the game, particularly against the run, where he developed a reputation second to none in the league.

While still at the top of his game, Addison used his leadership skills to spearhead an effort to improve pension and security benefits for all AFL players. Named the first president of the American Football League Players Association early in 1964, Addison proved to be extremely instrumental in obtaining for AFL players viable pension, medical, and insurance plans. Largely through his efforts, AFL players received the same representation and protection accorded to their NFL counterparts, thereby enabling the infant circuit to compete for top talent and survive as a separate entity until the two leagues merged in 1970.

Although Addison failed to earn Pro Bowl or All-Pro honors in either 1965 or 1966, he remained one of the Patriots' most dependable players, continuing his string of six consecutive seasons without missing a start. Apparently on his way to extending his streak to seven, Addison sat out the final three games of the 1967 campaign after injuring his knee in a Week 11 loss to the New York Jets. Subsequently unable to fully recover from his second knee surgery, Addison was released by the Patriots on June 18, 1968, after team doctors advised him not to play again. He announced his retirement shortly thereafter, ending his eight-year career in Boston with a total of 16 interceptions in 106 regular-season games. Among his five All-AFL nominations was one First-Team selection, which he garnered in 1961. Four years after Addison retired, Patriot fans awarded him a spot on the franchise's All-1960s Team. He lived another 40 years, passing away at his home in Bluffton, South Carolina, on June 14, 2011, some two months after celebrating his 75th birthday.

CAREER HIGHLIGHTS

Best Season

Addison established career highs with 5 interceptions and 42 return yards in 1962. However, he had his finest all-around season one year earlier, when he earned First-Team All-Pro honors for the only time in his career.

Memorable Moments/Greatest Performances

Addison played an integral role in securing victory for the Patriots in the 1963 AFL Eastern Division Championship Game when he made a key play early in the fourth quarter. With the Pats in front 26-8 and Buffalo on the verge of making it a two-touchdown game, Addison tackled Bills quarterback Jack Kemp for a loss near the Patriots' goal line on fourth down, ending any hopes Buffalo had of mounting a comeback.

Addison experienced one of his most memorable moments on October 6, 1962, when he recorded the only touchdown of his career, returning an interception of a Lee Grosscup pass 12 yards for a score during a 43-14 victory over the New York Titans.

NOTABLE ACHIEVEMENTS

- Started every game from 1961 to 1966 (84 straight games).
- 1963 AFL Eastern Division champion.

- Five-time AFL All-Star selection (1960, 1961, 1962, 1963 & 1964).
- 1961 First-Team All-AFL selection.
- Four-time Second-Team All-AFL selection (1960, 1962, 1963 & 1964).
- Member of Patriots' 1960s All-Decade Team.

23

Jim Nance

(Courtesy Fenway Park Diaries)

The first Patriots running back to rush for more than 1,000 yards in a season, Jim Nance surpassed that magical figure in both 1966 and 1967, making him the only player in AFL history to accomplish the feat in back-to-back seasons. With 1,458 yards rushing in the first of those campaigns, the powerful Nance set a Patriots record that stood for nearly 30 years, further distinguishing himself by rushing for more yards in a season than any other player in the 10-year history of the AFL. Nance's extraordinary performance earned him league MVP honors, a spot in the Pro Bowl, and the first of two straight First-Team All-Pro selections. Although injuries ended up having a profound impact on Nance's career, limiting him to only seven seasons in Boston, he remains the Patriots' second-leading all-time rusher more than 40 years after he played his last game for them. Nance also continues to hold the franchise record for most touchdowns scored on the ground, earning in the process a spot on the Pats' 50th Anniversary Team and a place in their Hall of Fame.

Born in Indiana, Pennsylvania, on December 30, 1942, James Solomon Nance attended Indiana High School, before moving on to Syracuse University, where he starred at running back and won two NCAA heavyweight wrestling championships, losing only one of 92 matches in three varsity wrestling seasons. After Nance received All-America honors twice while playing for the Orangemen, the Chicago Bears selected him in the fourth round of the 1965 NFL Draft, with the 45th overall pick. Nance, though, instead chose to sign with the Boston Patriots, who selected him with the 151st overall pick, in the 19th round of the AFL Draft.

Although Nance scored 5 touchdowns as a rookie, he failed to distinguish himself in his first year of pro ball, rushing for only 321 yards, and averaging just 2.9 yards per carry. However, he established himself as the AFL's dominant running back in his second season, leading the league with 1,458 yards rushing, 11 rushing touchdowns, and 1,561 yards from scrimmage, en route to earning consensus Player of the Year honors. Nance followed that up by winning his second consecutive rushing title in 1967, this time carrying the ball for 1,216 yards and 7 touchdowns. By rushing for more than 1,000 yards for the second straight season, Nance became the only player in AFL history to accomplish the feat. He also joined San Diego's Paul Lowe as the only players in league history to reach the 1,000-yard plateau more than once. Nance's exceptional performance earned him Pro Bowl and First-Team All-Pro honors for the second straight time.

A classic fullback who stood 6'1" tall and weighed nearly 250 pounds, Nance possessed a powerful frame that enabled him to bounce off tacklers and drag others along with him. Yet, he also had outstanding quickness for a big man, often using his nimbleness to outmaneuver larger defenders at the point of attack.

Displaying a lack of timing and conditioning after reporting to camp late following a lengthy holdout prior to the start of the 1968 season, Nance suffered through an injury-marred campaign during which he rushed for only 593 yards. However, after undergoing surgery to repair his badly injured ankle during the subsequent offseason, Nance returned to the Patriots in 1969 tipping the scales at a relatively svelte 225 pounds. Although he failed to regain his earlier form, Nance managed to win AFL Comeback Player of the Year honors by finishing second in the league with 750 yards rushing. He also made a career-high 29 pass receptions and placed near the top of the league rankings with 6 rushing touchdowns.

Nance never again ranked among the AFL's elite running backs, rushing for a total of only 985 yards over the course of the next two seasons, before being traded to the Philadelphia Eagles prior to the start of the 1972 campaign. Having no desire to play in Philadelphia, Nance subsequently announced his retirement. However, after sitting out all of 1972, he attempted a comeback with the Jets the following year. Nance elected to leave New York after he rushed for only 78 yards as a backup with the Patriots' AFC East rivals in 1973. He then spent the next two seasons playing in the World Football League, splitting his time there between the Houston Texans and the Shreveport Steamer. Although Nance experienced a considerable amount of success in the WFL, establishing himself as the league's all-time leading rusher by gaining just over 2,000 yards on the ground over the course of his two seasons there, he called it quits for good when the league folded at the conclusion of the 1975 campaign. Excluding his time in the WFL, Nance ended his playing career with 5,401 yards rushing, 133 pass receptions for another 870 yards, a total of 46 touchdowns, and a rushing average of 4.0 yards per carry. His total of 5,323 yards rushing as a member of the Patriots places him second only to Sam Cunningham in franchise history. Meanwhile, his 45 rushing touchdowns remain a team record.

Unfortunately, poor health plagued Nance throughout much of his post-football life. After suffering a heart attack and stroke in 1983, he overcame paralysis in his left leg and arm to live another nine years, before passing away at only 49 years of age on June 16, 1992. Following Nance's death, Patriots executive officer Sam Jankovich released a statement that said, "We are all saddened by the loss of Jim Nance. As a player, Jim was a tough, powerful running back. He gave it everything he had on the field. And, in his lifetime, he battled back from adversity."

Patriots owner Robert Kraft also addressed Nance's passing, saying in a prepared statement, "He (Nance) was an attraction. He brought fans to the games, and that was very important in building a loyal fan base. Four decades later, we still have many season ticket holders who became fans of the Patriots in the 1960s because of players like Jim Nance. The fact that he still holds some prominent rushing records 38 years after his playing career speaks volumes."

The Patriots inducted Nance into their Hall of Fame 17 years later, in 2009, making him the 14th player, and the first running back, to be so honored. That very same year, Nance earned the honor of being named to the Pats' 50th Anniversary Team.

PATRIOT CAREER HIGHLIGHTS

Best Season

Nance had a big year for the Patriots in 1967, leading the AFL for the second straight time in yards rushing (1,216), rushing attempts (269), and rushing yards per game (86.9). He also placed among the leaders with 7 rushing touchdowns, 1,412 yards from scrimmage, and a 4.5-yard rushing average. Still, there is little doubt that Nance had the finest season of his career one year earlier. In addition to setting an AFL record in 1966 by gaining 1,458 yards on the ground, Nance led the league with 299 rushing attempts, 11 rushing touchdowns, 1,561 yards from scrimmage, and 104.1 rushing yards per game, en route to earning AFL MVP honors. Nance's average of 104.1 rushing yards per game remains a Patriots record.

Memorable Moments/Greatest Performances

Nance performed brilliantly a number of times during his banner year of 1966, having his breakout game on September 18, when he helped the Patriots even their record at 1-1 by carrying the ball 24 times, for 126 yards and 1 touchdown, during a 24-10 victory over the Broncos in Denver.

On October 30, Nance rushed for 2 TDs and a career-high 208 yards during a 24-21 home win over the Raiders. A true workhorse, Nance carried the ball 38 times over the course of the contest.

Nance helped the Patriots record another close victory four weeks later, on November 27, leading them to a 20-14 road win over the Dolphins by carrying the ball 23 times, for 133 yards and 1 touchdown. His 27-yard TD run midway through the third quarter ended up providing the winning margin, with the Dolphins subsequently scoring the game's final 14 points.

Nance rushed for 109 yards and 1 touchdown during a big 14-3 win over the Bills the following week that gave the Patriots sole possession of first place in the AFL's Eastern Division with only two games remaining on the schedule. The fullback made arguably the game's biggest play late in the first quarter, when, on a third-and-two situation from his own 35 yard line, he rammed over left guard, knocked away two defenders, and spun off a third, en route to recording a career-long 65-yard touchdown that gave the Patriots a 7-3 lead.

Nance ripped off another long touchdown run the very next week, scoring from 57 yards out during a 38-14 win over the Houston Oilers. He finished the day with 146 yards on 17 carries.

Nance also turned in a pair of epic performances the following year, with the first of those coming on September 24, 1967, when he carried the ball 34 times, for 185 yards and 1 touchdown, during a 23-0 win over the Bills. Later in the year, on December 17, he rushed for 164 yards and 2 touchdowns during 41-32 loss to the Dolphins.

Nance surpassed 100 yards rushing for the final time in his career on November 16, 1969, when he led the Patriots to a 25-14 win over the Cincinnati Bengals by carrying the ball 24 times for 125 yards.

NOTABLE ACHIEVEMENTS

- Rushed for more than 1,000 yards twice (1966 & 1967).
- Scored 11 touchdowns in 1966.
- Led AFL in: rushing yards twice; rushing touchdowns once; rushing attempts three times; rushing yards per game twice; all-purpose yards once; and yards from scrimmage once.
- Holds AFL single-season record for most rushing yardage (1,458 in 1966).
- Only AFL back to surpass 1,000 yards rushing in consecutive seasons (1966 & 1967).
- Holds Patriots career record for most rushing touchdowns (45).
- Ranks among Patriots all-time leaders in: rushing yardage (2nd); rushing average (9th); total touchdowns scored (6th); and total points scored (10th).
- 1966 AFL MVP.
- 1969 AFL Comeback Player of the Year.
- Two-time AFL Pro Bowl selection (1966 & 1967).
- Two-time First-Team All-AFL selection (1966 & 1967).
- 1969 Second-Team All-AFL selection.
- Named to Patriots' 50th Anniversary Team in 2009.
- Inducted into Patriots Hall of Fame in 2009.

24

Raymond Clayborn

(Courtesy Boston.com)

The fact that Raymond Clayborn spent his first few seasons in New England playing opposite Mike Haynes in the Patriots' defensive backfield likely prevented him from receiving as much credit as he deserved for his outstanding defensive work. But, with the departure of Haynes in 1983, Clayborn assumed a more prominent role in the Pats' secondary, subsequently establishing himself as one of the AFC's premier cover corners. After previously playing in Haynes' shadow, Clayborn appeared in the Pro Bowl three times between 1983 and 1986, also earning All-AFC honors in three of those four seasons. By the time he left New England at the conclusion of the 1989 campaign, Clayborn had recorded a total of 36 interceptions, tying him with Ty Law for the most in franchise history. He also amassed a total of 555 interception return yards, placing him second only to Law in team annals. An outstanding kickoff returner as well, Clayborn returned three kickoffs for touchdowns early in his career, before surrendering his kickoff duties to focus exclusively on shutting down opposing wide receivers. Clayborn's exceptional all-around play eventually earned him spots on the Patriots' All-1970s Team, All-1980s Team, and 35th Anniversary Team.

Born in Fort Worth, Texas, on January 2, 1955, Raymond Dean Clayborn attended Green B. Trimble Technical High School, before enrolling at the University of Texas at Austin. A three-year starter at Texas, Clayborn performed so well for the Longhorns that the Patriots selected him in the first round of the 1977 NFL Draft, with the 16th overall pick. In spite of his reputation, though, Clayborn failed to earn a starting job his first year in the league, spending most of his rookie campaign returning kickoffs and sitting on the bench behind starting cornerbacks Mike Haynes and Bobby Howard. Looking back at the early stages of his career, Clayborn said:

> You have to remember that, when I came out of Texas, I really wasn't versed in playing man-to man, even zone for that matter. We played an old, traditional cover-3. It was a running-type conference, the style for this conference. They didn't have the intricate passing games that they had in the pros. So, I actually didn't start my first year. I played behind Bobby Howard, who was an 11-year veteran in 1977 when I came up here with the Patriots. He was a technician. He was a guy that was a teacher, and they told me to follow him, to watch him and the things that he did. I think Mike would feel the same way too. Bobby Howard was a guy that you could look back on and say he helped us out tremendously with confidence, technique and fundamentals of the game.

While learning the intricacies of playing cornerback at the professional level, Clayborn made the most of his opportunity to return kickoffs, scoring three times on kickoff returns and averaging a league-leading 31 yards per return as a rookie, en route to earning First-Team All-NFL honors from *Pro Football Weekly*. Clayborn replaced Howard as the starting left cornerback the following year, displaying tremendous promise by intercepting 4 passes, which he returned for 72 yards. He followed that up by leading the Patriots with 5 picks in both 1979 and 1980, establishing himself during that time as arguably the best "number 2" corner in the league.

Having refined the technique he employed throughout the remainder of his career, Clayborn later discussed the manner in which he used his six-foot, 190-pound frame to impose his will on opposing receivers at the line of scrimmage, stating, "I definitely preferred man-to-man (coverage). I wanted to get up in people's faces. I wanted to challenge them on every play, whether it be a run or pass, because most of the time when it was a run play and you're right up on them, they're going to block you, so I had to get aggressive with them, and I tried to do the same in pass coverage; try to force them off what they wanted to do, and try to guide them into what I wanted them to do."

Clayborn continued to play left cornerback one more year, before switching sides with Haynes prior to the 1982 campaign. Clayborn spent the rest of his career at right cornerback, assuming the additional responsibility of covering the opposing team's top wide receiver when Haynes left for Los Angeles the following season. Although he failed to record an interception in 1983, Clayborn did an excellent job on the right side of New England's defense, earning his first Pro Bowl berth and Second-Team All-AFC honors.

After another solid season in 1984, Clayborn had arguably his best year in 1985, recording a career-high 6 interceptions, one of which he returned for a touchdown. His outstanding performance earned him a spot in the Pro Bowl and his lone Second-Team All-NFL selection. Clayborn made his final Pro Bowl appearance the following year, also earning First-Team All-AFC honors by recording 3 interceptions and 2 fumble recoveries. He spent three more seasons in New England, intercepting another 7 passes, to give him a career total of 36 picks that remains a team record. In addition to amassing 555 yards on interception returns, Clayborn returned 57 kickoffs for 1,538 yards and 3 touchdowns.

After leaving the Patriots, Clayborn joined the Cleveland Browns, with whom he spent the next two seasons before retiring in 1991. Reflecting on his final days in New England, Clayborn said, "The Patriots were in turmoil . . . total chaos. I was so happy to get out of there. The league was threatening, and eventually took over the payroll, because the Sullivans had gone into bankruptcy. Mr. Kraft had bought the stadium in '87 in bankruptcy after the Michael Jackson fiasco."

Clayborn assumed numerous jobs following his retirement, before eventually landing the position of NFL Uniform Program Representative for the Houston Texans. A prostate cancer survivor, he currently resides in the Houston suburb of Katy.

Although Clayborn has yet to be inducted into the Patriots Hall of Fame, Ty Law, who admitted to chasing the former's records during his time in New England, believes that the time has come for his predecessor to be recognized for his accomplishments, stating:

> Raymond Clayborn, you look at this guy and why hasn't he been there in the Hall of Fame. His numbers speak for themselves. And you see his highlights and you're like, 'Man, if he didn't get in, how the hell am I going to get in?' That's what you think about as a player when you see some of the greats. . . . Not trying to take away anything from yourself, but you can't but help look at a guy like that and think to say it's his time. He deserves it. He's waited long enough.

PATRIOT CAREER HIGHLIGHTS

Best Season

Clayborn made a tremendous impact as a kickoff return specialist in his rookie campaign of 1977, finishing third in the NFL with 869 return yards, and leading the league with 3 special team touchdowns and a 31.0-yard return average, both of which remain franchise records. However, he had his finest season as a cornerback in 1985, when he helped the Patriots advance to the Super Bowl by recording a career-high 6 interceptions, en route to earning Second-Team All-NFL honors from the Newspaper Enterprise Association.

Memorable Moments/Greatest Performances

Clayborn established a Patriots record that still stands by returning three kickoffs for touchdowns in 1977. His first came in Week 3, going 100 yards for a score during a 30-27 loss to the Jets on October 2. Five weeks later, on November 6, Clayborn scored 6 points when he returned a kickoff 93 yards during a 24-14 loss to the Buffalo Bills. Although the Patriots ended up blowing an 18-point lead to the Baltimore Colts in the regular-season finale, Clayborn returned the second-half kickoff 101 yards, temporarily putting his team up 21-3. However, led by Bert Jones, the Colts mounted a comeback, eventually prevailing 30-24.

Clayborn intercepted two passes in one game for the only time in his career on October 12, 1980, recording two of New England's four picks during a 34-0 victory over Miami.

Almost exactly four years later, during a 17-16 win over the Browns on October 7, 1984, Clayborn recorded the longest interception return of his career, running 85 yards after picking off a Paul McDonald pass before finally being brought down deep inside Cleveland territory.

The month of October proved to be an excellent one for Clayborn, who scored his only touchdown on an interception return on October 13, 1985, when he helped the Patriots defeat Buffalo 14-3 by returning an errant Vince Ferragamo pass 27 yards for the game's final score.

Clayborn continued to display his penchant for making big plays in October when, on October 18, 1987, he returned a blocked field goal attempt 71 yards for a touchdown during a 21-7 victory over the Houston Oilers.

Clayborn turned in one of his finest all-around performances in the 1985 AFC Championship Game, helping to lead the Patriots to a 31-14 win over the rival Miami Dolphins by intercepting one Dan Marino pass and defending against six others. The victory, which sent New England to the Super Bowl, ended an 18-game losing streak to the Dolphins in the Orange Bowl. When asked which of his interceptions he remembers most, Clayborn responded without hesitation, "The one in the AFC Championship Game against those Miami Dolphins, and Dan Marino, and those 'Marks Brothers.' I got one to stop a drive they had going, and it just really felt great to get at that particular time, and to lead us into Super Bowl XX."

Yet, the most infamous incident of Clayborn's career actually occurred off the field, in the Patriots' locker room, following a lopsided 56-3 victory over the Jets on September 9, 1979. Despite his team's dominating performance, Clayborn remained in a foul mood after suffering through a bad week of practice during which he scuffled with teammates on two separate occasions. Clayborn, who continued to vent his frustration by snapping at writers and bumping into them on purpose following the contest, agitated Will McDonough of the *Boston Globe* with his actions, prompting the legendary writer to say, "Hey, Ray, there's no need to do that." When Clayborn responded by jabbing his finger in McDonough's face and poking him in the eye, the latter punched him twice, knocking him into a laundry cart, which caused him to fall to the floor. Word of the incident spread quickly, with some accounts stating that McDonough had knocked Clayborn "out cold" with a single punch, while others described more of a scuffle between the two men. Either way, McDonough became a hero to his colleagues in the press, while Clayborn ended up being cast as a villain.

NOTABLE ACHIEVEMENTS

- Recorded at least 5 interceptions three times.
- Returned one interception for a touchdown.
- Returned 3 kickoffs for touchdowns.
- Led NFL with 3 kickoff return touchdowns and 31-yard kickoff return average in 1977.
- Finished third in NFL with 869 kickoff return yards in 1977.
- Tied for first all-time on Patriots with 36 career interceptions (Ty Law).
- Ranks second in Patriots history with 555 interception return yards.
- Holds Patriots single-season records for highest kickoff return average (31.0) and most kickoffs returned for touchdowns (3), both in 1977.
- 1985 AFC champion.
- Three-time Pro Bowl selection (1983, 1985 & 1986).
- 1985 Second-Team All-Pro selection.
- Two-time First-Team All-AFC selection (1977 & 1986).
- Three-time Second-Team All-AFC selection (1983, 1985 & 1988).
- Member of Patriots' All-1970s Team.
- Member of Patriots' All-1980s Team.
- Named to Patriots' 35th Anniversary Team in 1994.

25

Willie McGinest

(Courtney George A. Kitrinos)

An extremely versatile player who excelled at both linebacker and defensive end over the course of his career, Willie McGinest proved to be one of the Patriots' most dynamic defenders during his 12 years in New England. Third on the Pats' all-time sack list, McGinest tackled opposing quarterbacks behind the line of scrimmage at least 9 times in four different seasons, en route to amassing a total of 78 sacks as a member of the team. Particularly effective in big games, McGinest recorded a total of 16 sacks in

10 postseason contests with the Patriots, establishing himself in the process as the NFL's all-time sack leader in playoff history. An outstanding team leader as well, McGinest served as one of the Pats' defensive co-captains his last several years in New England, helping them create an NFL dynasty that saw them capture four AFC championships and win three Super Bowls between 1996 and 2004. Although McGinest spent the final three years of his playing career with the Cleveland Browns after leaving the Patriots at the conclusion of the 2005 campaign, he remains one of the most iconic players in franchise history and an adopted son of New England.

Born in Long Beach, California, on December 11, 1971, William Lee McGinest Jr. attended Long Beach Polytechnic High School, where he garnered all-state honors in football and basketball. A 14-point scorer on the basketball court during the 1989–90 season, McGinest excelled even more on the gridiron, earning All-American recognition from *Super Prep, Blue Chip, and Tom Lemming* magazines as a linebacker in 1989. Courted by numerous colleges following his graduation from Long Beach Polytechnic, McGinest ultimately chose to enroll at the University of Southern California. A three-year starter at defensive end for the Trojans, McGinest earned All-Pac-10 Conference honors three straight times and All-American acclaim as a senior, when he was a finalist for the Lombardi Award, presented annually to the best lineman or linebacker in college football.

Subsequently selected by the Patriots with the fourth overall pick of the 1994 NFL Draft, McGinest spent the early part of his rookie campaign platooning with Dwayne Sabb at left outside linebacker, before taking over as the full-time starter at the position during the season's second half. Playing well in his first year as a pro, McGinest recorded 4 ½ sacks and 43 tackles (29 solo), en route to earning All-Rookie recognition by *Pro Football Weekly*. The 1776 Quarterback Club also named him their 1994 Rookie of the Year.

The 6'5", 270-pound McGinest developed into one of the AFC's elite outside linebackers in his sophomore campaign of 1995, registering 88 tackles and a team-leading 11 sacks. Nevertheless, New England's coaching staff elected to deploy him primarily as a defensive lineman the following year, moving him to right defensive end, the same position he played in college. Excelling in his new role, McGinest earned Pro Bowl honors by making 9 ½ sacks and 67 tackles, 49 of which were unassisted.

Adversely affected by injuries in each of the next two seasons, McGinest appeared in a total of only 20 games in 1997 and 1998, recording just 5 ½ sacks and 64 tackles over the course of those two campaigns. Healthy again in 1999, he made 76 tackles and a team-leading 9 sacks.

After playing right defensive end almost exclusively from 1996 to 1999, McGinest shifted to the other side of the Patriots' defense in 2000, spending most of his remaining years in New England splitting his time between left defensive end and left outside linebacker. Wherever McGinest lined up, though, he did an outstanding job, using his exceptional ability, tireless work ethic, and strong locker room presence to establish himself as one of the Patriots' team leaders. Commenting on his dedication to his chosen profession, McGinest said, "I've got a commitment to this game like no other. I've been playing it since I was 8 years old."

While McGinest's hard work and outgoing personality helped him develop into one of the stronger voices in the Patriots' locker room, his dynamic playmaking ability enabled him to gradually evolve into one of the cornerstones of the team's defense. After being voted defensive co-captain for the 2000 season by his teammates, McGinest became one of the men new head coach Bill Belichick relied on most heavily for leadership both on and off the field in subsequent seasons.

Shifting back and forth between linebacker and defensive end from 2000 to 2003, McGinest played well at both positions, averaging 6 sacks and 55 tackles over the course of those four seasons, in helping the Patriots win two Super Bowls. He then spent his final two seasons in New England at left outside linebacker, performing particularly well in 2004, when he made 9 ½ sacks and 51 tackles for a Patriots team that captured its third Super Bowl title in four years.

Yet, in spite of the success McGinest experienced in New England, the Patriots elected to release him on March 9, 2006. The 34-year-old veteran subsequently signed with the Cleveland Browns, reuniting him with head coach Romeo Crennel, who had earlier served as the Patriots' defensive coordinator during McGinest's stint in New England. While in Cleveland, McGinest lent a strong veteran presence to the Browns' locker room, serving as a mentor to the team's young linebacking corps that included Kamerion Wimbley and D'Owell Jackson. McGinest announced his retirement at the conclusion of the 2008 campaign, ending his career with 86 sacks, 802 tackles (583 solo), 5 interceptions, 16 forced fumbles, 17 fumble recoveries, and 4 defensive touchdowns.

Following his retirement, McGinest became an NFL analyst at Fox Sports and ESPN, before assuming a similar position with the NFL Network. Since joining the latter station, McGinest has become a regular member of the cast on the program *NFL Total Access*, where he uses his wisdom and engaging personality to entertain and enlighten viewers.

PATRIOT CAREER HIGHLIGHTS

Best Season

McGinest earned two Pro Bowl selections over the course of his career, with the first of those coming in 1996, when he helped the Patriots capture the AFC title by making 9 ½ sacks, scoring 2 defensive touchdowns, and recording 67 tackles. He made the AFC Pro Bowl roster for the second time in 2003, when he again helped the Pats win the Conference championship by registering 5 ½ sacks and 67 tackles. However, McGinest actually played his best ball for the Patriots in 1995 and 1999. In addition to leading the team with 9 sacks in the second of those campaigns, McGinest recorded 76 tackles—the second highest total of his career. He performed even better in 1995, though, establishing career highs with 11 sacks and 88 tackles (70 solo) for a Patriots team that finished the season just 6-10.

Memorable Moments/Greatest Performances

McGinest recorded the first multiple-sack game of his career on October 23, 1995, getting to Buffalo quarterback Jim Kelly twice during a 27-14 victory over the Bills. Although the Patriots lost their next game to Carolina 20-17 in overtime, McGinest had another big day, making a season-high 11 tackles. McGinest continued to establish himself as a force to be reckoned with on November 12, when he sacked Dan Marino twice and forced a fumble during a 34-17 win over Miami.

McGinest earned AFC Defensive Player of the Week honors for the first time on October 27, 1996, when he helped the Patriots defeat Buffalo 28-25 by making seven tackles, defending two passes, sacking Bills quarterback Jim Kelly once, and returning his first career interception 46 yards for the game-winning touchdown. He scored the second touchdown of his career five weeks later during a 45-7 pasting of the San Diego Chargers on December 1, when he recovered a fumble in the end zone.

McGinest began the 1999 campaign in style, earning AFC Defensive Player of the Week honors for the second time in his career by recording two sacks, forcing a fumble, and scoring a touchdown by recovering another fumble in the end zone, in leading the Patriots to a 30-28 victory over the Jets in the regular-season opener.

McGinest scored the fourth and final touchdown of his career on December 20, 2003, when he rumbled 15 yards into New York's end zone after intercepting a Chad Pennington pass during a 21-16 Patriots' win over the Jets.

Three weeks earlier, McGinest made one of the most memorable plays of the Patriots' 2003 season when he preserved their 38-34 victory over the Colts by stopping Indianapolis running back Edgerrin James just short of the goal line with 11 seconds remaining in the game.

In weeks 7 and 8 of the 2001 season, McGinest became the first Patriots player to record multiple sacks in consecutive games since Chris Slade accomplished the feat eight years earlier, doing so during a 31-20 loss to Denver on October 28 and a 24-10 win over Atlanta on November 4.

An outstanding big-game player throughout his career, McGinest saved some of his finest performances for the postseason. En route to establishing a Patriots record by recording an NFL-leading 5 sacks during the 2003 postseason, McGinest sacked Tennessee quarterback Steve McNair three times during New England's 17-14 divisional playoff victory over the Titans on January 10, 2004. However, that effort paled in comparison to the dominating performance he turned in against the Jaguars in the first round of the 2005 playoffs. In leading the Patriots to a 28-3 victory over Jacksonville in their wild-card round matchup played on January 7, 2006, McGinest recorded 8 tackles and sacked Jaguars quarterbacks Byron Leftwich and David Garrard 4 ½ times, eclipsing in the process two NFL postseason records—most sacks in a game and most career postseason sacks (16).

NOTABLE ACHIEVEMENTS

- Finished in double-digits in sacks once (11 in 1995).
- Made more than 75 tackles twice (1995 & 1999).
- Scored four defensive touchdowns during career.
- Led Patriots in sacks six times.
- Ranks third all-time on Patriots with 78 career sacks.
- Holds NFL postseason records for most sacks in one game (4 ½) and most career sacks (16).
- Four-time AFC champion (1996, 2001, 2003 & 2004).
- Three-time Super Bowl champion (XXXVI, XXXVIII & XXXIX).
- Two-time Pro Bowl selection (1996 & 2003).
- Member of Patriots' 1990s All-Decade Team.
- Member of Patriots' 2000s All-Decade Team.

26

Tedy Bruschi

(Courtesy Karen Cardoza)

The inspirational leader of the Patriots for nearly a decade, Tedy Bruschi became renowned for his relentless work ethic, on-field intensity, and exceptional leadership ability that prompted his teammates to elect him defensive co-captain in each of his final seven seasons in New England. Considered to be the consummate Patriot by head coach Bill Belichick, who called the linebacker the "perfect player" at his retirement press conference in 2009, Bruschi often set the tone for his teammates on the playing field, leading them to eight division titles, five AFC Championships, and three Super Bowl titles in his 13 years with the club. A smart and instinctive player, Bruschi surpassed 100 tackles five times, leading the Patriots in that category on three occasions. Bruschi also had a knack for making big plays in critical situations, becoming in 2003 the only player in NFL history to return four consecutive interceptions for touchdowns. Bruschi's solid all-around play earned him one Pro Bowl selection, two All-Pro nominations, spots on the Patriots' 2000s All-Decade Team and 50th Anniversary Team, and a place in their Hall of Fame. Meanwhile, his dedication and perseverance enabled him to win AP NFL Comeback Player of the Year honors in 2005, just months after he suffered a stroke that would have ended the career of someone with less determination.

Born in San Francisco, California, of Italian and Filipino parents on June 9, 1973, Tedy Lacap Bruschi attended Roseville High School, where he lettered in football, wrestling, and track and field (shot put), earning all-conference honors on the gridiron as a defensive tackle. After enrolling at the University of Arizona, Bruschi spent the next four years anchoring the Wildcats' defensive line, amassing a total of 185 tackles and tying the NCAA Division I-A sack record by recording 52 sacks. Recognized as a consensus First-Team All-American in 1994 and 1995, Bruschi received the additional honor of winning the 1995 Morris Trophy as the Pac-10 Conference's best defensive lineman.

Subsequently selected by the Patriots in the third round of the 1996 NFL Draft, with the 86th overall pick, the 6'1", 247-pound Bruschi moved to linebacker as a pro, spending most of his rookie campaign playing on special teams and being used as a pass rush specialist. Performing well in his somewhat limited role, Bruschi finished his first year in the league with four sacks, one forced fumble, and 11 tackles.

After seeing his playing time gradually increase over the next two seasons, Bruschi became a full-time starter in 1999, manning the right outside linebacker position in New England's 4-3 defense, and finishing second on the team with 107 tackles (71 solo). He followed that up with another solid performance in 2000, once again finishing second on the team in tackles, this time with 106.

Shifted to middle linebacker in 2001, Bruschi handled his new post well, placing third on the team with 75 tackles (54 solo), despite starting only 9 of the 15 games in which he appeared due to an assortment of injuries. After being voted defensive co-captain by his teammates for the first time in his career prior to the start of the 2002 campaign, Brusci once again found himself being hampered by injuries. Yet, even though he appeared in just 11 games for the Patriots, Bruschi ranked among the team leaders with 66 tackles and 4 ½ sacks. He also intercepted two passes, both of which he returned for touchdowns—the first two of his career.

Starting all 16 games for the Patriots for the first of two consecutive times in 2003, Bruschi had a big year for the eventual Super Bowl champions, earning Second-Team All-Pro honors by recording a career-high and team-leading 131 tackles (79 solo), registering two sacks, forcing three fumbles, and intercepting three passes, two of which he returned for touchdowns. He followed that up by finishing second on the team with 122 tackles (76 solo) in 2004, while also recording 3 ½ sacks and intercepting another three passes for a Patriots team that went on to win its second straight Super Bowl. Bruschi's strong performance earned him Second-Team All-Pro honors for the second consecutive time and his lone Pro Bowl selection.

Unfortunately, just 10 days after celebrating the winning of Super Bowl XXXIX with his teammates, Bruschi experienced a life-changing event of a far more serious nature that threatened to bring his playing career to a premature end. Taken to the hospital with symptoms that included temporary numbness, blurred vision, and headaches, the 31-year-old linebacker was diagnosed as having suffered a mild stroke brought on by a congenital heart defect that leaves a small hole in the wall separating the left and right atria of the heart. Partially paralyzed as a result, Bruschi entered Massachusetts General Hospital, after which he spent the next several months undergoing rehab at Spaulding Rehabilitation Hospital in Boston.

Although Bruschi initially announced that he intended to sit out the 2005 NFL season, he made a remarkable recovery, prompting the Patriots to announce on October 16, 2005, that he had been medically cleared to resume playing football. Rejoining his teammates on the practice field three days later, Bruschi was activated for the Patriots' October 30 contest with the Buffalo Bills. Displaying only a minimal amount of rust after his long layoff, Bruschi helped the Pats register a 21-16 victory over Buffalo by making seven tackles, en route to earning AFC Defensive Player of the Week honors. He subsequently started all but one of New England's remaining eight regular-season games, recording a total of 62 tackles and two sacks over the course of the campaign. The circumstances under which Bruschi made his return enabled him to win the NFL Comeback Player of the Year Award, an honor he shared with Carolina Panthers wide receiver Steve Smith. Bruschi also received the Ed Block Courage Award and the Maxwell Football Club's Spirit Award.

Despite missing the first game of the 2006 season after undergoing surgery to repair a broken bone he suffered at the start of training camp,

Bruschi ended up making significant contributions to a New England team that won its fourth straight AFC East title. In addition to leading the Pats with 112 tackles (54 solo), he recorded 1 ½ sacks and the last of his 12 career interceptions. Bruschi followed that up by registering two sacks and a team-leading 92 tackles (64 solo) in the ensuing campaign, before seeing his production fall off somewhat in 2008 due to an assortment of injuries that limited him to 12 starts.

Choosing to announce his retirement prior to the start of the 2009 season, Bruschi made his decision official at a press conference held on August 28, with Patriots head coach Bill Belichick and team owner Robert Kraft standing by his side. Upon learning of Bruschi's decision, Belichick stated, "I've had the privilege of coaching a lot of great players and leaders in the National Football League, and I'll just put Tedy up there with all of them, and above all of them. There's no player that I think epitomizes more of what I believe a player should be on the field, off the field, really, in every situation."

In 189 regular-season games over the course of his career, Bruschi recorded 1,063 tackles (675 solo) and 30 ½ sacks. Including the postseason, he played in a total of 211 games, 144 of which the Patriots won, giving them a .682 winning percentage in those contests. Their postseason record with Bruschi in the lineup was a sparkling 16-6.

Following his retirement, Bruschi joined ESPN, where he assumed the role of an NFL analyst. While serving in that capacity, he became the 19th player and 21st member of the Patriots Hall of Fame when the team announced the results of a popular fan vote on May 21, 2013. Bruschi's induction ceremony took place during halftime of a Thursday Night Football game between the Patriots and Jets on September 12, 2013.

CAREER HIGHLIGHTS

Best Season

Bruschi had his first big year for the Patriots in 1999, when, playing on the outside, he made his first career interception and recorded 107 tackles, two sacks, and one forced fumble. Bruschi earned Second-Team All-Pro honors and made his lone Pro Bowl appearance in 2004, when, after moving to the inside a few years earlier, he registered 3 ½ sacks and placed second on the team with 122 tackles and three interceptions. However, Bruschi played his best ball for the Patriots one year earlier, concluding the 2003 campaign with two sacks, three interceptions, two of which he returned for touchdowns, three forced fumbles, and a career-high 131 tackles and 14 passes defended.

Memorable Moments/Greatest Performances

Bruschi scored the first of his five career touchdowns in just the fifth game of his rookie campaign of 1996 while playing on special teams. Scooping up a loose ball after teammate Larry Whigham blocked a Greg Montgomery punt, Bruschi returned it four yards for a TD that gave the Patriots a commanding 46-22 fourth-quarter lead over the Baltimore Ravens. Although two late scores by Baltimore closed the gap considerably, the Pats ended up winning the game 46-38.

Bruschi intercepted his first pass as a pro later that year when he picked off a Mark Brunell pass and returned it 12 yards during New England's 20-6 win over Jacksonville in the AFC Championship Game. Two weeks later, he sacked Brett Favre twice during the Patriots' 35-21 loss to Green Bay in Super Bowl XXXI.

Known for his penchant for making big plays, Bruschi returned four of his 12 career interceptions for touchdowns, with his first such score coming during a 27-20 loss to the Oakland Raiders on November 17, 2002, when he picked off a Rich Gannon pass late in the third quarter and returned it 48 yards for New England's first TD of the game. Bruschi accomplished the feat again just two weeks later during a 20-12 win over the Detroit Lions, giving the Pats an early 10-0 lead by intercepting an errant Joey Harrington pass and returning it 27 yards for a touchdown.

Bruschi scored the third defensive touchdown of his career on September 14, 2003, when he turned an interception against Philadelphia's Donovan McNabb into an 18-yard scoring play during a 31-10 victory over the Eagles. Bruschi also recorded a sack and three tackles during the contest, en route to earning AFC Defensive Player of the Week honors. Bruschi was again named the conference's top defensive player in Week 14, when he made six tackles and returned an interception five yards for the Patriots' only touchdown during a 12-0 win over Miami. Bruschi's TD pick made him the only player in NFL history to return four consecutive interceptions for touchdowns.

Bruschi earned AFC Defensive Player of the Week honors three times in 2004, with his two most notable performances coming in the regular-season finale against San Francisco and the Divisional Playoff against Indianapolis. In leading the Patriots to a 21-7 victory over the 49ers, Bruschi recorded a career-high 16 tackles. During a 20-3 win over the Colts two weeks later, he made eight tackles, forced a fumble, and recovered two others.

Nevertheless, Bruschi's return to the playing field on October 30, 2005, after suffering a stroke just eight months earlier, would have to be considered the most emotional and memorable moment of his career. After receiving a warm ovation from the Gillette Stadium crowd, which welcomed him back after his lengthy absence, Bruschi inspired his teammates by making seven tackles, in leading them to a 21-16 victory over Buffalo.

NOTABLE ACHIEVEMENTS

- Surpassed 100 tackles five times.
- Led Patriots in tackles three times.
- Scored four defensive touchdowns during career.
- Led NFL with two interceptions returned for touchdowns in 2003.
- Only player in NFL history to return four consecutive interceptions for touchdowns.
- Five-time AFC champion (1996, 2001, 2003, 2004 & 2007).
- Three-time Super Bowl champion (XXXVI, XXXVIII & XXXIX).
- 2004 Pro Bowl selection.
- Two-time Second-Team All-Pro selection (2003 & 2004).
- Two-time Ed Block Courage Award winner (2000 & 2005).
- 2005 AP NFL Comeback Player of the Year.
- Member of Patriots' 2000s All-Decade Team.
- Named to Patriots' 50th Anniversary Team in 2009.
- Inducted into Patriots Hall of Fame in 2013.

27

Mike Vrabel

(Courtesy Barry Lenard)

Another member of the Patriots linebacking corps in each of their Super Bowl championship seasons, Mike Vrabel proved to be one of the team's most versatile players. Whether lining up as an inside or outside backer, or occasionally as an extra tight end on offense, Vrabel did an outstanding job for the Pats, making significant contributions to teams that won six AFC East titles and four conference championships over the course of his eight seasons with the club. Playing well against both the run and the pass, Vrabel regularly finished among the Patriots' leaders in tackles and sacks, leading them in each category at different times. He also excelled as a pass-receiving specialist in short-yardage goal-line situations, making eight TD receptions, none of which went for more than two yards. Vrabel's solid all-around play ended up earning him one Pro Bowl selection, one First-Team All-Pro nomination, and spots on *Sports Illustrated*'s 2000s All-Decade Team, the Patriots' 2000s All-Decade Team, and the Patriots' 50th Anniversary Team.

Born in Akron, Ohio, on August 14, 1975, Michael George Vrabel attended Walsh Jesuit High School in Cuyahoga Falls, Ohio, where he first made a name for himself as the star of the Warriors football team. After accepting an athletic scholarship to Ohio State University, Vrabel spent the next four years playing defensive end for the Buckeyes, earning consensus First-Team All-American honors as a senior in 1996 and recognition as the Big Ten Defensive Lineman of the Year in both his junior and senior years.

Selected by the Pittsburgh Steelers in the third round of the 1997 NFL Draft, with the 91st overall pick, Vrabel subsequently found himself stuck behind the other members of Pittsburgh's outstanding linebacking corps, which included at different times Greg Lloyd, Levon Kirkland, Earl Holmes, Carlos Emmons, Jason Gildon, and Joey Porter. Relegated mostly to backup duty and special teams play, Vrabel recorded just seven sacks and 36 tackles over the course of the next four seasons, before signing with the Patriots as an unrestricted free agent on March 16, 2001.

Vrabel earned a starting job on the Patriots' defense shortly after he arrived in New England, using his versatility to rapidly develop into one of head coach Bill Belichick's favorite players. Blessed with good size, outstanding intelligence, and exceptional instincts, the 6'4", 261-pound Vrabel laid claim to the starting left linebacker position in New England's 4-3 defense early in the season, after which he went on to register 63 tackles (40 solo), three sacks, nine passes defended, and the first two interceptions of his professional career. He continued his strong all-around play the following season, finishing the year with 82 tackles (58 solo), 4 ½ sacks, one interception, and two forced fumbles.

With the Patriots switching to a 3-4 defense in 2003, they shifted Vrabel to right outside linebacker, where he assumed more of a pass-rushing role. Excelling at his new post, Vrabel led the team with 9 ½ sacks, even though he appeared in only 13 games due to injury. Continuing to display the multi-faceted nature of his game, Vrabel also recorded 52 tackles, two interceptions, four forced fumbles, and four passes defended. Manning the same position again in 2004, Vrabel started 15 of New England's 16 games. Although he failed to register any interceptions or forced fumbles, he helped the Patriots capture their third AFC championship in four years by placing second on the team with 5 ½ sacks, while also finishing fourth on the squad with 71 tackles (54 solo). Vrabel subsequently performed extremely well during New England's successful Super Bowl run, recording two sacks and 16 tackles, recovering a fumble, and even catching a touchdown pass during the Patriots' three postseason victories.

With inside backers Chad Brown and Monty Beisel failing to distinguish themselves during the early stages of the 2005 campaign, the Patriots shifted Vrabel to the interior of their defense, assigning him the task of playing right-inside linebacker for the first time in his career. Responding well to the challenge of playing a new position, Vrabel recorded 4 ½ sacks, two interceptions, and a team-leading and career-high 108 tackles (73 solo). Occasionally inserted into the Patriots' offense as an eligible receiver when the team drove the ball down close to the opponent's goal line, Vrabel also proved to be a favorite target of Tom Brady in such situations, making three TD catches for a total of four yards over the course of the campaign. Vrabel made a total of eight receptions during his time in New England, all of which went for touchdowns.

After making 4 ½ sacks, 89 tackles (54 solo), and a career-high three interceptions in 2006, while splitting his time between right-inside and right-outside linebacker, Vrabel had arguably his finest season in 2007. Switching sides with Rosevelt Colvin, Vrabel moved to left-outside linebacker, where he earned his lone Pro Bowl and First-Team All-NFL selections by recording 77 tackles, four forced fumbles, and a career-high 12 ½ sacks. Vrabel spent one more year in New England, making 62 tackles, four sacks, and the final interception of his career, before being dealt, along with Matt Cassel, to the Kansas City Chiefs for a second round pick in the 2009 NFL Draft that the Patriots eventually used to select Patrick Chung. Vrabel remained in Kansas City the next two seasons, recording just two sacks and a total of 100 tackles, before announcing his retirement on July 10, 2011, to become the linebackers coach at his alma mater, Ohio State. He ended his career with 740 tackles (511 solo), 57 sacks, 11 interceptions, 19 forced fumbles, 9 fumble recoveries, and 11 touchdowns, 10 of which came on pass receptions. As a member of the Patriots, Vrabel recorded 604 tackles (411 solo), 48 sacks, 11 interceptions, 13 forced fumbles, 5 fumble recoveries, and 9 of his 11 touchdowns.

Upon learning of Vrabel's retirement, Patriots chairman and CEO Robert Kraft issued a statement that read as follows:

> Mike Vrabel was a key contributor to the most successful era in Patriots franchise history and I will forever be grateful. His performance in Super Bowl XXXVIII was MVP worthy, and his touchdowns in back-to-back Super Bowls helped us win three championships in four years. During his Patriots career, there was no player more respected for his football intellect, and more revered for his leadership by his teammates than Mike. He was elected a team captain by his peers and is a player who I think everyone knew was destined to become a coach after his NFL playing career was over. I am thrilled for Mike and his family that his first coaching opportunity allows him to return home to coach at his alma mater, a school that he has always passionately supported. I am sure this is a dream come true for Mike, and will be the start of a long and successful coaching career at Ohio State. I know I'll be rooting for him. Mike is a true Patriot.

Vrabel's role at Ohio State changed slightly in 2012, when new head coach Urban Meyer made him the team's defensive line coach. Vrabel continued to serve in that capacity until 2014, when the Houston Texans hired him as their new linebackers coach.

PATRIOT CAREER HIGHLIGHTS

Best Season

Vrabel had one of his finest all-around seasons in 2003, when he led the Patriots with 9 ½ sacks and recorded two interceptions, four forced fumbles, and 52 tackles. He also performed extremely well the previous year, registering 4 ½ sacks and finishing fifth on the team with 82 tackles (58 solo). But Vrabel played his best ball for the Patriots in 2005 and 2007, concluding the first of those campaigns with 4 ½ sacks, two interceptions, one of which he returned for his only defensive touchdown, and a career-high 108 tackles (73 solo). Furthermore, Vrabel, who found himself playing inside linebacker for the first time in his career, provided outstanding leadership to his teammates in the absence of Tedy Bruschi, who missed the first half of the season while recovering from a stroke he suffered during the offseason. Still, the 2007 campaign is generally considered to be the finest of Vrabel's career. In addition to serving as co-captain of a Patriots team that finished the regular season with a perfect 16-0 record, he recorded four forced fumbles, 77 tackles (55 solo), and 12 ½ sacks, which represented the highest total compiled by a Patriots player since Andre Tippett sacked opposing quarterbacks 12 ½ times 20 years earlier. Giving further credence to the notion that Vrabel had his best season in 2007 is the fact that he earned Pro Bowl and First-Team All-Pro honors for the only time in his career.

Memorable Moments/Greatest Performances

Vrabel turned in one of his most dominant performances as a member of the Patriots on October 26, 2003, when he recorded a career-high three sacks during a 9-3 win over the Cleveland Browns.

During a 31-21 victory over the New York Jets on December 26, 2005, Vrabel became the first player to register two offensive touchdowns and a sack in the same game since sacks became an official NFL statistic in 1982, accomplishing the feat by making a pair of one-yard TD grabs and sacking Jets quarterback Brooks Bollinger.

Vrabel played the finest all-around game of his career on October 28, 2007, when he helped lead the Patriots to a lopsided 52-7 victory over the Washington Redskins by making 13 tackles and recording three strip-sacks of Washington quarterback Jason Campbell, creating in the process three turnovers that the Pats turned into 17 points. He also recovered an on-side kick and scored an offensive touchdown during the contest, en route to earning AFC Defensive Player of the Week honors. Such efforts later prompted the NFL Network to award Vrabel a #7 ranking on its list of the 10 Most Versatile Players in NFL History.

As noted earlier, Vrabel made eight touchdown receptions during his time in New England. He made the first of those during a 21-14 loss to the San Diego Chargers on September 29, 2002, when he lined up as a tight end and grabbed a one-yard pass from Tom Brady. However, Vrabel scored easily the two most memorable touchdowns of his career on the sport's grandest stage, hauling in TD passes from Brady in consecutive Super Bowls. In arguably his finest moment, Vrabel gave the Patriots a 29-22 lead over the Carolina Panthers late in the fourth quarter of Super Bowl XXXVIII when he hooked up with Brady on a one-yard scoring play. Although Carolina tied the score less than two minutes later, the Pats ended up winning the game on a 41-yard Adam Vinatieri field goal with just nine seconds remaining in regulation. Vrabel also recorded two sacks of Panthers quarterback Jake Delhomme. Vrabel was at it again in Super Bowl XXXIX, registering a sack of Donovan McNabb and scoring a touchdown on a two-yard pass from Brady, in helping the Patriots defeat the Philadelphia Eagles 24-21. Vrabel's catch, which he made despite being held by Philadelphia's

Jevon Kearse, was subsequently pictured on the cover of the *2005 NFL Record and Fact Book*.

NOTABLE ACHIEVEMENTS

- Finished in double-digits in sacks once (12 ½ in 2007).
- Surpassed 100 tackles once (108 in 2005).
- Led Patriots in sacks twice.
- Led Patriots with 108 tackles (73 solo) in 2005.
- Scored one defensive touchdown during career.
- Made eight receptions, all for touchdowns, as a member of the Patriots.
- Four-time AFC champion (2001, 2003, 2004 & 2007).
- Three-time Super Bowl champion (XXXVI, XXXVIII & XXXIX).
- Ranks fourth all-time on Patriots with 48 career sacks.
- AFC Defensive Player of the Month for December 2003.
- 2007 Pro Bowl Selection.
- 2007 First-Team All-Pro selection.
- Member of *Sports Illustrated*'s 2000s All-Decade Team.
- Member of Patriots' 2000s All-Decade Team.
- Named to Patriots' 50th Anniversary Team in 2009.

28

Irving Fryar

Irving Fryar in Miami Dolphins uniform.
(Courtesy Joe Schilp)

The first wide receiver ever selected with the first overall pick of the NFL Draft, Irving Fryar never quite lived up to his advanced billing during his time in New England. Immaturity, a lack of foresight, and personal problems off the field all prevented Fryar from reaching his full potential in his nine seasons with the Patriots. In fact, it wasn't until Fryar joined New England's foremost rival—the Miami Dolphins—that he truly developed into an elite NFL wide-out. Nevertheless, Fryar accomplished enough over the course of his nine seasons with the Patriots to earn a prominent place in these rankings. In addition to doing an outstanding job of returning punts, he surpassed 50 receptions three times and 1,000 receiving yards once, en route to placing among the team's all-time leaders in both categories. Fryar also ranks among the Patriots' all-time leaders in all-purpose yards and touchdowns scored. A member of the Pats' 1985 AFC Championship squad, Fryar earned his lone Pro Bowl selection that year by making 39 receptions for 670 yards and 7 touchdowns, rushing for another score, returning two punts for touchdowns, amassing 1,256 all-purpose yards, and leading the NFL with a 14.1 yard punt-return average. In all, Fryar made more than 350 receptions as a member of the Patriots, gained nearly 6,000 yards through the air, scored a total of 42 touchdowns, and amassed almost 8,500 all-purpose yards. Those are the figures that eventually earned him a spot on the Patriots' 50th Anniversary Team, as well as the 28th overall position in these rankings.

Born in Mount Holly, New Jersey, on September 28, 1962, Irving Dale Fryar attended Rancocas Valley Regional High School, where he starred in both baseball and football, earning All-County and All-State honors in the latter. After fielding scholarship offers from several universities following his graduation from Rancocas Valley, Fryar eventually settled on Nebraska. While in college, Fryar excelled as a wide receiver and punt returner under Coach Tom Osborne, capping his collegiate career with selections to the Big Eight First-Team and the Kodak All-American Team. The success Fryar experienced at Nebraska prompted the Patriots to select him with the first overall pick of the 1984 NFL Draft, even though questions concerning the quality of his character abounded following an incident in which he broke down the door to his girlfriend's apartment.

In spite of his lofty draft status, Fryar started only three games for the Patriots his first year in the league, spending most of his rookie season returning punts and backing up Stanley Morgan and Stephen Starring at wide receiver. Concluding the 1984 campaign with modest numbers for such a highly-touted collegiate player, Fryar amassed a total of 347 punt-return yards and made just 11 receptions, for 164 yards and one touchdown

After beating out Starring for the starting spot opposite Morgan the following year, Fryar became a far more significant contributor. In addition to making 39 receptions for 670 yards and 7 touchdowns, he finished second in the NFL with 520 punt-return yards, scoring twice in that fashion, and leading the league with an average of 14.1 yards per return. Fryar's outstanding all-around play earned him Pro Bowl and Second-Team All-NFL honors.

However, Fryar failed to make an appearance in the Patriots' 31-14 victory over the Miami Dolphins in the 1985 AFC Championship Game due to his involvement in the first of a series of bizarre incidents that came to define the nine turbulent years he spent in New England. Shortly before the Patriots' meeting with Miami, Fryar's wife slashed him with a kitchen knife after he knocked her down during a domestic dispute, cutting two of his fingers and, thereby, keeping him out of the title tilt.

Although Fryar compiled impressive numbers again the following season, making 43 receptions for 737 yards and 6 touchdowns, while also amassing another 366 yards on punt returns, his troubles continued when he smashed his car after leaving Sullivan Stadium prior to the conclusion of a contest against the Buffalo Bills. Upset over being forced to leave the game with an injury, Fryar left the stadium at halftime in his Mercedes sports coupe, only to smash the vehicle at a fork in the road not far from the Patriots' practice facility. He later admitted that the accident occurred because he failed to pay proper attention to his driving while talking on his car phone.

Fryar experienced other off-field problems during his time in New England, including being arrested for carrying an array of weapons in his trunk after being stopped for speeding by a New Jersey state trooper, and being hauled in again for brandishing a handgun following a fracas at a Providence nightclub. Nevertheless, Fryar eventually went on to establish himself as the Patriots' "go-to" receiver following the departure of Stanley Morgan at the conclusion of the 1989 campaign. After failing to make more than 33 receptions or accumulate more than 537 receiving yards in any of the three previous seasons, Fryar emerged as the Patriots' top offensive threat in 1990, leading them with 54 catches and 856 receiving yards. He followed that up with a banner year in 1991 during which he established new career highs in receptions (68) and receiving yards (1,014). Fryar then made 55 catches, for 791 yards and 4 touchdowns in 1992, before being dealt to the Miami Dolphins at season's end. Fryar left New England having made a total of 363 receptions, for 5,726 yards and 38 touchdowns. He also carried the ball 35 times for 188 yards and one touchdown, gained 2,055 yards returning punts, and accumulated 495 yards on kickoff returns, amassing in the process a total of 8,464 all-purpose yards that places him fifth in franchise history.

Playing with Dan Marino in Miami seemed to agree with Fryar, who made more than 60 receptions in each of the next three seasons and surpassed 1,000 receiving yards twice, en route to earning his second and third

Pro Bowl selections. Fryar had his best season for the Dolphins in 1994, when he made 73 catches for 1,270 yards and 7 touchdowns. Acquired by the Eagles prior to the start of the 1996 campaign, Fryar continued his outstanding play in Philadelphia, topping 80 receptions and 1,000 receiving yards in two of the next three seasons, and earning two more Pro Bowl nominations, before moving on to Washington, where he spent his final two years before retiring at the end of 2000. Fryar concluded his playing career with 851 receptions, for 12,785 receiving yards and 84 touchdowns. He also returned three punts for touchdowns and scored one rushing TD. By amassing a total of 12,785 receiving yards over the course of his career, Fryar became just the eighth player in NFL history to reach the 12,000-yard plateau.

Unfortunately, Fryar continued to run afoul of the law after his playing career ended. After founding New Jerusalem House of God in 2003 and subsequently spending the next several years serving as their pastor, Fryar allegedly used his church to perpetrate a $690,000 mortgage fraud scheme. The allegations made against him in 2013 claim that he falsified his mother's income on mortgage applications, stating that she made thousands of dollars a month as an event coordinator for the church. Indicted on counts of conspiracy and theft by deception, Fryar and his 80-year-old mother pleaded not guilty to all charges, with their lawyer claiming that they were the victims of a scam, and not the perpetrators. If convicted, Fryar faces 5 to 10 years in prison and a $150,000 fine.

PATRIOT CAREER HIGHLIGHTS

Best Season

Fryar compiled his best pass-receiving totals for the Patriots in 1991, when he surpassed 1,000 receiving yards for the only time as a member of the team. Functioning almost exclusively as a wide-out for the first time in his career, Fryar made 68 receptions, for 1,014 yards and 3 touchdowns. However, he made his greatest overall impact in New England in 1985, when he earned his lone Pro Bowl and Second-Team All-NFL selections as a Patriot. In addition to accumulating 670 yards on 39 pass receptions, Fryar rushed for 27 yards and amassed another 559 yards on special teams, compiling in the process a total of 1,256 all-purpose yards. He also made 7 touchdown receptions, rushed for one score, and returned two punts for touchdowns, en route to leading the league with an average of 14.1 yards per punt return.

Memorable Moments/Greatest Performances

One of the NFL's most dangerous punt returners his first few years in the league, Fryar returned three punts for touchdowns over the course of his career, with all of those coming as a member of the Patriots. Fryar scored his first special-teams touchdown on September 22, 1985, helping the Patriots defeat Buffalo 17-14 by returning a John Kidd punt 85 yards for what proved to be the game-winning touchdown. Fryar's 85-yard return ended up being the longest in the NFL all season. Fryar nearly matched his earlier effort seven weeks later, when he returned a punt 77 yards for a touchdown during a 34-15 victory over the Indianapolis Colts. He also recorded a 5-yard TD reception during the contest. Fryar registered his final special-teams touchdown the following season, returning a punt 59 yards for a score during a 25-17 win over the Atlanta Falcons on November 2, 1986.

Fryar also had a number of huge pass-receiving days for the Patriots, with the first of those coming on October 13, 1985, when he made six receptions for 132 yards and a touchdown during a 14-3 victory over the Buffalo Bills. Fryar's 16-yard TD hookup with Steve Grogan in the third quarter provided the winning margin.

Although the Patriots ended up losing to the Jets 31-24 on October 12, 1986, Fryar had a big game, making three receptions for 126 yards and one touchdown, with his scoring play covering 69 yards. Five weeks later, Fryar helped the Patriots overcome a 28-16 fourth-quarter deficit to the Los Angeles Rams by hauling in two late TD passes from Tony Eason, with the last of those being a 25-yard reception that came in the game's closing minutes.

Fryar made the longest reception of his career on October 30, 1988, when he scored from 80 yards out during a 30-7 home win over the Chicago Bears. He finished the day with three catches for 122 yards.

Fryar had one of his best pass-receiving days as a member of the Patriots on October 20, 1991, when he helped the Pats defeat Minnesota 26-23 in overtime by making nine receptions for 161 yards. He had another big game four weeks later against the Jets, making eight catches for 143 yards and a touchdown during a 28-21 home loss. Fryar continued his outstanding 1991 campaign by making six receptions for 134 yards and a touchdown during a 16-13 victory over the Buffalo Bills on November 24. He scored the Patriots' only touchdown of the game late in the second quarter when he hooked up with quarterback Hugh Millen on a 50-yard pass play.

Fryar had his last big game for the Patriots on October 4, 1992, when he made eight receptions for 165 yards and two touchdowns during a 30-21 loss to the Jets. His scoring plays covered 20 and 38 yards.

NOTABLE ACHIEVEMENTS

- Caught more than 50 passes three times, topping 60 receptions once (68 in 1991).
- Surpassed 1,000 receiving yards once (1,014 in 1991).
- Averaged 18.5 yards per reception in 1989.
- Surpassed 1,000 all-purpose yards three times.
- Returned 3 punts for touchdowns.
- Led NFL with 14.1 yard punt-return average in 1985.
- Finished second in NFL with 520 punt return yards in 1985.
- Ranks among Patriots all-time leaders in: pass receptions (6th); receiving yardage (4th); touchdown receptions (7th); all-purpose yards (5th); and touchdowns scored (tied-9th).
- 1985 AFC champion.
- 1985 Pro Bowl selection.
- 1985 Second-Team All-Pro selection.
- Named to Patriots' 50th Anniversary Team in 2009.

29

Vince Wilfork

(Courtesy Keith Allison)

One of only two Patriot players to have a hand in each of the team's last two Super Bowl victories (Tom Brady is the other), Vince Wilfork has been an integral member of the New England defense for the past 11 seasons. An outstanding team leader who plays the game with an edge, Wilfork does much of the dirty work on the interior of the Patriots' defensive line, eating up space with his massive 6'2", 350-pound frame, taking on multiple blockers on virtually every play, and creating lanes that enable his teammates to bring down opposing ball carriers. Although Wilfork's contributions to the success of the team typically go unnoticed by the casual observer, bringing him little in the way of personal on-field glory, they have gained him a considerable amount of respect throughout the league, earning him five Pro Bowl selections and five All-Pro nominations over the course of his career. Meanwhile, the Patriots and their fans have shown their appreciation to Wilfork by awarding him spots on the franchise's 2000s All-Decade Team and 50th Anniversary Team.

Born in Boynton Beach, Florida, on November 4, 1981, Vince Lamar Wilfork attended Santaluces Community High School in nearby Palm Beach County, where he lettered in football, wrestling, and track and field. After earning Second-Team All-American honors from *USA Today* in football, and becoming Florida State 4A state champion in the shot put and discus throw as a senior, Wilfork moved on to the University of Miami. While playing for the Hurricanes, Wilfork assumed a part-time role his first two seasons, before becoming a full-time starter in his junior year, when he earned All-Big East Conference First-Team honors by recording 64 tackles and a team-leading 20 quarterback hurries. Yet, before emerging as one of the nation's premier defensive tackles, Wilfork nearly decided to quit football, recalling years later, "Everything wasn't perfect for me growing up. But I had a mother growing up who worked so hard that I only saw her in the mornings before school. I had a father who came to my practices, came to my games, and who was always there for the both of them. My dad died after a long struggle with diabetes in the summer of 2002. Six months later my mom died of a stroke. I was going to quit football. I was going to quit on a lot of things."

Choosing instead to continue pursuing his dream of playing in the NFL, Wilfork performed so well as a junior at Miami that he entered the 2004 NFL Draft ranked as the Number 2 defensive tackle (behind only Tommie Harris) after he decided to forego his final year of collegiate eligibility. Compared by some pro scouts to fellow Miami alumnus Warren Sapp, Wilfork ended up being selected by the Patriots in the first round of the draft, with the 21st overall pick.

Sharing nose tackle duties with veteran Keith Traylor his first year in the league, Wilfork had a solid rookie campaign, recording 42 tackles (27 solo), two sacks, and two fumble recoveries, in helping the Patriots capture their second consecutive AFC Championship and Super Bowl title. Wilfork's strong play prompted the Pats to release Traylor at season's end, making Wilfork the full-time starter at the position. He subsequently went on to contribute significantly to New England's third straight AFC East title by making 54 tackles (40 solo) in his second year in the league.

After another solid year in 2006 (50 tackles), Wilfork earned Pro Bowl and Second-Team All-Pro honors for the first time in 2007 by making 48 tackles (36 solo) and two sacks for a Patriots team that finished the regular season with a perfect 16-0 record. He followed that up by recording a career-high 66 tackles (45 solo) in 2008, although the Patriots' failure to make the playoffs likely prevented him from receiving postseason honors once more. Wilfork then began a string of four straight seasons in which he appeared in the Pro Bowl. He also earned All-Pro honors in each of those years, being named to the First Team in 2012 and the Second Team the other three years.

Nevertheless, in spite of his outstanding play, Wilfork found himself at odds with the Patriots front office at the conclusion of the 2009 campaign when his contract expired. Seeking a long-term deal and threatening to hold out if the team placed a franchise tag on him, Wilfork told the *South Florida Sun-Sentinel* that it would be "a dream come true" to play for either the Tampa Bay Buccaneers or the Miami Dolphins. Subsequently assigned the non-exclusive version of the franchise tag by the Patriots on February 22, 2010, Wilfork re-signed with New England less than two weeks later for $40 million over five years, with more than half the money being guaranteed. Looking back years later at the contentious negotiations, Wilfork states, "Oh yeah, it sure looked like, for a minute, that my Patriots time was up. I got way too personal in it. I took everything involved in those talks way too personal. But this is where I am supposed to be."

After re-signing with the Patriots, Wilfork continued his streak of four straight seasons in which he earned Pro Bowl and All-Pro honors, averaging 52 tackles and 3 sacks during that time. More importantly, Wilfork helped the Patriots capture the AFC East title each year and advance to the Super Bowl once more, contributing greatly to the success of the team throughout the period with his exceptional leadership and intimidating brand of defense.

A Patriots' defensive co-captain since 2008, Wilfork has remained one of the team's most respected players, stating this past season, "I continue to work. I demand it from my teammates and they demand it from me. . . . And the day I stop being that disciplined, I think it's time for me to call it quits. But my teammates depend on me too much for me to sit down and say, 'I'm okay, I've been doing it for so long. I don't have to do it.' I do everything they do and probably a little bit more, and I think that's one thing my teammates really love from me is that I put the work in."

Wilfork added, "I'm not one of those guys that tells them what to do and I sit back and don't do it. I'm right with them. If he's a rookie or he's not a rookie, his vet is going to be right with him, working with him. And I think that's one of the things my teammates love for me the most is because I actually cherish the time that we have together and try to lend a hand when I can for those guys. So I'm going to continue to work until I don't have to work anymore, but this is what I love to do."

Speaking of the overall impact that Wilfork has had on his teammates, Patriots' defensive coordinator Matt Patricia suggested, "He's great for us. He's obviously one of our strongest leaders and a guy that I can really turn to week in and week out to show our younger players and say: 'This is how you practice. This is how you prepare. This is what it means to be a professional. This is what it means to stay in the league this long by doing things the right way.' And he does it every single day. It shows the young guys the examples that he sets and the standard that he sets. I'm very fortunate to have him."

Linebacker Jamie Collins added, "Vince is the ultimate veteran, man. We need guys like that around the locker room, especially when you're a leader on the field. It just leads to younger guys that want to be just like him and have the success he has had."

While Wilfork is beloved by his teammates, he is both feared and respected by his opponents for the physicality of his game and the anger he displays from time to time. A space-eater who closes up would-be running lanes, Wilfork is excellent at penetrating opposing offenses and freeing up other defenders to make plays. Although listed at 325 pounds, he weighs closer to 350, making it extremely difficult for opposing linemen to move him off the line of scrimmage. Wilfork also possesses a mean streak that occasionally causes him to engage in extracurricular activities on the field. In 2007 alone, the NFL levied four fines against him that ended up costing him a total of $27,500.

Wilfork saw his string of four consecutive Pro Bowl and All-Pro selections come to an end in 2013 after he tore his right Achilles' tendon in Week 4 while trying to maneuver past Atlanta guard Justin Blalock. Placed on injured reserve for the remainder of the year, Wilfork appeared in only four games, making a total of just nine tackles. After the Patriots finished 26th in the NFL in total yards allowed in 2013, Wilfork's return in 2014 helped them advance 13 notches in the rankings, into the number 13 position. Starting all 16 regular-season contests for the Pats, Wilfork recorded 53 tackles (28 solo)—his highest total since 2010. Taking note of Wilfork's strong play over the course of the campaign, Seattle Seahawks center Max Unger commented before Super Bowl XLIX, "Vince has been playing the game at maybe the highest level anybody has in the last 10 years."

Seahawks offensive tackle Russell Okung opined, "Vince is a tough player. He really brings it. We know that. I mean, he really brings it. He is a passionate player who knows football, knows what it takes. We have to match his intensity. We know that."

Seattle head coach Pete Carroll also praised Wilfork, stating, "He's a monster of a guy; such a worker. He is really tough to knock off the ball. He has a penchant for making plays. We have got to find a way to throw him off his mark. We have got to find a way to move him. And that is not going to be easy."

Although Wilfork ended up making just two tackles during the Patriots' 28-24 victory over Seattle in Super Bowl XLIX, he played a huge role in the win, clogging up the middle and allowing the other defenders around him to do a relatively good job of containing Marshawn Lynch and Russell Wilson.

Since Wilfork will celebrate his 34th birthday near the midway mark of the upcoming season, it remains to be seen how much longer he can continue to compete at an elite level. He will enter the 2015 campaign with career totals of 522 tackles (355 solo), 16 sacks, 3 interceptions, 23 passes batted down, 5 forced fumbles, 12 fumble recoveries, and one touchdown. A place in the Patriots' Hall of Fame likely awaits Wilfork when he eventually decides to retire.

CAREER HIGHLIGHTS

Best Season

Wilfork had his two finest statistical seasons for the Patriots in 2008 and 2010, recording two sacks each year and making a career-high 66 tackles in the first of those campaigns, before bringing down opposing ball-carriers 57 times two years later. However, he earned his lone First-Team All-Pro selection in 2012, when, in addition to recording 48 tackles and three sacks, he established career-highs by batting down six passes, forcing three fumbles, and recovering four others. Furthermore, Wilfork anchored a Patriots' defense that allowed the ninth-fewest rushing yards in the league, limiting opposing running backs to an average of 3.9 yards per carry. The Patriots ranked 15th and 11th in the NFL in rushing defense the other two years.

Therefore, since Wilfork's primary responsibility has always been to stop the run, he made his greatest overall impact in 2012.

Memorable Moments/Greatest Performances

Wilfork turned in the first dominant performance of his career on October 30, 2005, making nine tackles during a 21-16 victory over the Buffalo Bills.

Although the Patriots lost their 2009 first-round playoff matchup with the Baltimore Ravens 33-14, Wilfork played a tremendous game, recording a career-high 13 tackles.

Wilfork experienced one of his most memorable moments late in the third quarter of New England's 37-16 victory over the rival New York Jets in the first round of the 2006 postseason tournament when he recovered a Chad Pennington fumble near midfield and returned it 31 yards to the New York 15 yard line before being brought down by Jerricho Cotchery. The play resulted in a Stephen Gostkowski field goal that put the Patriots in front 23-13.

Wilfork recorded two sacks for the only time in his career in the 2010 regular-season finale, getting to Dolphin quarterbacks twice during the Patriots' 38-7 win over Miami.

Wilfork ironically recorded two of his three career interceptions just two weeks apart in 2011, picking off his first pass during a 35-21 win over the Chargers on September 18, and intercepting another pass during a 31-19 victory over Oakland on October 2. He returned those picks 28 and 19 yards, respectively. Wilfork registered his third interception this past season, picking off rookie QB Derek Carr during the Patriots' 16-9 win over Oakland.

Wilfork scored his only career touchdown on December 11, 2011, when he recovered a Rex Grossman fumble in the end zone to give the Patriots an early 7-0 lead over Washington in a game they eventually won 34-27.

Yet, Wilfork's most noteworthy accomplishment took place off the playing field, occurring shortly after the Patriots defeated Indianapolis in the AFC Championship Game on January 18, 2015. Noticing an overturned SUV while on his way home from Gillette Stadium, Wilfork helped pull the driver to safety. Recounting his role in assisting the injured motorist, Wilfork explained, "I think anybody would do the same thing. I saw the lady in there and asked her if she was okay; could she move. She grabbed my hand, and I kind of talked her through it. It wasn't a big deal;

it was seeing someone that needed help and helping. I was just trying to get her to safety."

NOTABLE ACHIEVEMENTS

- Has surpassed 50 tackles five times.
- Has led Patriots defensive linemen in tackles twice.
- Has scored one defensive touchdown during career.
- Four-time AFC champion (2004, 2007, 2011 & 2014).
- Two-time Super Bowl champion (XXXIX & XLIX).
- Five-time Pro Bowl selection (2007, 2009, 2010, 2011 & 2012).
- 2012 First-Team All-Pro selection.
- Four-time Second-Team All-Pro selection (2007, 2009, 2010 & 2011).
- Member of Patriots' 2000s All-Decade Team.
- Named to Patriots' 50th Anniversary Team in 2009.

30

Adam Vinatieri

Adam Vinatieri in Indianapolis Colts uniform.
(Courtesy of Sgt. Brian Ferguson, U.S. Air Force)

The greatest clutch kicker in NFL history, Adam Vinatieri acquired the nickname "Iceman" during his time in New England for his ability to excel under pressure. In his 10 years with the Patriots, Vinatieri kicked 18 game-winning field goals with less than one minute remaining, doing so three times in the postseason, including twice in the Super Bowl. Also frequently referred to as "Automatic Adam" for his consistency and dependability, Vinatieri successfully converted 81.9 percent of his field goal attempts as a member of the Patriots, making him the league's fifth most accurate kicker in history as of 2005, his last year in New England. Along the way, Vinatieri kicked more field goals (263) than anyone else in franchise history, with his total of 1,158 points as a member of the Pats placing him second only to Stephen Gostkowski in team annals. The holder of numerous NFL postseason records as well, Vinatieri can lay claim to appearing in more games (30), scoring more points (234), and kicking more field goals (56) than any other player in playoff history. A member of the Patriots' 50th Anniversary Team, Vinatieri also earned a spot on the Pro Football Hall of Fame 2000s All-Decade Team with his clutch kicking. The ageless Vinatieri has continued his success since leaving New England, winning two more AFC titles and another Super Bowl as a member of the Indianapolis Colts, making him a key contributor to six Conference and four Super Bowl championship teams.

Born in Yankton, South Dakota, on December 28, 1972, Adam Matthew Vinatieri attended Central High School in Rapid City, South Dakota, where he lettered in football, basketball, soccer, wrestling, and track. After beginning his career on the gridiron as a backup quarterback and middle linebacker, Vinatieri gradually transitioned to placekicker due to his lack of size. Originally recruited to kick for Army following his graduation from Central High, Vinatieri elected to leave West Point after just two weeks when he realized that a career in the military did not suit his personality. Returning to his home state, Vinatieri enrolled at South Dakota State University, where he spent the next four years serving as the football team's placekicker and punter. Although Vinatieri later admitted, "My college stats were less than great," he ended up winning two Division II titles and establishing himself as SDSU's all-time scoring leader.

After going undrafted by the NFL, Vinatieri spent the fall of 1995 honing his kicking skills under the watchful eye of Doug Blevins, a kicking guru confined to a wheelchair for life by cerebral palsy. Stating years later, "At that point, I was committed to doing everything and anything I could to try and get in the league," Vinatieri worked ceaselessly with Blevins, who vastly improved the youngster's performance by correcting the flaws in his technique. Ready for a professional tryout following his work with Blevins, Vinatieri ended up securing a job with the Amsterdam Admirals of the now-defunct World League of American Football (later rebranded as NFL Europe), for whom he spent the 1995 campaign serving as placekicker and punter.

Invited to training camp the following year by Patriots' head coach Bill Parcells, primarily to provide competition for 16-year veteran Matt Bahr,

Vinatieri surprised everyone by winning the starting job. After being told by Parcells, "I'm going to give you an opportunity to show me what you've got, and either you're going to shine, or you're going to pack your shit and get out of here," Vinatieri had a solid rookie campaign, converting 27 of 35 field goal attempts, en route to scoring a total of 120 points that placed him sixth in the league rankings. Vinatieri further endeared himself to Parcells by chasing down and tackling Dallas's Herschel Walker on a kickoff return, prompting his head coach to tell him, "You're not a kicker—you're a football player!"

Vinatieri continued to perform well for the Patriots over the course of the next five seasons, finishing among the NFL's top scorers three times, including 1997, when he successfully converted 25 of 29 field goal attempts, giving him an 86.2 field goal percentage that ranked as the fifth-highest mark in the league. He also scored 127 points the following year, placing him sixth in the league rankings.

However, Vinatieri failed to gain national recognition until the 2001 postseason, when he began to build his reputation as a superb clutch performer. With the Patriots and Oakland Raiders battling one another under blizzard conditions in the first round of the playoffs, Vinatieri calmly kicked a 45-yard field goal with only 32 seconds remaining in regulation to knot the score at 13-13. He subsequently sent the fans at Foxboro Stadium home happy when he gave the Pats a 16-13 victory by converting a 23-yard field goal attempt 6:35 into overtime. Vinatieri performed heroically again two weeks later when he kicked a 48-yard field goal as time expired, to give the Patriots a 20-17 upset win over the St. Louis Rams in Super Bowl XXXVI.

Vinatieri followed that up by earning Pro Bowl and First-Team All-Pro honors for the first time in 2002 by successfully converting 27 of 30 field goal attempts, compiling in the process a league-leading 90 percent field goal percentage. Although Vinatieri subsequently suffered through an uncharacteristically inconsistent 2003 campaign that saw him post a career-low 73.5 field goal percentage, he again came up big when it mattered most, giving the Patriots a 32-29 victory over Carolina in Super Bowl XXXVIII by kicking a 41-yard field goal with only four seconds remaining in regulation.

Vinatieri then put together arguably his finest season in New England, converting 31 of 33 field goal attempts in 2004, en route to leading the league in field goals made, points scored (141), and field goal percentage (93.9). Vinatieri's exceptional performance earned him Pro Bowl and First-Team All-Pro honors for the second time.

A tremendously focused and dedicated professional, Vinatieri described the approach he takes to his craft when he revealed:

> I get very upset about wasting kicks or wasting practice time. I don't ever go out without a purpose. I don't necessarily say, "This is a game winner." I feel like every single time you step on the field, it's a potential game-winning situation. You don't know how the game is going to end. There are games that end 21-20. That extra point that you kicked in the second quarter maybe is the difference. Every single time I step on the field to kick, I take it real serious in the sense that there's never a wasted "rep" ever. It is always, hey, every time I step on the field, I'm expected to put points on the board to help our team, increase our lead, win a game, whatever the situation may be. For me, I don't care if it's the first quarter or with two seconds left on the clock; it's serious business every single time I step out there.

After another solid year in 2005 in which he successfully converted 80 percent of his field goal attempts, Vinatieri grew weary of the gamesmanship previously displayed by the New England front office, which presented him with numerous unsatisfactory contract offers and placed several franchise tags on him through the years. Seeking more than the three-year deal the Patriots offered him at season's end, Vinatieri changed agents and put himself on the open market. The Indianapolis Colts subsequently came calling, signing the 10-year veteran to a five-year contract, with a $3.5 million signing bonus.

Upon announcing his departure from New England, Vinatieri stated, "When the Colts called, I told my agent, 'Let's not screw around.' I told him, 'If Indy is interested, let's get this done.'" He added that he had no regrets about not giving the Patriots a chance to match the offer.

Vinatieri has remained one of the NFL's most accurate kickers since joining the Colts nearly a decade ago, connecting on 86 percent of his field goal attempts, including surpassing the 90 percent mark on two occasions. He had his two best years for the Colts in 2010 and 2014, successfully converting 26 of 28 field goal attempts and all 51 extra point attempts in the first of those campaigns, before missing just one of 31 field goal attempts while also converting all 50 extra point attempts this past season. Vinatieri's career-high and league-leading 96.8 field goal percentage in 2014 earned him First-Team All-Pro honors for the third time in his career.

Heading into 2015, Vinatieri has converted 83.7 percent of the field goals he has attempted over the course of his career. Displaying his remarkable consistency, he has also converted 56 of 67 postseason attempts, including five of six from at least 50 yards out, giving him a postseason percentage of 83.6. Vinatieri currently ranks fourth in NFL history in points scored (2,146), fourth in field goals made (478), and fifth in extra points made (710).

PATRIOT CAREER HIGHLIGHTS

Best Season

Vinatieri earned the first of his All-Pro selections as a member of the Patriots in 2002, when he converted 27 of 30 field goal attempts, en route to scoring 117 points and leading all NFL kickers with a 90 percent field goal average. However, he performed even better in 2004, when he compiled a league-leading 93.9 field goal percentage by successfully converting 31 of 33 field goal attempts. Vinatieri also converted all 48 of his point-after-touchdown attempts (PATs), en route to compiling a career-high 141 points that led the NFL.

Memorable Moments/Greatest Performances

Vinatieri helped lead the Patriots to victory by kicking at least four field goals in a game on nine occasions, one of which took place on October 12, 1997, when he split the uprights four times during a lopsided 33-6 victory over the Buffalo Bills. Vinatieri's three-pointers included a season-long 52-yarder.

Some two months later, on December 7, Vinatieri proved to be the difference during a 26-20 win over the Jacksonville Jaguars, connecting from 44, 41, 33, and 39 yards out.

Vinatieri recorded four field goals in one game three times in 1998, doing so during wins over Kansas City on October 11 and Miami on November 23, and also connecting four times against St. Louis during the Patriots' 32-18 loss to the Rams on December 13. In the last contest, Vinatieri split the uprights from 55 yards out, registering in the process the second-longest three-pointer of his career.

Vinatieri had another huge game on November 10, 2002, when his four field goals helped the Patriots edge out the Chicago Bears 33-30. Vinatieri's 57-yard field goal early in the second quarter proved to be the longest of his career.

Vinatieri turned in arguably his finest all-around performance on November 7, 2004, when he helped lead the Pats to a 40-22 victory over

St. Louis by kicking four field goals and completing a four-yard TD pass to Troy Brown on a fake field goal attempt. The following week, Vinatieri recorded a career-high five field goals during a 29-6 win over the Buffalo Bills.

Although Vinatieri gained much of his notoriety for his ability to excel under the extreme pressure of the postseason, he also demonstrated during his time in New England a propensity for coming up big in the clutch during the regular season, delivering 15 late game-winning kicks. Vinatieri revealed his coolness under pressure for the first time in just his fourth NFL game, giving the Patriots a 28-25 win over Jacksonville on September 22, 1996, by kicking a 40-yard field goal in overtime. The three-pointer was Vinatieri's fifth of the game.

Vinatieri delivered his second game-winning kick in overtime nearly one year later, when he gave the Pats a 27-24 win over the New York Jets on September 14, 1997, by splitting the uprights from 34 yards out during the overtime session

Vinatieri kicked game-winning field goals in the closing moments of contests twice in 1998, doing so for the first time on October 4, when he connected from 27 yards out with only six seconds remaining in regulation to give the Patriots a 30-27 win over New Orleans. He again came through with just six seconds left on the clock on December 20, converting a 35-yard field goal attempt to give the Pats a 24-21 victory over San Francisco.

Vinatieri helped the Patriots get off to a 4-0 start in 1999 by winning each of their first two games in the closing moments. After giving the Pats a 30-28 victory over the Jets in the regular- season opener by kicking a 23-yard field goal as time expired, Vinatieri connected from 26 yards out with only 1:30 left on the clock the following week, to help the Patriots defeat Indianapolis 31-28.

Vinatieri again proved to be the hero of two contests in 2000, converting a 22-yard field goal with just six seconds remaining in regulation, to give the Pats a 16-13 win over Cincinnati on November 19, before splitting the uprights from 24 yards out with only 23 seconds remaining in overtime, to give the Patriots a 13-10 win over Buffalo on December 17.

Vinatieri delivered two game-winning kicks in overtime in 2001, giving the Patriots a 29-26 victory over San Diego on October 14 by converting a 44-yard field goal attempt with 11 minutes remaining in the overtime session, before connecting from 23 yards out nearly six minutes into overtime, to give the Pats a 12-9 win over Buffalo on December 16.

Vinatieri duplicated that effort the following year, kicking two game-winning field goals of 35 yards, to give the Patriots overtime wins of

41-38 over Kansas City on September 22, 2002, and 27-24 over Miami in the regular-season finale.

Vinatieri delivered another game-winning kick in overtime on November 23, 2003, when he connected from 28 yards out as time expired in the overtime session, to give the Pats a 23-20 victory over the Houston Texans.

Vinatieri also gave the Patriots a pair of late wins in his final season in New England, kicking a 43-yard field goal with just five seconds remaining in regulation during a 23-20 victory over Pittsburgh on September 25, and splitting the uprights from 29 yards out with only 20 seconds remaining on the clock during a 31-28 win over Atlanta on October 9.

Nevertheless, Vinatieri will always be remembered most fondly by Patriots fans for his clutch postseason performances, the first of which came on January 19, 2002, in the final game ever played at Foxboro Stadium. With the Patriots facing the Oakland Raiders in a divisional playoff contest that came to be known as the "Tuck Rule Game," Vinatieri tied the score at 13-13 with only 32 seconds remaining in regulation by kicking a 45-yard field goal in horrible conditions that included a frigid wind and a driving snowstorm. He subsequently delivered the game-winning 23-yard field goal nearly nine minutes into overtime, to put the Patriots in the AFC Championship Game. Two weeks later, Vinatieri gave the Patriots their first NFL championship by kicking a 48-yard field goal as time expired, enabling them to edge out the favored St. Louis Rams 20-17 in Super Bowl XXXVI.

Vinatieri again came up big in the 2003 postseason, first sending the Patriots to the AFC title game by delivering a 46-yard field goal with 4:11 remaining in regulation, to give them a 17-14 victory over the Tennessee Titans in their divisional playoff matchup. Vinatieri proved to be the difference once more three weeks later, kicking a 41-yard field goal with just four seconds remaining on the clock, to give the Patriots a 32-29 win over Carolina in Super Bowl XXXVIII.

NOTABLE ACHIEVEMENTS

- Scored at least 100 points 10 straight times, surpassing 120 points three times and 140 points once (141 in 2004).
- Converted at least 90 percent of field goal attempts twice.
- Led NFL in: points scored once; field goal percentage twice; and field goals made once.
- Holds Patriots career record for most field goals made (263).
- Ranks second all-time on Patriots in points scored (1,158).

- Ranks among NFL career leaders in: points scored (4th) and field goals made (4th).
- Holds NFL career postseason records for most: games played (30); points scored (234); field goals made (56); and field goals made in Super Bowls (7).
- Shares NFL single-game postseason record for most field goals made (5).
- Four-time AFC champion (1996, 2001, 2003 & 2004).
- Three-time Super Bowl champion (XXXVI, XXXVIII & XXXIX).
- Two-time Pro Bowl selection (2002 & 2004).
- Two-time First-Team All-Pro selection (2002 & 2004).
- Two-time First-Team All-AFC selection (2002 & 2004).
- Two-time Golden Toe Award winner (2002 & 2004).
- 2004 NFL Alumni Special Teams Player of the Year.
- Member of Patriots' 1990s All-Decade Team.
- Member of Patriots' 2000s All-Decade Team.
- New England Patriots' 50th Anniversary Team.
- Pro Football Hall of Fame 2000s All-Decade Team.

31

Rob Gronkowski

(Courtesy Ronny Leber)

The fact that injuries have kept Ron Gronkowski off the playing field for significant periods of time in two of his first five NFL seasons is the only thing that prevented him from finishing much higher in these rankings. A matchup nightmare for opposing defenses due to his rare combination of size, speed, and strength, Gronkowski has already established himself as one of the most dominant offensive players in Patriots history when he is healthy. The 6'6", 265-pound freight train known affectionately to his teammates as "Gronk" has surpassed 80 receptions and 1,000 receiving yards in two of his three full seasons, setting a new NFL record for tight ends by gaining 1,327 yards through the air in 2011. That same year, Gronkowski caught a league-leading 17 touchdown passes, making him the first tight end in NFL history to top the circuit in that category. Gronkowski has scored at least 10 touchdowns in four of his five NFL seasons, placing him second all-time among Patriots players in TDs scored. He also ranks among the franchise's all-time leaders in pass receptions (9th), receiving yardage (9th), and points scored (7th). Gronkowski's stellar play has helped the Patriots win two AFC championships and one Super Bowl, earning him three Pro Bowl selections and three First-Team All-Pro nominations in the process.

Born in Amherst, New York, on May 14, 1989, Robert Paxton Gronkowski was raised in nearby Williamsville, about 11½ miles northeast of Buffalo. While attending Williamsville North High School, Gronkowski displayed his tremendous all-around athletic ability by starring in football and basketball, excelling on both offense and defense on the gridiron, while also shining as a center on the basketball court. After spending three years at Williamsville North, during which time he earned All-Western New York First Team and All-State Second-Team honors as a junior, Gronkowski moved with his family to suburban Pittsburgh, where he attended Woodland Hills High School as a senior. Gronkowski continued his success at Woodland Hills, setting himself up for a number of scholarship offers by earning numerous individual accolades, including Super Prep All-American, Prep Star All-American, Associated Press Class 4-A All-State, and *Pittsburgh Post-Gazette* "Fabulous 22" honors. Subsequently recruited by Arizona, Clemson, Louisville, Maryland, Ohio State, and Syracuse, the fun-loving Gronkowski ultimately settled on the University of Arizona, due in no small part to its reputation as a "partying" school.

Gronkowski spent two of his three years at the University of Arizona playing for the Wildcats football team, starring at tight end in his freshman and sophomore years. However, after earning Associated Press Third-Team All-American and All-Pac-10 First-Team tight end honors as a sophomore by setting single-game, single-season, and career school records for most catches, receiving yards, and touchdowns scored by a tight end, Gronkowski sat out the entire 2009 campaign while recovering from offseason back surgery.

With several NFL teams concerned over Gronkowski's health, he ended up sliding to the second round of the 2010 NFL Draft after foregoing his final year of collegiate eligibility, enabling the Patriots to select him with the 42nd overall pick. Proving to be a steal at that spot, Gronkowski made significant contributions to a New England team that compiled a 14-2 record during the 2010 regular season. Despite sharing playing time with Aaron Hernandez, Gronkowski made 42 receptions, for 546 yards and 10 touchdowns, becoming in the process the first rookie tight end since the NFL-AFL merger to score as many as 10 TDs.

Taking over as the full-time starter in 2011, Gronkowski greatly increased his offensive production, concluding his sophomore campaign with 90 receptions, for 1,327 yards and a league-leading 17 TD catches. He also scored another touchdown on the ground, giving him a total of 18 TDs that placed him second in the league only to Philadelphia's LeSean McCoy, who scored 20 times. Gronkowski's 1,327 receiving yards, 17 touchdown catches, and 18 total touchdowns all established new single-season NFL records for tight ends, earning him Pro Bowl and First-Team All-Pro honors for the first time in his career.

Gronkowski's unique physical gifts made him the league's finest all-around player at his position in just his second season. Although rivaled by New Orleans Saints tight end Jimmy Graham as a pass-catcher, Gronkowski possessed superior blocking skills from the time he first entered the league. He also displayed an aggressiveness and mean streak that his Saints counterpart lacked, often using his formidable 6'6", 265-pound frame to bulldoze his way through opposing defensive backs, who he typically shrugged off with ease once they attempted to bring him down in the open field. Meanwhile, his outstanding speed enabled him to create separation against opposing linebackers, and even many of the league's faster safeties. Gronkowski's size, speed, soft hands, and aggressive attitude prompted former NFL quarterback and current analyst for Showtime's *Inside the NFL*, Boomer Esiason, to comment, "Nobody, I mean nobody on planet Earth, can cover Rob Gronkowski."

Unfortunately, Gronkowski did not subsequently prove to be much of a factor for the Patriots when they faced the New York Giants in Super Bowl XLVI. After making three touchdown receptions during New England's 45-10 rout of the Denver Broncos in their Divisional playoff matchup, Gronkowski suffered a serious ankle injury while being tackled by Ravens safety Bernard Pollard during the Pats' 23-20 win over Baltimore in the AFC Championship Game. Although Gronkowski managed to play the entire game against the Giants, he made just two receptions for 26 yards, with his limited effectiveness contributing significantly to New York's 21-17 victory over the Pats.

Despite needing surgery to repair the ligaments he strained in his ankle during New England's victory over Baltimore in the 2011 playoffs, Gronkowski signed a six-year, $54 million contract extension with the Patriots on June 8, 2012, making him the highest-paid tight end in NFL history. However, after making 55 receptions for 790 yards and 11 touchdowns over the course of the first 11 games of the 2012 campaign en route to earning Pro Bowl and All-Pro honors for the second straight time, Gronkowski broke his left forearm late in the fourth quarter of the Pats' 59-24 win over Indianapolis, forcing him to the sidelines for the remainder of the regular season. After having his forearm surgically repaired, Gronkowski attempted to return to the team for the playoffs, but ended up suffering a setback when he reinjured his forearm during New England's first-round win over the Houston Texans. A second operation on the injured limb followed shortly thereafter, with two more procedures eventually having to be done as well after doctors discovered an infection in the forearm.

Gronkowski's injury woes continued in 2013, when, after undergoing back surgery in June, he tore the ACL and MCL in his right knee in a game against the Cleveland Browns in Week 14. Sidelined for the remainder of the year, Gronkowski concluded the campaign with only 39 receptions, 592 receiving yards, and four touchdowns, in just seven games.

Having undergone ACL/MCL surgery during the offseason, Gronkowski saw somewhat limited action in the first few games of the 2014 campaign as he continued to work his way back into top condition. His old self by the midway point of the season, Gronkowski ended up making 82 receptions, for 1,124 yards and 12 touchdowns, becoming in the process the first tight end in NFL history to catch at least 10 touchdown passes in four different seasons. Gronkowski's exceptional performance earned him NFL Comeback Player of the Year honors and his third Pro Bowl and First-Team All-Pro selections. He subsequently played well for New England in the postseason, totaling 16 receptions, 204 receiving yards, and three touchdowns in the Patriots' three playoff games, in helping them capture their eighth AFC Championship and fourth Super Bowl title.

Taking note of Gronkowski's return to top form prior to his team's first-round playoff matchup with the Patriots, Ravens safety Will Hill discussed the matchup problems that the big tight end presents to opposing defenses when he said, "It's not just a one-man job; it's a team effort. He's not a slow guy. If you try to play off him, you're just giving him what he needs. If you play up, he has the strength to get through people. He's a beast. He has a lot of aggression."

Baltimore head coach John Harbaugh commented "He's one of the best. He's big. He's fast. He's tough. He's nasty. He gets the ball in his hands and he wants to punish people. Run after catch, he's trying to run everybody he can over. He's just a gifted guy, and they get him the ball, and they get him the ball quickly, and they give him the ball downfield."

Harbaugh added, "He's unique in the sense that he's so big and so fast. He has a unique ability to beat coverage, and there really are not too many matchups you can put on him, zone or man. I guess you could bracket him and put him in a vice, kind of like you do on punts, but he's just a big, strong, fast guy. He has great hands. He's tough. He's very unique."

In comparing Gronkowski to New Orleans Saints tight end Jimmy Graham, the league's other premier player at the position, Ravens defensive coordinator Dean Pees suggested:

> They are different style of guys. They are both big, talented tight ends. They flex them out, both. The biggest thing with Rob is the fact that he's just so big and can body you up. The problem with him in a seam route is he's so big Tom (Brady) is going to put it up over your head and let him go get it. That's always going to be the problem. He's a guy that, if you contact him downfield, he's generally going to win, because he's going to knock down a 190-pound guy, as big as he is.

Even though Gronkowski's gregarious manner, carefree attitude, and hard-partying ways have caused many people to view him as someone who lacks total dedication to his profession, he is actually quite serious about perfecting his craft on the field. Patriots head coach Bill Belichick explains: "I think Rob has worked really hard on all areas of his game: running game, passing game and all the things involved with that, red area, play action, third down, different locations that he's been aligned in, in the backfield, on the line, flexed outside. He's developed a lot of different aspects to his game. He'll just try to continue to be able to threaten the defense in different ways."

Gronkowski will enter the 2015 campaign with career totals of 308 receptions, 4,379 receiving yards, and 55 touchdowns. Since he will be only 26 years of age at the start of the season, he figures to add significantly to those numbers in the future, as long as he is able to remain relatively healthy. That being the case, it seems likely that Gronkowski will eventually assume a much higher place in these rankings.

CAREER HIGHLIGHTS

Best Season

Even though Gronkowski played extremely well for the Patriots this past season (82 receptions, 1,124 receiving yards, 12 touchdowns), there is little doubt that he had the best season of his young career in 2011, when, in addition to scoring 18 touchdowns and leading the NFL with 17 TD catches, he finished fifth in the league with 90 receptions and sixth in the circuit with 1,327 receiving yards. Gronkowski's 17 touchdown receptions, 18 touchdowns, and 1,327 receiving yards all established new single-season NFL records for tight ends, with his 17 TD grabs making him the first tight end ever to lead the league in that category.

Memorable Moments/Greatest Performances

Gronkowski had his breakout game for the Patriots in Week 10 of his 2010 rookie campaign, catching five passes, for 72 yards and three touchdowns, during a 39-26 win over the Steelers in Pittsburgh. Gronkowski hooked up with Tom Brady on scoring plays that covered 19, 9, and 25 yards. He recorded the first 100-yard receiving day of his career in that year's regular-season finale, making six receptions, for 102 yards and one touchdown, during New England's 38-7 home win over Miami.

Gronkowski turned in a number of exceptional performances over the course of his historic 2011 campaign, with the first of those coming on September 25, when he made seven receptions, for 109 yards and two touchdowns, during a 34-31 loss to the Bills. He had another huge game against the Jets in Week 10, catching eight passes, for 113 yards and two touchdowns, in helping the Patriots defeat New York 37-16. Gronkowski again scored twice the following week against Kansas City, helping the Patriots rout the Chiefs 34-3 by making four receptions for 96 yards, with his 52-yard TD catch-and-run representing the longest play of his career. Gronkowski established a new single-season NFL record for most touchdowns scored by a tight end two weeks later against Indianapolis by scoring his 12th, 13th, and 14th TDs of the year during a 31-24 victory over the Colts. Gronk earned AFC Offensive Player of the Week honors the following week by making six receptions, for a career-high 160 yards, and scoring another two touchdowns during a 34-27 win over the Washington Redskins. Gronkowski's scoring plays covered 11 and 37 yards. He also hooked up with Tom Brady on a 50-yard catch-and-run during the contest.

Gronkowski added to his record totals by making eight receptions, for 108 yards and two touchdowns, during the Patriots' 49-21 victory over Buffalo in the regular-season finale.

Before injuring himself in the ensuing contest against Baltimore, Gronkowski continued his success in the first round of the 2011 playoffs, helping the Patriots record a lopsided 45-10 victory over the Denver Broncos by making 10 receptions, for 145 yards and three touchdowns.

Gronkowski also had a couple of big games in 2012, making eight receptions, for 146 yards and two touchdowns, during a 45-7 pasting of the St. Louis Rams on October 28, before hooking up with Tom Brady seven times, for 137 yards and two touchdowns, during a 59-24 mauling of the Indianapolis Colts three weeks later.

Despite appearing in only seven games in 2013, Gronkowski turned in a pair of dominant performances, making nine catches, for 143 yards and one touchdown, during a 55-31 victory over Pittsburgh on November 3, and helping the Patriots defeat Houston, 34-31, four weeks later by making six receptions, for 127 yards and one touchdown, including a season-long 50-yard catch-and-run.

After playing limited snaps during the early stages of the 2014 campaign, Gronkowski broke out against Chicago in Week 8, making nine receptions, for 149 yards and three touchdowns, during a lopsided 51-23 victory over the Bears. Gronkowski's scoring plays covered 6, 2, and 46 yards. He also had a big game against the Ravens in the first round of the playoffs, helping the Patriots record a come-from-behind 35-31 victory by making seven receptions, for 108 yards and one touchdown, which covered 46 yards. After subsequently having a relatively quiet day against Indianapolis in the AFC Championship Game (3 receptions, 28 yards, 1 TD), Gronkowski performed well against Seattle in Super Bowl XLIX, making six receptions, for 68 yards and one touchdown.

NOTABLE ACHIEVEMENTS

- Has caught more than 80 passes twice, surpassing 90 receptions once (90 in 2011).
- Has topped 1,000 receiving yards twice.
- Has scored at least 10 touchdowns four times.
- Led NFL with 17 touchdown receptions in 2011.
- Finished second in NFL with 18 touchdowns in 2011.

- Finished fifth in NFL with 90 receptions in 2011.
- Ranks among Patriots all-time leaders in: pass receptions (9th); receiving yardage (9th); touchdown receptions (2nd); touchdowns scored (2nd); and points scored (7th).
- First tight end to lead NFL in touchdown receptions (17 in 2011).
- Holds NFL single-season records for most touchdown receptions (17), touchdowns scored (18), and receiving yards (1,327) by a tight end, all in 2011.
- Two-time AFC champion (2011 & 2014).
- Super Bowl XLIX champion.
- Three-time Pro Bowl selection (2011, 2012 & 2014).
- Three-time First-Team All-Pro selection (2011, 2012 & 2014).
- 2014 NFL Comeback Player of the Year.

32

Babe Parilli

(Courtesy Mainline Autographs)

After being cast aside by the NFL, Babe Parilli went on to become one of the American Football League's most productive and colorful players as a member of the Boston Patriots. Winning the Pats' starting quarterback job shortly after arriving in Beantown early in 1961, Parilli ended up leading the Patriots to their first playoff appearance and a winning record in five of his first six seasons as their primary signal-caller. Before he left Boston at the conclusion of the 1967 campaign, Parilli passed for nearly 17,000 yards and threw 132 touchdown passes, placing him fourth in franchise history in both categories. Parilli also earned three Pro Bowl selections and one First-Team All-AFL nomination during his time in Boston, establishing a new league mark in 1964 by passing for 3,465 yards—the third highest total ever compiled in the 10-year history of the AFL. An exceptional holder as well, Parilli earned the nickname "Gold Finger" for his ability to place the ball in perfect position for Boston's longtime placekicker Gino Cappelletti.

Born in the Pittsburgh industrial suburb of Rochester, Pennsylvania, on May 7, 1930, Vito "Babe" Parilli attended the University of Kentucky, where he earned All-America honors quarterbacking the Wildcats under legendary coach Paul "Bear" Bryant. Expected to accomplish great things in the professional ranks as well, Parilli entered the NFL having been selected by the Green Bay Packers in the first round of the 1952 NFL Draft, with the fourth overall pick. However, the 22-year-old quarterback soon discovered that the success he experienced in college did not necessarily translate to the pro level.

Joining a poor Packers team that won only three games in 1951, Parilli spent most of his time in Green Bay splitting time at quarterback with Tobin Rote, compiling an overall mark of just 2-7 as a starter, completing just 44 percent of his passes, and throwing twice as many interceptions as touchdown passes. Released by the Packers at the end of the 1953 campaign, Parilli traveled north to the Canadian Football League, where he spent most of the next two seasons playing for the Ottawa Rough Riders. After also serving a brief stint in the military, Parilli returned to the NFL in 1956, appearing in five games with the Cleveland Browns before being traded back to the Packers. Parilli's time in Green Bay again proved to be short-lived, though, since the Packers cut him after he started a total of only five games over the course of the next two seasons. Spurned by the NFL for a second time, Parilli rejoined Ottawa in the CFL, spending all of 1959 playing north of the border, before electing to return to the States when the American Football League opened for business the following year.

The 30-year-old Parilli found himself competing for playing time with the much younger Tom Flores after he signed with the Oakland Raiders prior to the AFL's inaugural season. Making just two starts for the Raiders in 1960, Parilli experienced only moderate success, completing just under 50 percent of his passes for a total of 1,003 yards, while throwing 5 touchdown passes and 11 interceptions.

With Parilli's career apparently headed nowhere, things took a sudden turn for the better when an April 4, 1961, trade between the Raiders and

Patriots sent him and fullback Billy Lott to Boston for defensive tackle Hal Smith and running backs Alan Miller and Dick Christy. Platooned at quarterback with Butch Songin his first year in Boston, Parilli threw for 1,314 yards, tossed 13 touchdown passes and 9 interceptions, and led the AFL with a 52.5 completion percentage, in winning six of his eight starts under new head coach Mike Holovak. His confidence buoyed by his solid performance in 1961, Parilli got off to an even better start the following year, leading the Patriots to a 6-2-1 record in their first nine games, before a broken collar bone suffered during a Week 10 loss to the Houston Oilers shelved him for the remainder of the campaign. Parilli finished the season with 1,988 yards passing, 18 TD passes, just 8 interceptions, and a career-high 55.3 pass-completion percentage.

A return to full health enabled Parilli to earn his first All-Star selection in 1963, a season in which he led the Patriots to their first playoff appearance. Certainly, the numbers compiled by the 33-year-old quarterback over the course of that 1963 campaign could hardly be considered overwhelming. In addition to completing only 45.4 percent of his passes, he threw for just 2,345 yards, tossed only 13 touchdown passes, and finished second in the league with 24 interceptions. But Parilli provided the Patriots with outstanding leadership on offense, possessed a strong throwing arm, and excelled at play-action, which fit in well with coach Holovak's offensive scheme.

Although the Patriots failed to repeat as AFL Eastern Division champions in 1964, they finished the season with an exceptional 10-3-1 record, led by Parilli, who had the finest season of his career. Despite leading the league with 27 interceptions, Parilli also topped the circuit with 3,465 passing yards and 31 touchdown passes, earning in the process consensus First-Team All-AFL honors.

After briefly considering retirement during the subsequent offseason, Parilli ended up spending three more years in Boston, never again performing as well as he did in 1964, but still managing to post solid numbers in each of those campaigns. Particularly effective in 1966, Parilli led the Patriots to what turned out to be their last winning record for 10 seasons (8-4-2) by passing for 2,721 yards and 20 touchdowns, en route to earning his final All-Star selection.

Parilli left the Patriots at the end of the 1967 season and spent the final two years of his career backing up Joe Namath in New York. He left Boston having thrown for 16,747 yards and 132 touchdowns in his seven years with the Patriots. Parilli also tossed 138 interceptions, compiled a 47.2 completion percentage, and posted a passer rating of 64.8 during his time in Beantown, with the last two figures representing average marks for the era in which he played. The Patriots compiled an overall record of 44-32-7 between 1961 and 1967 with Parilli calling the signals. During that same period, they posted a mark of 6-7-2 with someone else taking the snap from center.

While serving as Joe Namath's backup his last two seasons, Parilli earned a championship ring when the Jets upset the heavily favored Baltimore Colts in Super Bowl III, defeating them by a score of 16-7. During his time in New York, Parilli furthered his reputation as one of the game's great holders by helping Jets placekicker Jim Turner score a then-record 145 points on field goals and extra points in 1968. Parilli announced his retirement the following year, concluding his career with 22,681 total passing yards, 178 touchdown passes, 220 interceptions, a 46.6 completion percentage, and an overall quarterback rating of 59.6.

Following his retirement, Parilli began a successful coaching career that saw him serve as quarterbacks coach for the Steelers, Broncos, and Patriots. While coaching for the Steelers in 1972 and 1973, he tutored a young Terry Bradshaw. Parilli also later worked with Craig Morton during Denver's 1977 AFC championship run, and with Steve Grogan after he returned to the Patriots in 1981. He also held various head-coaching positions, serving as top man on the New York Stars of the World Football League in 1974, and assuming the same position on the Chicago Winds the following year, before coaching several Arena Football League teams from 1981 to 1993.

Yet, Parilli will always be remembered most for the seven years he spent in Boston; years that he later admitted presented a number of challenges. Reflecting back on his time with the Patriots, Parilli noted, "The New York Giants had been big in New England for years. They were New England's team. Their games were televised in New England for some time before we came along. So starting a new team in Boston was not easy."

Parilli added, "We had great fans, but they were hard fans. They used to cheer when I got hurt. We did have to prove ourselves."

PATRIOT CAREER HIGHLIGHTS

Best Season

Parilli might well have gone on to post the best overall numbers of his career in 1962 had his season not been cut short by a broken collar bone he suffered during a Week 10 loss to Houston. Performing more efficiently than at any other point in his career, Parilli established career-high marks in pass-completion percentage (55.3) and quarterback rating (91.5). He also passed for almost 2,000 yards, threw 18 TD passes, and tossed only 8 interceptions. But, with Parilli having to sit out the final four games of that 1962 campaign, he ended up compiling easily his best numbers two years later. Even though he failed to finish near the top of the AFL rankings in either pass-completion percentage (48.2%) or passer rating (70.8) in 1964, Parilli led all league quarterbacks with 3,465 yards passing and 31 touchdown passes. In addition to establishing a new single-season AFL record for most passing yardage, Parilli set a Patriots record for most touchdown passes in a season that stood until 2007, when Tom Brady finally surpassed it. He also finished first among AFL quarterbacks in 4th-quarter comebacks (3) and game-winning drives (3). Parilli's exceptional performance earned him the second of his three Pro Bowl selections and his only First-Team All-AFL nomination.

Memorable Moments/Greatest Performances

Parilli played the finest 15 minutes of football of his career on October 6, 1962, throwing 3 second-quarter touchdown passes during a 43-14 mauling of the New York Titans. After hooking up with wide receiver Jim Colclough on a 63-yard scoring play early in the period, Parilli tossed a 13-yard TD pass to running back Ron Burton. He concluded the offensive outburst with a 36-yard strike to his favorite target, Gino Cappelletti. Parilli finished the day 14 of 23, for 234 yards and 3 touchdowns. He also ran with the ball twice for 29 yards.

After being hobbled by injuries the previous few weeks, Parilli turned in one of his finest performances on October 18, 1963, leading the Patriots to a 40-21 win over the Denver Broncos by completing 21 of 31 passes, for 358 yards and 2 touchdowns. Parilli's scoring passes went to Gino Cappelletti (24 yards) and Tony Romeo (31 yards).

Parilli had another big game one month later, helping the Patriots forge a 24-24 tie with the Kansas City Chiefs on November 17, 1963, by passing for 354 yards and one touchdown. He also scored a TD himself on a one-yard run.

However, Parilli experienced his finest moment of the 1963 campaign when the Patriots defeated Buffalo 26-8 in the AFL Eastern Division Championship Game. Even though Parilli's accuracy over the course of the contest left something to be desired (he completed just 14 of 35 passes), he used the swing pass to perfection, enabling him to finish the afternoon with 300 yards and 2 touchdowns, including a 59-yarder to Larry Garron that the running back took the distance after catching the ball near midfield.

Parilli had one of the biggest days of his career on October 16, 1964, when he threw for 422 yards and 4 touchdowns during a 43-43 tie with the Oakland Raiders. After hooking up with Jim Colclough on a 36-yard TD pass in the second quarter, Parilli tossed two TD passes to Larry Garron and another to Art Graham in the second half.

Parilli continued to perform well in his banner year of 1964, passing for 256 yards and running for a career-high 96 yards and 2 touchdowns during a 25-24 win over the Houston Oilers on November 6. He again frustrated Houston's defense three weeks later, passing for 336 yards and 3 touchdowns, in leading the Patriots to a 34-17 victory over the Oilers on November 29. Parilli's TD passes went for 26 yards to Larry Garron, 80 yards to Art Graham, and 20 yards to Jim Colclough. Parilli posted big numbers again the following week, when he passed for 300 yards and 3 touchdowns during a 31-24 win over the Kansas City Chiefs on December 6. Over the course of the contest, Parilli connected with Gino Cappelletti from 58 yards out and Art Graham from 3 yards out, before tossing a 39-yard scoring strike to Graham.

Parilli closed out the 1966 campaign in style, playing exceptionally well in Boston's final two games of the season. After completing 15 of 21 passes, for 256 yards and 3 touchdowns, in leading the Patriots to a 38-14 victory over Houston on December 11, Parilli passed for 379 yards and 3 touchdowns during a 38-28 loss to the Jets in the regular-season finale.

Parilli had the last truly big day of his career on October 15, 1967, when he threw a career-high 5 touchdown passes during a 41-10 pasting of the Miami Dolphins. He finished the game with 16 completions in only 20 passing attempts, for a total of 281 yards. Parilli hooked up with Larry Garron twice, from 17 and 41 yards out, and with tight end Jim Whalen three times, on scoring plays of 9, 9, and 41 yards.

NOTABLE ACHIEVEMENTS

- Passed for more than 3,000 yards once (3,465 in 1964).
- Topped 20 touchdown passes twice, surpassing 30-mark once (31 in 1964).
- Posted quarterback rating in excess of 90.0 once (91.5 in 1962).
- Led AFL quarterbacks in: passing yardage once; touchdown passes once; pass completion percentage once; pass interception percentage

once; fourth-quarter comebacks three times; and game-winning drives twice.

- Ranks among Patriots all-time leaders in: passing yardage (4th); pass completions (4th); and touchdown passes (4th).
- One of only 20 men to play all 10 AFL seasons.
- 1963 AFL Eastern Division champion.
- Three-time AFL Pro Bowl selection (1963, 1964 & 1966).
- 1964 First-Team All-AFL selection.
- 1966 AFL All-Star Game MVP.
- Member of Patriots' 1960s All-Decade Team.
- Inducted into Patriots Hall of Fame in 1993.

33

Jon Morris

(Courtesy Fenway Park Diaries)

The greatest center in Patriots history, Jon Morris spent his first four years in Boston snapping the ball to Babe Parilli, the man who immediately preceded him on this list. An outstanding all-around athlete who possessed size, speed, strength, and agility, Morris anchored the Patriots' offensive line from 1964 to 1972, establishing himself during that time as one of the AFL's premier linemen. A true ironman, Morris missed only one game his first nine years in the league, en route to appearing in a total of 130 regular-season games as a member of the Patriots—the eighth most in team history. Particularly effective from 1964 to 1970, Morris earned Pro Bowl honors in each of his first seven seasons, also earning in the process spots on the AFL's All-Time Team and the Patriots' 50th Anniversary Team.

Born in Washington, D.C., on April 5, 1942, Jon Nicholson Morris starred in baseball, football, and basketball while attending Gonzaga College High School in his home state, before enrolling at the College of the Holy Cross. Morris continued to display his athletic prowess in college, spending three seasons at Holy Cross playing center and linebacker on the school's football team. The Washington native had a banner year as a senior in 1963, earning All-America honors, being named Holy Cross Varsity Club Athlete of the Year and Lineman of the Year, and captaining the North Squad at the Senior Bowl.

Subsequently selected by Vince Lombardi's Green Bay Packers in the second round of the 1964 NFL Draft, with the 27th overall pick, Morris instead chose to sign with the Boston Patriots, who picked him in the fourth round of that year's AFL Draft, with the 29th overall selection. The 6'4", 254-pound Morris wasted little time in establishing himself as a starter in Boston, taking over immediately at center, en route to being named the Patriots' Rookie of the Year. Morris, who helped the Patriots improve their record from 7-6-1 to 10-3-1, also earned All-Star and Second-Team All-AFL honors his first year in the league.

Developing rapidly into one of Boston's team leaders, Morris again made Second-Team All-AFL and appeared in the Pro Bowl in his second season, earning recognition along the way as the Patriots' "Unsung Hero." The following year, Morris received the third of his seven consecutive Pro Bowl nominations, while also being named First-Team All-Pro for the only time in his career.

As Morris's list of honors continued to grow, he furthered his reputation as one of the sport's most durable players. Starting all but one game at center for the Patriots from 1964 to 1972, Morris appeared in 127 out of a possible 128 contests, including the playoffs. He also gained general recognition as one of the AFL's top two centers, usually being ranked behind only Oakland Raiders Hall of Famer Jim Otto.

Morris continued to play at an extremely high level for the Patriots until 1972, earning four more Pro Bowl selections and one more Second-Team All-AFL nomination. Morris's seven Pro Bowl appearances place him second in Patriots history, behind only John Hannah, who graced the AFC roster a total of nine times during his Hall of Fame career. In fact, after the

NFL and AFL merged at the conclusion of the 1969 campaign, Morris became the first Patriots player to represent the AFC in the Pro Bowl, joining Jim Otto at center on the 1970 AFC squad.

After losing his starting job in 1973, Morris remained in Boston one more year, eventually signing with the Detroit Lions, with whom he spent the next three seasons. Showing that he still had something left in the tank, Morris started every game at center for the Lions over the course of those three seasons, being voted the team's "Offensive Player of the Year" by his Lions teammates in 1975. Following his tenure in Detroit, Morris spent his final season serving as a backup on the Chicago Bears, before announcing his retirement at the end of 1978. In addition to his seven Pro Bowl selections and four All-Pro nominations, Morris eventually landed Second-Team honors on the AFL's All-Time All-Star Team (Jim Otto made the First Team) and a spot on the Patriots' All-1960s Team. The Patriots also acknowledged the many contributions he made to their success through the years by inducting him into their Hall of Fame in 2011.

Following his retirement, Morris entered into a career in broadcasting, serving as the color commentator on Patriots radio broadcasts from 1979 to 1987. He also later did color analysis of NFL games for NBC television.

PATRIOT CAREER HIGHLIGHTS

Best Season

The Washington Touchdown Club honored Morris as the top athlete of his home state in 1967. Nevertheless, the Patriots center had his finest season one year earlier, earning First-Team All-AFL honors for the only time in his career. Further strengthening the case for 1966 is the tremendous amount of success that Jim Nance had over the course of the campaign, running for a league-leading 1,458 yards behind an offensive line anchored by Morris.

Memorable Moments/Greatest Performances

Morris displayed a knack for falling on loose balls over the course of his career, recovering 3 fumbles during his time in Boston. Two of those recoveries proved to be critical, with the first of them occurring on October 23, 1964, when Morris scooped up a fumble by running back Ron Burton during a 24-7 victory over the Kansas City Chiefs. Morris also helped preserve a 27-27 tie with the Chiefs on November 20, 1966, when he recovered a fumble by running back Larry Garron.

However, as an offensive lineman, Morris usually found himself living vicariously through the success of others, experiencing most of his greatest moments when the men who ran behind him accomplished something truly extraordinary. That being the case, he arguably turned in his finest performance on October 30, 1966, when he helped create gaping holes in Oakland's defensive front, enabling Patriot running backs to amass a total of 281 yards on the ground during a 24-21 home win over the Raiders. Jim Nance proved to be the biggest beneficiary of Morris's exceptional blocking, rushing for a career-high 208 yards.

NOTABLE ACHIEVEMENTS

- Appeared in 125 consecutive games with Patriots from 1964 to 1972.
- First Patriots player to appear in NFL Pro Bowl.
- Seven-time Pro Bowl selection (1964–1970).
- 1966 First-Team All-AFL selection.
- Three-time Second-Team All-AFL selection (1964, 1965 & 1969).
- AFL Hall of Fame All-1960s Second Team.
- Named to Patriots' 50th Anniversary Team in 2009.
- Inducted into Patriots Hall of Fame in 2011.

3 4

Lawyer Milloy

Lawyer Milloy playing as a Seattle Seahawk
(Courtesy of Jeffrey Beall)

A hard-hitting safety who never missed a game in his seven seasons with the Patriots, Lawyer Milloy proved to be one of the NFL's best players at his position during his time in New England, earning four Pro Bowl selections, two All-Pro nominations, and three All-AFC selections. An outstanding run-stuffer, Milloy amassed well in excess of 100 tackles on five occasions, en route to finishing first on the team in that category four straight times. Doing a solid job in pass coverage as well, Milloy recorded a total of 19 interceptions for the Patriots, placing him 12th in franchise history. Milloy's exceptional all-around play helped the Pats win two AFC championships and one Super Bowl, earning him in the process a place on both their 1990s and 2000s All-Decade Teams.

Born in St. Louis, Missouri, on November 14, 1973, Lawyer Marzell Milloy attended Lincoln High School in Tacoma, Washington, where he starred in football, baseball, and basketball. A teammate of future NFL quarterback Jon Kitna at Lincoln, Milloy earned *Parade* magazine high school All-American honors in his senior year by rushing for 1,056 yards and 15 touchdowns as a tailback, while also intercepting seven passes as a safety. At the same time, Milloy excelled in baseball to such a degree that the Cleveland Indians drafted him as a pitching prospect upon his graduation from Lincoln High.

Choosing instead to further his education, Milloy accepted an athletic scholarship from the University of Washington, where he continued to star in baseball, prompting the Detroit Tigers to eventually select him in the 19th round of the 1995 MLB Draft. However, after earning First-Team All-Pac-10 and consensus First-Team All-American honors as a safety for the Huskies in 1995, Milloy elected to pursue a career in football instead.

Selected by the Patriots in the second round of the 1996 NFL Draft, with the 36th overall pick, Milloy wasted little time in establishing himself as a key member of New England's defensive secondary, starting the final 10 games of the regular season and all three playoff games at strong safety as a rookie. Displaying the outstanding all-around ability that made him one of the league's top safeties, Milloy finished his first NFL season with 84 tackles (54 solo), two interceptions, eight passes defensed, one sack, two forced fumbles, and one fumble recovery. He followed that up with a strong sophomore campaign in which he finished second on the team with 112 tackles (82 solo) and three interceptions.

Rapidly developing into one of the Patriots' most consistent players, Milloy began a string of four consecutive seasons in 1998 in which he led the team in tackles, averaging 119 stops per season over that stretch of time. He also finished first on the team in interceptions twice, totaling 14 picks from 1998 to 2001. Milloy perhaps played his best ball for the Patriots in 1998 and 1999, recording 120 tackles (79 solo) and a career-high six interceptions in the first of those campaigns, before amassing 120 tackles (91 solo), picking off four passes, and registering two sacks the following year. In addition to making the AFC Pro Bowl roster and earning First-Team All-AFC honors in 1998, 1999, and 2001, Milloy earned First-Team All-Pro honors in 1999. He also made Second-Team All-Pro in 1998. Milloy's outstanding play throughout the period prompted his teammates to elect him defensive co-captain prior to the 2001 season.

Milloy had another solid year in 2002, earning the last of his four Pro Bowl selections by finishing third on the Patriots with 94 tackles (65 solo). However, after failing to come to terms on a new contract with the team, Milloy was released by the Patriots just five days before the start of the 2003 NFL season, bringing to an end his exceptional seven-year run in New England.

Taken aback by Milloy's release, the remaining members of the Patriots initially found it extremely difficult to accept the fact that their longtime teammate would no longer be lining up alongside them. Speaking in the Patriots' locker room after learning the news, a stunned Tedy Bruschi lamented, "Has it ever been this quiet in here? I don't think it has. I think 'shocked' is the word. . . . You sort of just shake your head and ask yourself, 'Why?'"

In addressing the situation, head coach Bill Belichick stated, "Today is a day that nobody is happy about. This isn't the way we wanted this story to end. This is the hardest player that I have had to release. It was the hardest situation that I've had to go through like this, here or anywhere else."

Over the course of his seven seasons in New England, Milloy appeared in every Patriots game, starting all but the first six contests of his rookie campaign. During that time, he made 764 tackles (538 solo), 19 interceptions, and seven sacks, forced seven fumbles, recovered seven others, and scored one defensive touchdown. Milloy finished no lower than fourth on the team in tackles in any of his seven years in New England.

Signed by the Bills shortly after being released by the Patriots, Milloy spent the next three years in Buffalo, continuing his solid play at the safety position. In addition to surpassing 100 tackles in two of those campaigns, he recorded a total of eight sacks and three interceptions for the Bills, before being released by them as well in a salary cap-related move. Subsequently signed by Atlanta, Milloy started all but one game for the Falcons over the course of the next three seasons, averaging 94 tackles and intercepting a total of three passes during that time, before spending his final two seasons with the Seattle Seahawks. He announced his retirement at the conclusion of the 2010 campaign, ending his career with 1,438 tackles (1,033 solo), 25 interceptions, and 21 sacks, making him a member of the select 20/20 club.

During his time in Seattle, Milloy served as a mentor to young safeties Earl Thomas and Kam Chancellor, treating them as both friends and students. Admitting that he entered the league with little knowledge of Milloy's background, Thomas, who Seattle selected with the 14th overall pick of the 2010 NFL Draft, later revealed, "The first time I met him (Milloy), he asked me my name. I have to be honest—I didn't know who he was."

Thomas continued, "It was crazy, once I did my research, to see what a great player he was, and how much he had accomplished in the game. I mean, he was a great player. He is a future Hall of Famer. But here he was that first day, just being a humble guy, taking time out for little old me. He didn't have to do that, but I really appreciated it."

Meanwhile, Chancellor disclosed that Milloy taught him a great deal about being a professional, emphasizing to him the importance of studying film and learning his assignments. He also said that Milloy taught him how to be a leader, and how to take control of the other members of the secondary.

Discussing how Milloy's absence affected him the first few months after he announced his retirement, Chancellor stated, "Without Lawyer, we don't really have that older guy to really guide you like we had last year. Lawyer brought that intensity to the field. And every time I had a question, he answered it for me. He taught me the steps."

Chancellor added, "It was good having Lawyer around because he's like a legend, man. He was one of those faces that was feared. It's kind of hard to believe he went that many years, the way he hit. I feel blessed to have been behind a guy like that."

PATRIOT CAREER HIGHLIGHTS

Best Season

Milloy had an outstanding all-around year for the Patriots in 2000, leading the team with 121 tackles (90 solo) and three forced fumbles, and tying for the team lead with two interceptions. He again played extremely well the following season, earning Pro Bowl and First-Team All-AFC honors by recording 113 tackles (77 solo), two interceptions, and three sacks. Still, it would be difficult to argue with the notion that Milloy had his two finest seasons in 1998 and 1999. In addition to making 120 tackles (79 solo) in the first of those campaigns, Milloy registered a sack and a career-high six interceptions, one of which he returned 30 yards for the only defensive touchdown of his career. He followed that up by making another 120 tackles (91 solo) in 1999, while also recording two sacks, two fumble recoveries, and a team-leading four interceptions. Milloy earned Pro Bowl and First-Team All-AFC honors both years. However, while only the Associated Press named him Second-Team All-Pro in 1998, Milloy earned unanimous

First-Team All-Pro recognition the following season, being accorded that honor by the *Sporting News* as well. That being the case, 1999 is the choice here for Milloy's best season.

Memorable Moments/Greatest Performances

Although the Patriots lost their November 17, 1996, matchup with the Denver Broncos 34-8, Milloy recorded his first career interception during the game, picking off a John Elway pass and returning it 14 yards.

Milloy scored the only defensive touchdown of his career on September 20, 1998, when he intercepted a Steve McNair pass late in the fourth quarter and returned it 30 yards for a TD, clinching in the process New England's 27-16 victory over the Tennessee Oilers. He also recorded eight tackles during the contest.

Six weeks later, on November 1, Milloy helped preserve a 21-16 victory over the Indianapolis Colts by picking off Peyton Manning twice in the final two minutes of the game. Milloy's exceptional performance enabled him to win AFC Defensive Player of the Week honors.

Milloy also played exceedingly well in New England's 24-21 win over San Francisco on December 20, 1998, recording a season-high 14 tackles.

Milloy began the 1999 campaign in grand fashion, intercepting a Vinny Testaverde pass and making eight tackles during a 30-28 win over the Jets. He turned in another outstanding effort in Week 7 against Denver, helping the Patriots edge out the Broncos 24-23 by recording a season-high 14 tackles. However, Milloy saved arguably his finest all-around performance of the year for the regular-season finale, registering an interception, a sack, and 10 tackles during a 20-3 win over the Baltimore Ravens.

Milloy played superbly against the Bengals on November 19, 2000, helping the Patriots edge out Cincinnati 16-13 by picking off a Scott Mitchell pass and making a team-leading 14 tackles.

Milloy experienced two of his finest moments during the 2001 postseason, en route to helping the Patriots claim their first Super Bowl title. With the Pats clinging to a 24-17 lead over Pittsburgh late in the fourth quarter of the AFC Championship Game, Milloy picked off a Kordell Stewart pass at the New England 39-yard line and returned it to midfield. The Patriots subsequently held on to the ball for the final 2:02 of regulation, enabling them to advance to the Super Bowl. The following week, against St. Louis in Super Bowl XXXVI, Milloy recorded seven tackles and led the team with three passes defensed, in helping the Pats defeat the Rams by a score of 20-17.

NOTABLE ACHIEVEMENTS

- Intercepted 6 passes in 1998.
- Surpassed 100 tackles five times.
- Led Patriots in tackles four straight times (1998–2001).
- Returned one interception for a touchdown.
- Ranks 12th all-time on Patriots with 19 career interceptions.
- Two-time AFC champion (1996 & 2001).
- Super Bowl XXXVI champion.
- Four-time Pro Bowl selection (1998, 1999, 2001 & 2002).
- 1999 First-Team All-Pro selection.
- 1998 Second-Team All-Pro selection.
- Three-time First-Team All-AFC selection (1998, 1999 & 2001).
- Member of Patriots' 1990s All-Decade Team.
- Member of Patriots' 2000s All-Decade Team.

35

Randy Moss

(Courtesy Keith Allison)

Perhaps the most naturally-gifted wide receiver ever to play in the NFL, Randy Moss also proved to be one of the league's most controversial and polarizing figures throughout his 14-year career, which he spent with five different teams. The target of criticism from the time he first entered the NFL due to a number of incidents that occurred earlier in his private life, Moss added further fuel to the fire by frequently conducting himself in an inappropriate and unprofessional manner during his years in Minnesota, Oakland, New England, Tennessee, and San Francisco. Yet, through it all, the enigmatic wide receiver remained one of the league's most potent offensive weapons—one that opposing defenses both feared and respected. After earning five Pro Bowl selections, four First-Team All-NFC nominations, and three First-Team All-Pro selections as a member of the Minnesota Vikings, Moss reached the pinnacle of his career with the Patriots in 2007, when, en route to earning Pro Bowl and All-Pro honors for the final time, he caught 98 passes for 1,493 yards and established a new single-season NFL record by recording 23 touchdown receptions. Moss also played extremely well for the Pats in each of the next two seasons, totaling more than 150 receptions, for nearly 2,300 yards and 24 touchdowns, before wearing out his welcome in New England during the early stages of the 2010 campaign. Even though Moss wore a Patriots uniform for just a little over three seasons, he ranks among the franchise's all-team leaders in five different offensive categories, establishing himself during that time as the most dangerous wide-out ever to perform for the team.

Born in Charleston, West Virginia, on February 13, 1977, Randy Gene Moss grew up in nearby Rand, where he attended DuPont High School. While at DuPont, Moss demonstrated the extraordinary athletic ability that eventually earned him the nickname "The Freak" by excelling in football, basketball, baseball, and track. In addition to twice being named West Virginia Player of the Year in basketball, Moss led the DuPont Panthers to back-to-back state championships in football, starring at wide receiver and defensive back, while also serving as the team's kicker, punter, and primary return man on kickoffs and punts. An outstanding student as well, Moss also served as a member of the school's debate team.

Yet, in spite of the tremendous success he experienced at DuPont, Moss had to complete his high school education at Cabell Alternative School after being expelled by DuPont for pleading guilty to misdemeanor battery charges stemming from an incident that occurred on March 23, 1995, when he supported a friend in a hallway fight against a white student who allegedly used racist remarks towards his companion. Convicted of sending the student to the hospital by kicking him repeatedly, Moss began his 30-day jail sentence on August 1, 1995, spending three days behind bars at the South Central Regional Jail in Charleston, before having the remainder of his sentence suspended until he completed his freshman year in college.

After originally signing a letter of intent to attend the University of Notre Dame, Moss found his enrollment application denied due to his troubles with the law, prompting him to enroll at Florida State instead.

However, Seminoles head football coach Bobby Bowden soon revoked his scholarship when Moss tested positive for smoking marijuana shortly after he turned himself in to jail to complete the remainder of his 30-day sentence.

Dismissed from Florida State and sentenced to an additional 60 days in prison, Moss ultimately transferred to Marshall University, where he spent the next two years starring at wide receiver and kickoff returner. After leading Marshall to a perfect record and the Division I-AA title as a freshman in 1996, Moss teamed up with future New York Jets quarterback Chad Pennington the following year to lead the Thundering Herd to the Mid-American Conference title in their first year as a Division I-A entity. In addition to earning All-America honors both years, Moss won the Fred Biletnikoff Award as the nation's top wide receiver and placed fourth in the Heisman Trophy balloting in 1997, finishing behind only Charles Woodson, Peyton Manning, and Ryan Leaf.

Electing to turn pro following the conclusion of the 1997 campaign, Moss entered the 1998 NFL Draft as one of the year's most highly touted prospects. However, with questions regarding the quality of his character abounding, Moss ended up lasting until the 21st overall pick, when the Minnesota Vikings finally selected him. Entering the league with a huge chip on his shoulder, Moss proclaimed that the teams that passed on him "will regret it once they see what kind of a player I am, and what kind of a guy I really am."

Living up to his words, Moss took the NFL by storm, earning Pro Bowl, First-Team All-Pro, and AP Offensive Rookie of the Year honors in 1998 by making 69 receptions, for 1,313 yards and a league-leading 17 touchdowns. His fabulous performance helped the Vikings set a new NFL record (since broken) by scoring 556 points, en route to finishing the season with a 15-1 record. Yet, Moss still managed to draw a considerable amount of criticism from many quarters by squirting a referee with a water bottle during Minnesota's 30-27 overtime loss to Atlanta in the NFC Championship Game.

Blessed with exceptional speed, outstanding leaping ability, good size, and large, soft hands, the 6'4", 215-pound Moss proved to be too much for opposing defensive backs to contend with. Able to run past virtually any defender, Moss outleaped those backs he found himself unable to outrun. Commenting on Moss's extraordinary natural ability, Brian Billick, who served as an assistant under head coach Dennis Green in Moss's first two seasons in Minnesota, said, "Nobody, and I mean nobody, has all those physical skills Randy has. They just don't. That kid loves to play football."

Moss compiled similarly impressive numbers in each of the next two campaigns, concluding 1999 with 80 receptions for 1,413 yards and 11 touchdowns, before making 77 catches for 1,437 yards and a league-leading 15 TD grabs in 2000. Although Moss subsequently failed to make the NFC Pro Bowl roster for the first time in his young career in 2001, he had another extremely productive year, making 82 receptions for 1,233 yards and 10 touchdowns. In spite of the success he experienced on the playing field, though, Moss again raised a number of eyebrows around the league when he tested positive for marijuana under the NFL's substance abuse program in 2001, making him subject to additional random drug screening for the next two years.

After earning his fourth Pro Bowl selection in 2002 by making 106 receptions for 1,347 yards and seven touchdowns, Moss had his best season for the Vikings in 2003, finishing second in the NFL with 111 receptions and 1,632 receiving yards, while topping the circuit with 17 TD catches. Moss' brilliant effort earned him a spot on the NFC Pro Bowl roster for the fifth time and First-Team All-Pro honors for the third time.

Injuries and a somewhat apathetic attitude prevented Moss from reaching the same level of production in 2004, limiting him to only 13 games, 49 receptions, and 767 receiving yards, although he still managed to score 13 touchdowns. Angered by Moss' lackadaisical approach to his craft, the Vikings began to seriously consider trading him. The enigmatic wide receiver all but sealed his fate during Minnesota's 31-17 playoff win over the Packers on January 9, 2005, when, despite making four catches for 70 yards and two touchdowns, he further antagonized team management by making an obscene gesture towards the fans of Green Bay. After scoring his second touchdown of the contest, Moss trotted to the goalpost and feigned pulling down his pants, as if mooning those Packer fans situated behind the end zone. Taken aback by Moss' behavior, NFL on Fox announcer Joe Buck called it a "disgusting act."

The Vikings parted ways with Moss nearly two months later, sending him to the Oakland Raiders for linebacker Napoleon Harris and a pair of 2005 draft picks on March 3, 2005. Before Moss joined his new team, though, he once again raised the ire of the league office when he admitted during an August 2005 television interview with Bryant Gumbel that he smoked marijuana during his NFL career "every blue moon." When asked if he still used marijuana, Moss replied, "I might. I might have fun. And, you know, hopefully . . . I won't get into any trouble with the NFL by saying that, you know. I have had fun throughout my years and, you know, predominantly in the offseason."

Moss subsequently claimed that his words were taken out of context, stating, "That was really me talking in the past tense of way back in the beginning of my career and my childhood—especially in high school and college." Nevertheless, the league office expressed its dissatisfaction with Moss, putting him on a tighter leash than ever.

Despite gaining 1,005 yards on 60 pass receptions in 2005, Moss suffered through two subpar seasons in Oakland, frequently displaying his dissatisfaction with the Raiders' poor performance by failing to put forth a 100 percent effort. Playing for an Oakland team that posted a combined record of 6-26 in 2005 and 2006, Moss often appeared uninterested in the outcomes of games, admitting as much when he responded to questions about his dropped passes and lackluster effort by suggesting, "Maybe because I'm unhappy and I'm not too much excited about what's going on, so, my concentration and focus level tend to go down sometimes when I'm in a bad mood."

Moss's uninspired play ruffled the feathers of many of his peers, with former MVP quarterback Kurt Warner stating on one occasion, "Randy's just a guy I don't see eye to eye with. I take my responsibilities in this league a little differently."

Meanwhile, former Pro Bowl lineman Kyle Turley fumed, "As a player, I like Randy Moss. He's got incredible talent, and I think he's nasty. But, if he was on my team and he pulled the shit he pulls, I'd walk up to him on the sideline and punch him in the face."

Having grown weary of Moss' antics, Oakland completed a trade with the Patriots on the first day of the 2007 NFL Draft in which they sent the disgruntled wide receiver to New England for a fourth round selection in that year's draft. With Tom Brady subsequently restructuring his contract to create room under the salary cap for Moss, the latter expressed his glee over joining the Patriots when he said, "I'm still in awe that I'm a part of this organization. I think that he's (Bill Belichick) the kind of coach that can motivate me. He has a proven track record."

After sitting out the entire 2007 preseason with a hamstring injury he suffered during the first week of training camp, Moss ended up having a season for the ages. Forming a symbiotic relationship with his new quarterback, Moss combined with Brady to lead the Patriots to an all-time record 589 points and a perfect 16-0 record during the regular season. Along the way, Moss caught 98 passes, finished second in the league with 1,493 receiving yards, and set a new single-season NFL record by making 23 touchdown receptions, en route to earning his sixth Pro Bowl nomination and his fourth First-Team All-Pro selection.

Noting the enormous impact Moss made in New England, James Black, NFL Editor for *Yahoo! Sports*, wrote on November 4, 2007, "Every week, in addition to out-leaping at least one defender for a touchdown, Moss keeps making incredible one-handed grabs that make you mutter, 'How the heck did he come up with that?'"

Moss made an equally strong impression on his Patriot teammates, with Tom Brady stating on one occasion, "He was just born to be a football player."

Commenting on the positive attitude Moss brought with him to New England, Tedy Bruschi suggested, "He's done nothing but work hard and put the team first."

Ben Watson added, "Whenever you have a guy like Randy Moss, a guy who everybody in the league respects, and who has big-play capability every time he gets on the field, teams have to respect that."

Often praised by Brady and head coach Bill Belichick for his superior intellect, Moss also drew raves from NFL coach Scott Linehan, who said, "He has a tremendous football IQ. The guy has the ability to dominate a game even when he's not touching the ball."

Signed to a new three-year, $27 million deal by the Patriots after becoming a free agent at season's end, Moss compiled outstanding numbers in 2008 and 2009 as well, even though he spent the first of those campaigns catching passes from Matt Cassel instead of Tom Brady, who suffered a torn ACL in his left knee in the regular-season opener. After making 69 receptions for 1,008 yards and 11 touchdowns in 2008, Moss caught 83 passes for 1,264 yards and 13 touchdowns the following year, amassing in the process more than 1,000 receiving yards for the 10th and final time in his career.

Unfortunately, the 2009 campaign proved to be Moss' last full season in New England. After telling CBS Sports that he "did not feel wanted" by the Patriots when they failed to offer him a contract extension prior to the start of the 2010 regular season, Moss exchanged barbs with Tom Brady through the local media the next few weeks, prompting the Patriots to trade Moss back to Minnesota for a 2011 third-round draft pick four weeks into the campaign. Moss left New England having caught a total of 259 passes, for 3,904 yards and 50 touchdowns.

Moss's Vikings reunion proved to be short-lived, with Minnesota head coach Brad Childress electing to waive him less than four weeks later after he criticized Childress and his teammates during a press conference following the team's loss to the Patriots at Gillette Stadium. Subsequently claimed by the Titans, Moss spent the remainder of the year in Tennessee, making just six receptions for 80 yards in a part-time role. He then opted to sit out the 2011 season, before returning to the NFL as a member of the San Francisco 49ers the following year. After making only 28 receptions for 434 yards and three touchdowns as a backup with the 49ers in 2012, Moss announced his retirement, ending his career with 982 receptions, 15,292 receiving yards, and 157 touchdowns. Moss' 157 career TDs place him fourth in NFL history. He also ranks second in touchdown receptions, third in pass receiving yardage, and 10th in pass receptions. In addition to surpassing 1,000 receiving yards 10 times, Moss topped 100 receptions twice and scored at least 10 touchdowns on nine separate occasions.

Following his retirement, Moss accepted a position with Fox Sports 1, where he continues to serve as an analyst for that station's *Fox Football Daily Show*.

PATRIOT CAREER HIGHLIGHTS

Best Season

Although Moss also played well for the Patriots in each of the next two seasons, he clearly had his best year for them in 2007, when, in addition to finishing eighth in the NFL with 98 receptions, he placed second in the league with 138 points and a franchise-record 1,493 receiving yards. Meanwhile, his 23 TD receptions established a new single-season NFL record, breaking the previous mark of 22 set by Jerry Rice in the strike-shortened 1987 campaign. Moss' brilliant year included eight multi-touchdown games, nine 100-yard games, and six touchdown catches of 40 or more yards.

Memorable Moments/Greatest Performances

After sitting out the entire 2007 preseason with a hamstring injury, Moss began his Patriots career in style, making nine receptions for 183 yards and one touchdown during New England's 38-14 win over the New York Jets in the regular-season opener. Moss exhibited his still-blazing speed by running past three Jets defenders, in scoring from 51 yards out midway through the third quarter.

Moss had another huge game in Week 9, helping the Pats improve their record to 9-0 by catching nine passes for 145 yards and one touchdown during a come-from-behind 24-20 victory over Peyton Manning and the Colts in Indianapolis.

In New England's next game, played against Buffalo on November 18, Moss made a career-high four TD grabs during a 56-10 dismantling of the Bills. Moss, who finished the contest with 10 catches for 128 yards, scored all four touchdowns in the first half, connecting with Tom Brady from 43, 16, 6, and 17 yards out.

Moss, though, experienced his most memorable moment of the campaign in the regular-season finale against the New York Giants, hooking up with Tom Brady on scoring plays that covered 4 and 65 yards to establish a new single-season record for touchdown receptions. Moss's 65-yard TD grab, which put the Patriots ahead to stay with 11:15 remaining in the fourth quarter, also enabled Brady to break Peyton Manning's single-season record for most touchdown passes. New England ended up winning the contest 38-35, thereby finishing the regular season with a perfect 16-0 record.

Moss had his biggest game of the 2008 campaign in Week 12 against Miami, making eight receptions for 125 yards and three touchdowns during a 48-28 victory over the Dolphins. Moss' scoring plays went for 25, 8, and 29 yards.

Moss recorded the longest touchdown of his Patriots career in the next-to-last game of the 2008 regular season, hauling in a 76-yard TD pass from Matt Cassel during a 47-7 mauling of the Arizona Cardinals.

Moss also turned in a number of memorable performances in his final full season in New England, helping the Patriots overcome a 24-13 fourth-quarter deficit to Buffalo in the 2009 regular-season opener by making a career-high 12 receptions for 141 yards. Ben Watson scored two late touchdowns to give the Pats a 25-24 come-from-behind victory over their AFC East rivals.

Moss recorded the only interception of his career on October 11, 2009, when he picked off a "Hail Mary" pass thrown by Denver's Kyle Orton in the closing moments of the first half of a game the Broncos eventually won 20-17 in overtime.

At a snowy Gillette Stadium the very next week, Moss helped the Patriots record a lopsided 59-0 victory over the Tennessee Titans by making eight receptions for 129 yards and three touchdowns. Moss' first two scores, which covered 40 and 28 yards, came in the second quarter, helping Tom Brady set a record for most TD passes in a quarter (five).

Moss made one of his biggest plays of the 2009 campaign on November 8, when he scored from 71 yards out with only 3:27 left in the fourth quarter, to give the Patriots a 24-17 lead over Miami in a game they eventually won 27-17. Moss finished the day with six receptions for 147 yards and one touchdown.

Although the Patriots lost their prime time Sunday night matchup with Peyton Manning and the Colts the following week 35-34, Moss had another huge game, making nine receptions for 179 yards and two touchdowns. His 63-yard TD grab early in the second quarter moved him past Terrell Owens into sole possession of second place on the all-time career touchdown reception list.

NOTABLE ACHIEVEMENTS

- Caught more than 60 passes three times, topping 80 receptions twice and 90 receptions once.
- Surpassed 1,000 receiving yards three times, topping 1,400 yards once (1,493 in 2007).
- Scored more than 10 touchdowns three straight times, topping 20 TDs once (23 in 2007).
- Led NFL with 23 touchdowns in 2007.
- Finished second in NFL with 1,493 receiving yards and 138 points scored in 2007.
- Holds Patriots single-season records for most touchdown receptions (23 in 2007) and most touchdowns scored (23 in 2007).
- Ranks among Patriots all-time leaders in: pass receptions (14th); receiving yardage (11th); touchdown receptions (tied-3rd); touchdowns scored (tied-3rd); and points scored (tied-7th).
- 2007 AFC champion.
- Holds NFL single-season record for most touchdown receptions (23 in 2007).
- Ranks among NFL all-time leaders in: pass receptions (10th); touchdown receptions (2nd); receiving yards (3rd); and touchdowns scored (4th).
- 2007 Pro Bowl selection.
- 2007 First-Team All-Pro selection.
- 2007 Pro Football Writers Association Comeback Player of the Year.
- Member of Patriots' 2000s All-Decade Team.
- Pro Football Reference 2000s All-Decade First Team.
- Pro Football Hall of Fame 2000s All-Decade First Team.

36

Steve Grogan

(Courtesy George A. Kitrinos)

Known for his toughness and determination, Steve Grogan spent his entire 16-year NFL career with the Patriots, overcoming numerous injuries and challenges from other quarterbacks during that time to establish himself as one of the franchise's all-time leaders in every major statistical category for QBs. Even though Grogan started as many as 10 games in just six of his 16 seasons, he ranks second in Patriots' history in touchdown passes and third all-time in pass attempts, pass completions, and passing yardage. An outstanding runner as well, Grogan set an NFL record for quarterbacks by rushing for 12 touchdowns in 1976, en route to scoring a total of 35 times on the ground over the course of his career—a figure that places him fourth in team annals. Grogan's versatility, grittiness, and leadership helped the Patriots advance to the Super Bowl once and the playoffs five times, with the team compiling an overall record of 75-60 in games he started. Conversely, they finished just 47-60 during that same period with someone else calling signals. Grogan's contributions to the Patriots eventually earned him a spot on their 35th Anniversary Team and a place in their Hall of Fame.

Born in San Antonio, Texas, on July 24, 1953, Steven James Grogan starred in three different sports at Ottawa High School in Kansas, excelling in track and field, basketball, and football. After enrolling at Kansas State University, Grogan went on to establish himself as one of the school's all-time passing and total offense leaders, doing an outstanding job with both his arm and his legs. Impressed with Grogan's versatility and leadership skills, the Patriots selected him in the fifth round of the 1975 NFL Draft, with the 116th overall pick, even though they had made Heisman Trophy winner Jim Plunkett the draft's first overall selection just four years earlier.

Dissatisfied with Plunkett's play behind center, Patriots head coach Chuck Fairbanks turned the starting duties over to Grogan midway through his rookie campaign of 1975. Starting seven of the team's final eight games, Grogan experienced the usual growing pains of any first-year quarterback, compiling a record of 1-6, completing just over 50 percent of his passes for 1,976 yards, and throwing 11 touchdown passes and 18 interceptions. Nevertheless, he made enough of an impression on Fairbanks to prompt the coach to trade Plunkett at season's end.

Starting every game for the Patriots for the first of four straight times in 1976, Grogan led them to an 11-3 record and their first playoff appearance in 13 years. For his part, the second-year quarterback posted modest individual numbers, completing just 48 percent of his passes for only 1,903 yards, while tossing 18 touchdown passes and 20 interceptions. However, Grogan also ran for 397 yards and 12 touchdowns, establishing in the process a TD record for quarterbacks that stood for 35 years, until Carolina Panthers QB Cam Newton rushed for 14 scores in 2011.

Possessing surprising speed and quickness for a man his size, the 6'4", 210-pound Grogan added another dimension to the Patriots' offense with his ability to run with the ball. Discussing that particular aspect of his game years later with *ABC Sports Online*, Grogan noted:

> I was a pretty good athlete. We ran the ball a lot in high school, and, while at Kansas State, we ran the option offense. So I really didn't know much about the passing game when I came in the league, and, suddenly, halfway through my rookie year, I was starting for a National Football League team. I really didn't have any idea of what I was doing out there; I was just having fun. I'd drop back and, if my first or second options weren't there, I'd take off and run with it because it was something I had done most of my football career. I did that the first four or five years; then I had knee problems. I think one of the things I'm most proud of is that I was able to adapt my skills from being a running quarterback to a pocket passer later in my career when my running ability had diminished.

Grogan continued to make excellent use of his running ability over the course of the next three seasons, rushing for well over 300 yards each year, including a total of 539 yards in 1978 that helped the Patriots set a new single-season NFL rushing record. Although Grogan never developed into a pinpoint passer, he also gradually improved his passing skills, throwing for 3,286 yards and leading all NFL quarterbacks with 28 touchdown passes in 1979.

That 1979 campaign proved to be the last time Grogan started every game for the Patriots. After injuries began to take their toll on him the following year, he spent the next several seasons splitting time at quarterback with a number of young hopefuls that included Matt Cavanaugh, Tony Eason, Doug Flutie, and Tom Ramsey. Appearing in more than eight games in just two of his final 11 seasons, Grogan surpassed 2,000 yards passing only two more times, and tossed more than 10 TD passes just three more times. Yet, he continued to develop his passing skills, completing more than 55 percent of his passes on four occasions, after failing to reach that mark in any of his first five seasons. Grogan had his two best years during that period in 1980 and 1983, passing for 2,475 yards and 18 touchdowns in the first of those campaigns, before throwing for 2,411 yards and 15 touchdowns in the second.

Meanwhile, even though Grogan often found himself sitting on the sidelines his last several years in the league, he remained one of the Patriots' team leaders, taking the field whenever they needed a spark, and providing inspiration to his teammates with his mental and physical toughness. A favorite among fans and teammates alike, Grogan built his reputation largely on his grittiness, inspiring Nick Cafardo of the *Boston Globe* to write an article in 2003 that gave a partial listing of the injuries he sustained over the course of his 16-year career. Cafardo listed in his piece: "Five knee surgeries; screws in his leg after the tip of his fibula snapped; a cracked fibula that snapped when he tried to practice; two ruptured disks in his neck, which he played with for 1 ½ seasons; a broken left hand (he simply handed off with his right hand); two separated shoulders on each side; the reattachment of a tendon to his throwing elbow; and three concussions."

Grogan finally announced his retirement after appearing in only four games for a Patriots team that finished just 1-15 in 1990. He ended his career with 1,879 pass completions, 26,886 yards passing, 182 touchdown passes, 208 interceptions, a 52.3 completion percentage, and a quarterback rating of 69.6. Tom Brady and Drew Bledsoe are the only Patriot quarterbacks with more pass completions and passing yardage. Meanwhile, only Brady has thrown more touchdown passes as a member of the team. Grogan also ran for 2,176 yards and 35 touchdowns, compiling a rushing average of 4.9 yards per carry during his career. Although Grogan never earned Pro Bowl or All-NFL honors, he helped the Patriots advance to the postseason tournament five times. Before he joined them in 1975, the Pats made the playoffs just once in the previous 15 seasons.

CAREER HIGHLIGHTS

Best Season

Even though Grogan compiled mediocre passing numbers both years, he performed well for the Patriots in 1976 and 1978, leading them to records of 11-3 and 11-5, respectively. In addition to completing 48 percent of his passes for a total of 1,903 yards in 1976, Grogan threw 18 touchdown passes and 20 interceptions, en route to posting a passer rating of 60.6. However, he did much of his damage on the ground, rushing for 397 yards and 12 touchdowns. Two years later, Grogan completed 50 percent of his passes for 2,824 yards, tossed 15 touchdown passes and 23 interceptions, compiled a passer rating of 63.6, and rushed for five scores and a career-high 539 yards. Although the Patriots went just 6-6 in Grogan's 12 starts in 1983, he reached a much higher level of passing efficiency, completing 55.4 percent of his passes for 2,411 yards, throwing 15 touchdown passes and 12 interceptions, and compiling a passer rating of 81.4. He also rushed for 108 yards and 2 scores. Nevertheless, Grogan had his finest all-around season in 1979, when, despite completing only 48.7 percent of his passes for a Patriots team that finished 9-7, he established career highs with

3,286 passing yards and a league-leading 28 touchdown passes. Grogan also posted a passer rating of 77.4 and rushed for 368 yards and 2 touchdowns.

Memorable Moments/Greatest Performances

Grogan had his first big game for the Patriots on November 23, 1975, shortly after Chuck Fairbanks inserted him as the team's starting quarterback. Although the Pats lost to Buffalo 45-31, Grogan connected on 25 of 46 passes, for 365 yards and 2 touchdowns.

On October 18, 1976, Grogan led the Patriots to a lopsided 41-7 win over Joe Namath and the New York Jets by completing 14 of 23 passes, for 182 yards and a touchdown, and also rushing for 103 yards and one touchdown. Grogan's 41-yard touchdown run, which made the score 27-0 early in the third quarter, proved to be the longest of his career.

Grogan turned in one of his finest all-around performances during another one-sided victory over the Jets on October 29, 1978. In addition to carrying the ball three times for 32 yards, he completed 15 of 19 passes, for 281 yards and 4 touchdowns, connecting with Harold Jackson on scoring plays of 11 and 28 yards, Stanley Morgan from 30 yards out, and Russ Francis from 11 yards out.

Grogan again torched the Jets' defensive secondary on September 9, 1979, this time completing 13 of 18 passes, for 315 yards and a career-high 5 touchdowns, during a 56-3 home win over New York. In addition to hooking up with Harold Jackson three times on scoring plays of 49, 44, and 28 yards, Grogan connected with Stanley Morgan twice, on pass plays that covered 37 and 50 yards. Grogan posted a quarterback rating of 153.9 during the contest that remained the Patriots single-game mark until Drew Bledsoe compiled a perfect 158.3 rating against the Indianapolis Colts on December 26, 1993.

Grogan had another big game nearly two months later, on November 4, leading the Patriots to 26 unanswered points during a 26-6 victory over the Buffalo Bills. Grogan passed for 350 yards and 3 touchdowns during the contest, tossing a six-yard TD pass to Horace Ivory in the second quarter, before connecting with Stanley Morgan from 63 and 34 yards out in the second half.

Although the Patriots lost to Miami 39-24 four weeks later, Grogan again passed for 350 yards and 3 touchdowns, hooking up with Harold Jackson, Stanley Morgan, and Carlos Pennywell on scoring plays that covered 16, 38, and 13 yards, respectively.

Grogan turned in another outstanding effort in a losing cause on November 10, 1980, passing for 374 yards and 3 touchdowns during a 38-34 loss to the Oilers in Houston. With the Patriots trailing 24-6 at the end of the first half, Grogan led a second-half comeback that fell just a bit short, tossing a 39-yard TD pass to Harold Jackson in the third quarter, before connecting with Russ Francis from 21 and 15 yards in the fourth quarter.

After sitting on the bench behind a struggling Tony Eason the first five weeks of the 1985 campaign, Grogan assumed control of New England's offense in week 6, leading the Patriots to a 14-3 win over the Buffalo Bills by completing 15 of 19 passes, for 282 yards and one touchdown. The Patriots won each of their next five games as well with Grogan calling the signals for them, before the quarterback broke his leg during a 16-13 overtime loss to the New York Jets on November 24.

Despite once again being relegated to backup duties for much of 1986, Grogan performed exceptionally well whenever the coaching staff called upon him, completing 60.8 percent of his passes, throwing 9 touchdown passes and only 2 interceptions, and posting a career-best 113.8 quarterback rating. He turned in his finest effort of the season in one of his two starts, passing for 3 touchdowns and a career-high 401 yards during a 31-24 loss to the Jets. The Patriots scored all their points in the second half, with Grogan nearly leading them all the way back from a 24-0 halftime deficit by tossing a 44-yard TD pass to Stanley Morgan, a 69-yarder to Irving Fryar, and an 18-yard scoring strike to Cedric Jones.

Reclaiming his starting job during the latter stages of the ensuing campaign, Grogan led the Patriots to a 42-20 victory over the Jets on December 13, 1987, by throwing 4 touchdown passes and rushing for another score.

Grogan had his last big day for the Patriots in the 1989 regular-season finale, passing for 313 yards and one touchdown during a 24-20 loss to the Los Angeles Rams.

NOTABLE ACHIEVEMENTS

- Passed for more than 3,000 yards once (3,286 in 1979).
- Threw more than 20 touchdown passes once (28 in 1979).
- Rushed for more than 300 yards four times, topping 500 yards once (539 in 1978).
- Rushed for 12 touchdowns in 1976.
- Led NFL quarterbacks with 28 touchdown passes in 1979.

- Finished third in NFL with 13 touchdowns scored in 1976.
- Finished second among NFL quarterbacks with six game-winning drives in 1978.
- Ranks among Patriots career leaders in: passing yardage (3rd); completions (3rd); touchdown passes (2nd); and rushing touchdowns (4th).
- 1985 AFC champion.
- Member of Patriots' 1970s All-Decade Team.
- Member of Patriots' 1980s All-Decade Team.
- Named to Patriots' 35th Anniversary Team in 1994.
- Inducted into Patriots Hall of Fame in 1995.

37

Logan Mankins

(Courtesy Keith Allison)

A quiet leader on Patriot teams that won eight division titles and two AFC Championships, Logan Mankins proved to be one of the most indispensable members of the Pats' offense during his nine years in New England. Tough and durable, Mankins became a starter as soon as he joined the Patriots in 2005, starting every game for them at left guard in each of his first five seasons, before sitting out the first seven games of the 2010 campaign while holding out for a new contract. In all, Mankins missed only 14 games in his nine years with the Pats, displaying his toughness and determination in 2011 by playing virtually the entire season with a torn ACL in his right knee. A six-time Pro Bowler and six-time All-Pro selection, Mankins received the additional honor of being named to the Patriots' 50th Anniversary Team in 2009.

Born in Catheys Valley, California, on March 10, 1982, Logan Lee Mankins attended Mariposa High School, where he earned All-League and team MVP honors as a senior. Following his graduation from Mariposa, Mankins enrolled at Fresno State University, where he started every game for the Bulldogs at left tackle in three of the next four seasons, missing his entire junior year after tearing his ACL in preseason practice. Blocking for future NFL quarterback David Carr as a freshman, Mankins allowed just two sacks, earning in the process a spot on the *Sporting News*'s Freshman All-American First Team. Mankins performed even better in his final year at Fresno State, earning First-Team All-Western Athletic Conference and team MVP honors by recording a school record 82 knockdown blocks and not allowing a single sack or quarterback pressure the entire year. By being named MVP of the Bulldogs, Mankins became the first offensive lineman in school history to be accorded that honor.

Subsequently selected by the Patriots in the first round of the 2005 NFL Draft, with the 32nd overall pick, the 6'4", 307-pound Mankins soon found himself starting at left guard for the defending Super Bowl champions after Joe Andruzzi left the team via free agency. Beginning a string of 80 consecutive starts for the Pats, Mankins performed well at his new position his first year in the league, earning a spot on *Pro Football Weekly*'s 2005 All-Rookie Team. After another solid year in 2006, Mankins helped the Patriots advance to the Super Bowl for the fourth time in seven seasons in 2007 by allowing just one sack of Tom Brady the entire year. His outstanding performance earned him his first Pro Bowl selection and Second-Team All-Pro honors for the first of five times.

New England's failure to advance to the playoffs following the loss of Brady in the opening game of the 2008 campaign likely prevented Mankins from earning a return trip to the Pro Bowl. Nevertheless, he helped Patriots running backs amass 2,278 yards on the ground—the largest total compiled by the team since 1985. After being named to the Patriots' 50th anniversary team in August 2009, Mankins continued his string of 80 consecutive starts, appearing in every game for the Pats for the fifth straight season, en route to earning Pro Bowl and Second-Team All-Pro honors for the second time.

With Mankins becoming a restricted free agent following the 2009 season, the Patriots tendered him a one-year contract worth $3.26 million, making it necessary for any other team interested in acquiring his services to surrender their first and third-round draft picks to New England in return. Displeased with the Patriots' decision, Mankins refused to sign his tender, prompting them to ultimately lower his tender amount to 110 percent of his prior year's salary, or $1.54 million. A lengthy holdout ensued, with Mankins remaining unsigned through Week 7 of the regular season. Yet, even though he ended up starting just the final nine games, Mankins managed to earn Pro Bowl and First-Team All-Pro honors.

Not wishing to engage in another contentious contract negotiation with Mankins at the conclusion of the campaign, the Patriots assigned him the franchise tag on February, 14, 2011. After reporting to training camp a few months later, Mankins signed a six-year deal worth more than $60 million, making him the highest paid guard in the league.

Displaying tremendous tenacity and a desire to fulfill the obligations of his new contract, Mankins missed just one game in 2011, even though he tore the ACL in his right knee in the regular-season opener. Hiding his injury from the team the entire year, Mankins did not become fully aware of its severity until he tore the MCL in his left knee during New England's victory over Denver in the divisional playoffs. Yet, playing through the pain, Mankins started the AFC Championship Game vs. the Baltimore Ravens and the Super Bowl vs. the New York Giants. At season's end, he was accorded Pro Bowl honors for the fourth time and Second-Team All-Pro honors for the third time.

Despite missing six games due to injury in the ensuing campaign, Mankins earned Pro Bowl and Second-Team All-Pro honors in both 2012 and 2013. However, while the nine-year veteran remained an asset in the running game in the second of those years, he became less effective in pass protection due to his diminished ability to move well laterally. Asked to take a pay cut at the end of the year, Mankins refused, after which the Patriots traded him to Tampa Bay for tight end Tim Wright and a fourth-round pick in the 2015 NFL Draft shortly before the 2014 regular season got underway.

News of the deal spread quickly through the Patriots' locker room, with most of the players expressing their regret over Mankins' impending departure. Newly-signed free agent cornerback Darrelle Revis said, "I've only been here for a couple of months, but Mank is known around the league as being one of the best offensive linemen in the game. He's proven that, and he's done it for a long time."

In discussing his feelings upon learning of the trade, Mankins stated, "I didn't know it was going to happen the way it did. But it's not a shocker. Once you've been around this business long enough, anything is a possibility. It's a business first and foremost. Guys play it because they love it, but it is a business, and if you don't understand that it's a business, you're lying to yourself. You have to be prepared for whatever happens in this league at any time."

Mankins added, "We had discussions and couldn't come to a common ground. So they made the move they did."

Meanwhile, Buccaneers new head coach Lovie Smith looked forward to Mankins' arrival, saying, "He has a history of a certain type of play in the league. Most people say 'Logan Mankins—tough football player; real man; everybody loves him; great guy in your locker room.' . . . (He's) exactly what we need on our football team and, of course, in the offensive line room."

New Tampa Bay general manager Jason Licht, who worked in the Patriots front office from 2009 to 2011, chimed in, "We're very excited to acquire a player like Logan. We feel very fortunate. Logan is a very good player. I'm a first-hand witness to what he means in the locker room as well. His play on the field speaks for itself."

Despite choosing to part ways with Mankins, Patriots head coach Bill Belichick spoke glowingly of him, saying in a prepared statement, "Logan Mankins is everything we would ever want in a football player. It is hard to imagine a better player at his position, a tougher competitor or a person to represent our program. He is one of the all-time great Patriots and the best guard I ever coached. Logan brought a quiet but unmistakable presence and leadership that will be impossible to duplicate."

When asked if he had spoken with Tom Brady since news of the trade broke, Mankins said, "Yeah, I've talked to him. I've talked to probably 99 percent of the team. I'm not going to get into what we said. We were good friends. We spent a lot of time, a lot of years together. I'll miss Tom for sure. I'll miss a lot of those guys. I have a lot of good friends there. A lot of coaches I was good friends with. It's a sad day to not be with those guys. But I've got new teammates here I'm looking to develop relationships with, and I'll see how it goes."

Asked about his memories with the Patriots, Mankins added, "I had a lot of great ones. I had a lot of fun there. I had a lot of rough memories and great ones too. It's a place I'll always remember, and I have nothing bad to say about New England. I love that place. I'm moving on."

PATRIOT CAREER HIGHLIGHTS

Best Season

Although Mankins earned his lone First-Team All-Pro selection in 2010, it would be difficult to identify that as his finest season since he missed the first seven games of the campaign while trying to settle his contract situation. Mankins played extremely well in 2009, contributing significantly to a Patriots offensive line that allowed Tom Brady to be sacked a career-low 16 times. In addition to being named Second-Team All-Pro, Mankins made his second start for the AFC in the Pro Bowl, joining John Hannah as the only guards in franchise history to be so honored. Nevertheless, Mankins had probably his best year in 2007, when he permitted just one sack of Brady, en route to earning Pro Bowl and All-Pro honors for the first time in his career.

Memorable Moments/Greatest Performances

Although the Patriots ended up losing the 2006 AFC Championship Game to the Indianapolis Colts by a score of 38-34, Mankins experienced the most memorable moment of his career midway through the first quarter when he recovered a Laurence Maroney fumble in the end zone to give his team an early 7-0 lead. The touchdown remains the only one Mankins has scored over the course of his 10 NFL seasons.

NOTABLE ACHIEVEMENTS

- Started every game for Patriots from 2005 to 2009, making 80 consecutive starts during that time.
- Two-time AFC champion (2007 & 2011).
- Six-time Pro Bowl selection (2007, 2009, 2010, 2011, 2012 & 2013).
- 2010 First-Team All-Pro selection.
- Five-time Second-Team All-Pro selection (2007, 2009, 2011, 2012 & 2013).
- 2012 Ed Block Courage Award winner.
- Member of Patriots' 2000s All-Decade Team.
- Named to Patriots' 50th Anniversary Team in 2009.

38

Julius Adams

(Courtesy Mainline Autographs)

The longest-tenured player in Patriots history, Julius Adams spent his entire 16-year career in New England, playing every position along the defensive line at one time or another. A consistent and durable performer, Adams appeared in every game for the Patriots in 12 of his 16 seasons, at one point starting 57 consecutive games from his right defensive end position. Although Adams earned Pro Bowl honors just once, he established himself during his time in New England as one of the AFC's better pass-rushers, leading the Patriots in sacks four times, en route to amassing an "unofficial" total of 79 ½ career sacks that places him second only to Andre Tippett in team history. The big defensive end's consistently outstanding play also ended up earning him a spot on the Patriots' 50th Anniversary Team in 2009.

Born in Macon, Georgia, on April 26, 1948, Julius Thomas Adams Jr. attended Ballard High School, before enrolling at Texas Southern University. A four-year starter in college, Adams earned All-Conference honors in both 1968 and 1970, prompting the Patriots to select him in the second round of the 1971 NFL Draft, with the 27th overall pick.

Joining a Patriots team that finished the previous year with an embarrassing 2-12 record, Adams helped the Pats compile a mark of 6-8 in his rookie campaign of 1971, earning in the process a spot on the UPI All-Rookie team. After starting at right defensive tackle his first year, Adams spent a significant amount of time at left tackle and left end the next two seasons, before finally finding a permanent home at right defensive end in 1974. Leading the Patriots with 7 ½ sacks that year, Adams earned recognition as one of the NFL's top defensive linemen by *Pro QB* magazine.

Although Adams gained much of his notoriety as a result of his ability to pressure opposing quarterbacks, he also played the run extremely well, using his strength, quickness, and burly 6'3", 270-pound frame to ward off opposing blockers at the line of scrimmage. In describing his technique, Adams stated, "I was trained to attack. . . . I never 'read.' Every play is a rush."

After missing five games due to a foot injury in 1975, Adams started every game for the Patriots in each of the next two seasons, accumulating totals of 15 ½ sacks and 90 tackles over the course of those two campaigns. A shoulder injury subsequently shelved Adams for virtually all of 1978, but he returned the following year to appear in all 16 games for the Pats, although he started just two. Adams then began a string of 57 consecutive starts in 1980, earning his lone Pro Bowl selection that year by recording 59 tackles and a team-leading 9 quarterback sacks. He also performed extremely well in 1981, registering 54 tackles and 30 assists, en route to winning the Jim Lee Hunt Memorial Award, presented annually to the team's most outstanding lineman. After another solid year in 1982, Adams recorded 8 quarterback sacks and a career-high 83 tackles in 1983.

During the second phase of his career, Adams refined his technique somewhat, explaining, "Some people rely on their peripheral vision to see the ball move. They don't take their eyes off the quarterback. But I move my head and actually face the ball. In today's football, everybody's big and strong—not like when I started. But, if you can train yourself to come off the ball, you can do the job."

As to how he managed to keep pace with the younger players who joined the Patriots each year, Adams added, "When a rookie would come in, I tried to beat him in running, or at least keep up with him."

Though still a major contributor to the Patriots on defense, Adams pondered retirement during the 1984 season due to philosophical differences with head coach Ron Meyer, who took control of the team two years earlier. In addition to bringing with him a disciplinary attitude, Meyer attempted to install more of a "read and react" type of defense. Not wishing to gear his pass-rushing to the alignments presented by the opposing offensive linemen and running backs, Adams butted heads with Meyer, causing his playing time to gradually diminish. Looking back at that particular time in his career, Adams later said, "Meyer put me on the bench because I didn't play his type of football."

Fortunately for Adams, the Patriots replaced Meyer with Raymond Berry midway through the campaign, causing him to change his retirement plans. Electing to return to the Patriots in 1985, Adams regained his starting job and contributed 5 sacks to New England's AFC championship team. Although he announced his retirement at season's end, spending all of 1986 breeding cattle on his farm, Adams chose to return to the Patriots for one more year, leaving the game for good after appearing in 10 games during the strike-shortened 1987 campaign. Adams retired as the Patriots' all-time leader in games played (206) and "unofficial" quarterback sacks (79 ½), although he has since been passed in both categories.

Following his retirement, Adams initially spent most of his time on his farm breeding cattle, before eventually returning to the game as an assistant high school football coach in South Carolina. Yet, Adams' heart remains in New England, with the former defensive end proudly stating, "Deep down inside, I'm still a Patriot. It's exciting to see what they've done (in recent years). That's a superb team that just keeps coming back year after year. Those young men play as a unit. There's nobody on that team who is 'me-me-me.' It's all 'we.'"

CAREER HIGHLIGHTS

Best Season

Adams had an outstanding season in 1977, recording a career-high 9 ½ sacks and making 43 tackles. He also played extremely well in 1980, earning his only Pro Bowl selection by making 59 tackles, leading the Patriots with 9 sacks, and finishing second on the team with 13 quarterback pressures. Nevertheless, the feeling here is that Adams had his finest all-around season in 1983, when, in addition to leading all Patriots' defensive linemen with a career-high 83 tackles, he finished second on the team with 8 quarterback sacks and also placed third on the club with 7 QB pressures.

Memorable Moments/Greatest Performances

Playing in front of his hometown fans in Atlanta-Fulton County Stadium on December 4, 1977, Adams turned in the most dominant performance of his career, recording 4 ½ of New England's 8 sacks of Falcons quarterback Steve Bartkowski during a 16-10 Patriots victory. The 4 ½ sacks represented a career high for Adams.

Adams made one of the biggest plays of his career on December 12, 1982, when he blocked a Uwe von Schamann field goal attempt to help preserve a Patriots 3-0 win over bitter rival Miami.

Adams made another huge play in the 1984 regular-season finale against Indianapolis, helping the Patriots defeat the Colts 16-10 by blocking a Raul Allegre 42-yard field goal attempt that would have tied the score at 13-13 with only five minutes remaining in the fourth quarter. Adams, who received a game ball for his effort, made his only start of the season in that contest.

NOTABLE ACHIEVEMENTS

- Made 83 tackles in 1983.
- Led Patriots in sacks four times (1972, 1973, 1974 & 1980).
- Ranks second all-time on Patriots' "unofficial" list with 79 ½ quarterback sacks.
- Ranks third in Patriots history in games played (206).
- 1985 AFC champion.
- 1980 Pro Bowl selection.
- Member of Patriots' All-1970s Team.
- Member of Patriots' All-1980s Team.
- Named to Patriots' 50th Anniversary Team in 2009.

39

Matt Light

Matt Light (#72)
(Courtesy Scott Horrigan)

A key member of Patriot teams that won five AFC championships and three Super Bowls, Matt Light spent his entire 11-year career protecting the blind side of quarterback Tom Brady from his left tackle position. An outstanding blocker at the point of attack, Light helped give Brady time to survey the field, while also opening up huge holes for 1,000-yard rushers Antowaine Smith, Corey Dillon, and BenJarvus Green-Ellis. An extremely durable player as well, Light started every game for the Patriots in seven of his 11 seasons, doing so despite playing his entire career with a serious illness that would have forced many men to the sidelines. Light's tenacity, dedication, and mental toughness ended up earning him three trips to the Pro Bowl, one First-Team All-Pro selection, and spots on the Patriots' 2000s All-Decade Team and 50th Anniversary Team.

Born in Greenville, Ohio, on June 23, 1978, Matthew Charles Light attended Greenville High School, where he played football and competed in the shot-put in track and field, earning district champion and All-County honors in the latter sport. A two-way starter on the gridiron, Light played linebacker on defense and spent one season each at guard, tackle, and tight end on offense, being accorded Second-Team Division II All-State honors primarily on the strength of his defensive play.

After enrolling at Purdue University, Light spent four of the next five years playing for the Boilermakers football team, sitting out the 1997 campaign after undergoing surgery to repair an injured left shoulder. Once again displaying his versatility while at Purdue, Light played tight end as a freshman, before moving to left tackle when he returned from his injury two years later. As the Boilermakers left tackle, Light spent the final three years of his collegiate career blocking for future Super Bowl MVP quarterback Drew Brees, earning honorable All-Big Ten Conference recognition as a sophomore, Second-Team All-Big Ten honors as a junior, and First-Team All-Conference honors as a senior.

Subsequently selected by the Patriots in the second round of the 2001 NFL Draft, with the 48th overall pick, the 6'4", 305-pound Light moved seamlessly into New England's offensive line, starting the final 12 games of the season, en route to earning a spot on the *Football News* 2001 NFL All-Rookie Team. The following year, Light began a string of three straight seasons in which he started every game for the Patriots, establishing himself during that time as the anchor of an offensive line that helped the team win back-to-back Super Bowls.

After signing a six-year contract extension with the Pats worth $27 million in October 2004, Light saw his consecutive games played streak come to an end early in 2005, when he broke his leg against Pittsburgh in Week 3. However, after missing the remainder of the campaign, Light returned the following year to begin another string of starts that lasted 53 games. During that time, Light earned his first two Pro Bowl selections, making the AFC roster in both 2006 and 2007. In helping the Patriots compile a perfect 16-0 regular-season record in the second of those campaigns, Light also was accorded First-Team All-Pro honors for the only time in his career.

Having started every game for the Patriots in each of the three previous seasons, Light began the 2009 campaign in similar fashion, assuming his left tackle post the first five games of the year, before missing the next five contests after suffering an injury during a 20-17 overtime loss to Denver on October 11. Yet, displaying the same mental and physical toughness he demonstrated throughout his career, Light returned in Week 12 to begin another string of 37 consecutive starts that lasted until shortly before he announced his retirement at the conclusion of the 2011 season. He earned the last of his three Pro Bowl nominations in 2010, joining fellow Patriots offensive lineman Logan Mankins on the AFC roster. On July 19, 2012, less than three months after Light officially announced his retirement during a press conference at Gillette Stadium, he accepted a position with ESPN, where he continues to serve as an NFL analyst on the station's *SportsCenter, Sunday NFL Countdown, NFL Live, ESPN First Take, and NFL 32* programs.

During his retirement press conference, Light made public for the first time his career-long battle with Crohn's disease—an often debilitating inflammatory bowel disease that causes, among other things, severe abdominal pain, fatigue, and persistent diarrhea. In discussing his illness with *U.S. News* shortly thereafter, Light revealed:

> I was officially diagnosed in 2001, but I had started experiencing a lot of the symptoms during my freshman year in college. At the time, I didn't connect it with being anything more than the flu or a stomach virus. I just wasn't up to speed with issues like Crohn's disease, or any other type of bowel disease. By the time I got to the NFL as a rookie, I just knew something wasn't right. I was experiencing internal bleeding—it's very difficult to talk about, kind of embarrassing, but this is what happens. I started asking a lot of questions, got a full exam, and the doctors at Massachusetts General Hospital told me I was suffering from Crohn's disease.

Forced to remain in the hospital 30 days while fighting through complications that resulted from having a 13-inch section of his intestine removed during the summer of 2004, Light found it impossible to attend the Super Bowl ring ceremony the Patriots held at owner Robert Kraft's home in June of that year. Unable to eat anything throughout the entire ordeal, he lost 55 pounds, dropping to his lowest weight since high school. Yet, he somehow managed to make it to training camp less than two months later, giving most of the credit for his successful return to his doctors and loved ones when he stated:

> It was very difficult, but I had really good doctors and a really good support team. You're not the only one who goes through this—it's all the people around you, and you rely on them. When you have a family, you have to be healthy for them. I remember my wife coming into the hospital and showing me my Super Bowl ring for the first time. It's pretty wild to think you can get through all that and still get back out there and win another championship.

Light added, "When you go through tough things like this, it gives you a pretty awesome perspective on what's important and what really matters. I used to say to myself, 'Even though it's bad, you've been through worse, and you can battle back—it's not the end of the world.' If you give in to being negative, that's the easy route. My goal is to stay positive, because that's all you've got sometimes."

CAREER HIGHLIGHTS

Best Season

Starting all 16 games at left tackle in 2004, Light helped the Patriots average more than four yards per carry for the first time in 19 seasons, with Corey Dillon setting a single-season franchise record by rushing for 1,635 yards. Light and his linemates also performed extremely well in 2009, when they allowed Tom Brady to be sacked just 16 times over the course of the campaign (back-up QB Brian Hoyer was also sacked twice). Nevertheless, Light had his finest season for the Patriots in 2007, when he earned Pro Bowl honors and his lone First-Team All-Pro selection by helping them score a franchise-record 589 points, en route to posting a perfect 16-0 record during the regular season. The *Tuesday Morning Quarterback*—a column written by Gregg Easterbrook on ESPN.com—also named Light its Non-QB, Non-RB Most Valuable Player of the league.

Memorable Moments/Greatest Performances

Light turned in an exceptional effort against St. Louis in Super Bowl XXXVI, leading an offensive line that enabled Patriot running backs to rush for 133 yards on 25 carries (5.3 yards per carry) during a 20-17 win over the Rams.

Light also performed extremely well against Carolina in Super Bowl XXXVIII, anchoring a line that did not allow a single sack of Tom Brady, even though the Panthers defensive front included outstanding pass-rushers such as Julius Peppers, Mike Rucker, and Kris Jenkins. Rucker, who Light spent most of the game blocking, earned Pro Bowl honors during the regular season by making 58 tackles and placing among the league leaders with 12 sacks. However, he failed to record a sack and made just two tackles during the Patriots' 32-29 victory.

NOTABLE ACHIEVEMENTS

- Compiled streaks of 51 and 53 consecutive starts at different points during career.
- Five-time AFC champion (2001, 2003, 2004, 2007 & 2011)
- Three-time Super Bowl champion (XXXVI, XXXVII & XXXIX).
- Three-time Pro Bowl selection (2006, 2007 & 2010).
- 2007 First-Team All-Pro selection.
- 2007 *Tuesday Morning Quarterback* Non-QB, Non-RB NFL MVP Award winner.
- 2010 Madden Most Valuable Protectors Award winner.
- Pro Football Reference 2000s All-Decade Second Team.
- Member of Patriots' 2000s All-Decade Team.
- Named to Patriots' 50th Anniversary Team in 2009.

40

Curtis Martin

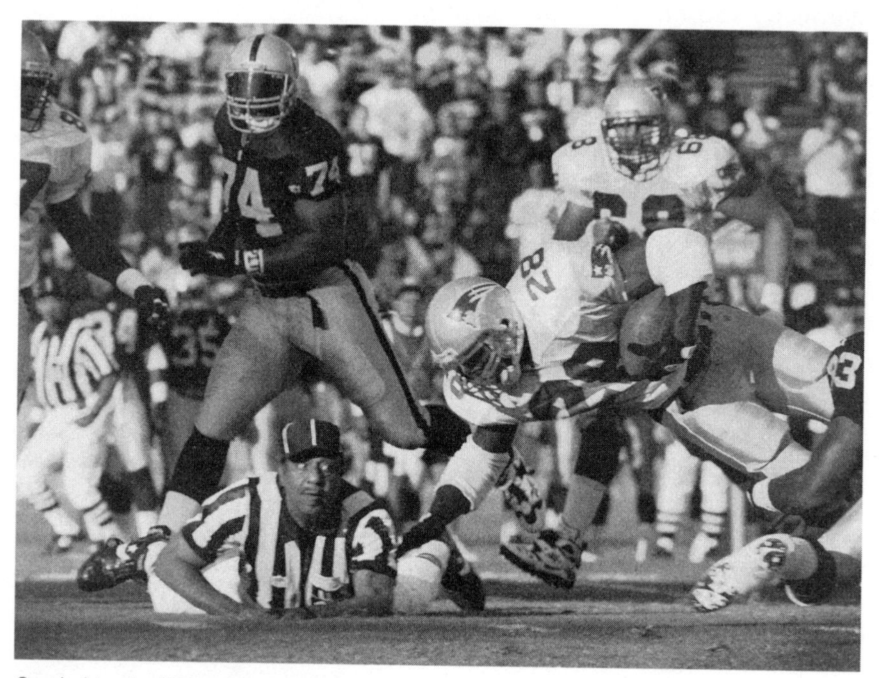

Curtis Martin (28) with the ball.
(Courtesy George A. Kitrinos)

Had Curtis Martin spent more than three seasons in New England, he unquestionably would have finished much higher in these rankings. Martin rushed for well over 1,000 yards each year he played for the Patriots, establishing a new franchise record (since broken) in 1995 by amassing an AFC-leading 1,487 yards on the ground. An outstanding pass receiver as well, Martin surpassed 30 receptions in each of his three seasons in New England, accumulating in the process well in excess of 1,400 yards from scrimmage each year, including a franchise record 1,748 yards in his rookie campaign of 1995. Martin performed at such a high level during his relatively brief stay in New England that he continues to rank among the team's all-time leaders in rushing yardage and rushing touchdowns. Meanwhile, his exceptional all-around play earned him two Pro Bowl selections and two All-AFC nominations as a member of the team. Martin continued to excel after he left the Patriots via free agency at the conclusion of the 1997 campaign, eventually becoming just the second player in NFL history to surpass 1,000 yards rushing in each of his first 10 seasons. Martin's consistency and durability ultimately enabled him to establish himself as the fourth leading rusher in the history of the league, earning him a well-deserved place in the Pro Football Hall of Fame.

Born in Pittsburgh, Pennsylvania, on May 1, 1973, Curtis James Martin Jr. lived through a difficult childhood that would have shattered the psyche of someone who lacked his inner strength. Abandoned by his alcoholic father at the age of five, Martin was raised solely by his mother, who worked two jobs to support the family. Reflecting back on his early years, Martin recalls, "When I was five years old, I remember watching him (my father) torture my mother. . . . I've watched my mother get punched in the face, get a black eye, and go to work with make-up on to provide for our family."

Experiencing the additional trauma of finding his grandmother murdered with a knife in her chest, young Curtis found himself constantly surrounded by violence while growing up in Pittsburgh's inner city, noting years later, "By the time I was 15, I had so many brushes with death."

After moving with his family to Point Breeze as a teenager, Martin began attending Taylor Alderdice High School, where he first began playing football as a senior at the insistence of his mother, who considered the sport a way of keeping her son away from crime and violence. Even though Martin later admitted, "I was never a football fan," he proved to be a natural on the gridiron, starring at both running back and linebacker in his one year of high school ball. Subsequently courted by several colleges following his graduation from Alderdice in 1991, Martin ultimately settled on the University of Pittsburgh since it accorded him the opportunity to remain close to home.

Martin, who Pittsburgh head coach Paul Hackett likened to Tony Dorsett, experienced a great deal of success whenever he took the field for the Panthers, once rushing for 251 yards against Texas. However, injuries plagued him for much of his collegiate career, causing him to fall to the third round of the 1995 NFL Draft, even though his slashing running style and 4.4 speed in the 40-yard dash made an extremely favorable impression on pro scouts. Having lost three running backs to free agency following the conclusion of the 1994 campaign, the Patriots proved to be the perfect fit for Martin, who the team selected with the 74th overall pick of the draft.

Martin soon quelled any concerns the Patriots may have had about his ability to remain healthy by appearing in all 16 games for them in 1995. In fact, he proved to be one of the NFL's most durable and dependable backs over the course of his career, missing only eight games in his 11 years in the league.

Martin ended up having a fabulous rookie season, rushing for more than 100 yards nine times, en route to leading the AFC with 1,487 yards gained on the ground. He also made 30 receptions, for another 261 yards, and finished sixth in the league with 15 touchdowns. Martin's exceptional all-around performance earned him the first of his five Pro Bowl selections, First-Team All-AFC honors, and recognition as the Associated Press NFL Offensive Rookie of the Year.

Martin continued his success in his sophomore campaign of 1996, earning Pro Bowl and Second-Team All-AFC honors by rushing for 1,152 yards, making 46 receptions for 333 yards, and finishing second in the league to Washington's Terry Allen with 17 touchdowns. He put together his third straight 1,000-yard season the following year, placing among the league leaders with 1,160 yards gained on the ground and 1,456 yards from scrimmage.

Unfortunately, the 1997 season proved to be Martin's last in New England. A free agent heading into 1998, Martin soon found himself being courted by the rival New York Jets and their head coach and general manager Bill Parcells, who had served as Martin's head coach his first two years in the league. Although the running back initially had reservations about playing in New York, especially for a division rival, the presence of Parcells eventually convinced him to sign the six-year $36 million contract the Jets offered him. Unwilling to match New York's offer, the Patriots allowed Martin to leave. However, they received as compensation the Jets' first and third round selections in the 1998 NFL Draft after filing a complaint with the NFL management council that New York's offer sheet violated the terms of the league's collective bargaining agreement since it included a clause that stated Martin would become an unrestricted free agent after one year if the Patriots chose to match the offer. Martin left New England having rushed for a total of 3,799 yards, caught 117 passes for another 890 yards, and scored a total of 37 touchdowns.

Martin spent the next eight seasons in New York, competing against his former team in the AFC East. During that time, he continued to build upon his legacy as one of the finest running backs of his generation, rushing for more than 1,000 yards in each of his first seven years with the Jets. In so doing, he became just the second running back in NFL history to surpass 1,000 yards rushing in each of his first 10 seasons (Barry Sanders was the first). Martin also joined Sanders, Walter Payton, and Emmitt Smith as the only players ever to rush for more than 14,000 yards in their career.

Although Martin performed exceptionally well his entire time in New York, earning three more Pro Bowl selections and three All-Pro nominations, he had three or four seasons that stood out from the rest. After finishing second in the league with 1,464 yards rushing in 1999, Martin rushed for 1,204 yards, made a career-high 70 receptions for another 508 yards, and scored 11 touchdowns in 2000. He followed that up by finishing second in the league in rushing again in 2001 by gaining 1,513 yards on the ground. Martin, though, had the finest season of his career in 2004, when he earned First-Team All-Pro honors for the only time by scoring 14 touchdowns and leading the NFL with 1,697 yards rushing.

Martin never again played a full season for the Jets. After suffering a knee injury in the second game of the 2005 campaign, he continued to play until the severity of the injury forced him to have season-ending surgery that kept him out of the final four contests. Martin finished the year with 735 yards rushing, failing to reach the 1,000-yard mark for the only time in his career. Unable to make a full recovery after being diagnosed with a bone-on-bone condition in his right knee, Martin subsequently chose to announce his retirement. With 14,101 yards to his credit, Martin ended his career as the NFL's fourth all-time leading rusher. He also scored 100 touchdowns and made 484 receptions for another 3,329 yards, placing him eighth on the all-time list with 17,430 yards from scrimmage. In addition to his five Pro Bowl selections and three All-Pro nominations, Martin earned All-AFC honors on four occasions.

Inducted into the Pro Football Hall of Fame in 2012, Martin revealed during his acceptance speech that he never truly loved the game, stating, "I have never been able to identify with the love and passion that many of my colleagues have. . . . I was forced to play football."

Moments later, Martin displayed the quality of his character when he added, "The only way I was going to be successful in this game called football is to play for a purpose bigger than myself." He then stated, "My greatest achievement in my life is helping nurture my mother from the bitter person she was to having a healthy mindset and forgive my father for everything he did to her."

Bill Parcells, who introduced Martin at his induction ceremony, expressed his admiration for the former running back when he said, "He has tremendous compassion for his fellow man. He's committed. He's very, very humble. He's the poster child for what the NFL's supposed to be. You maximize your ability. You make a smooth transition into society. And then you pass all those things along to other people. That's what this guy has done."

Meanwhile, Patriots owner Robert Kraft told ESPNNewYork.com: "The key to life is having quality people with you, and Curtis is right at the top of the heap as a quality individual, both the way he conducts himself personally and the way he played. I will forever have a warm spot in my heart for him. The Jets made a very wise decision by getting him. I just wish he were entering the Hall of Fame as 100 percent Patriot."

PATRIOT CAREER HIGHLIGHTS

Best Season

Martin had a big year for the Patriots in 1996, when he rushed for 1,152 yards, gained another 333 yards through the air, and scored a career-high 17 touchdowns, finishing second in the league in the last category. However, his rookie campaign of 1995 proved to be his finest in New England. In addition to leading the AFC with 1,487 yards rushing, Martin scored 15 touchdowns and amassed a total of 1,748 yards from scrimmage, earning in the process First-Team All-AFC and NFL Offensive Rookie of the Year honors.

Memorable Moments/Greatest Performances

Martin wasted little time in becoming a significant contributor to the New England offense, gaining 30 yards on his first NFL carry. He subsequently went on to make his professional debut a memorable one, carrying the ball 19 times for 102 yards, and scoring the game-winning touchdown, in helping the Patriots defeat Cleveland 17-14 on September 3, 1995.

Martin had another big game nearly two months later, on October 23, rushing for 127 yards and one touchdown during a 27-14 home win over the Buffalo Bills.

Martin again led the Patriots to victory on November 5, carrying the ball 35 times, for 166 yards and 2 touchdowns, during a 20-7 win over the Jets at Giants Stadium.

Martin rushed for 142 yards and scored another 2 touchdowns the following week, in helping the Pats defeat Miami 34-17.

Martin rushed for more than 100 yards against Buffalo's defense for the second time on November 26, when he gained 148 yards on the ground during a 35-25 Patriots victory over the Bills.

In another exceptional effort, Martin carried the ball 31 times, for 148 yards and 2 touchdowns, in leading the Patriots to a 31-28 win over the Jets on December 10. His one-yard TD run late in the fourth quarter provided the margin of victory.

Although the Patriots ended up losing to Pittsburgh by a score of 41-27 on December 16, Martin had one of his finest all-around games of the year, carrying the ball 20 times for 120 yards, and making 8 receptions for 62 yards and a touchdown.

Martin concluded his fabulous rookie campaign the following week by rushing for 103 yards and making 3 receptions for another 24 yards during a 10-7 loss to the Indianapolis Colts.

Martin also had a number of big days the following year, with the first of those coming on September 15, 1996, when he rushed for 92 yards, made 5 receptions for another 33 yards, and scored 3 touchdowns, in leading the Patriots to a 31-0 pasting of the Arizona Cardinals. Martin scored his touchdowns on a 13-yard reception from Drew Bledsoe, a one-yard run, and a seven-yard pass from Bledsoe.

One month later, on October 13, Martin carried the ball 17 times for a season-high 164 yards during a 27-22 home loss to the Washington Redskins. The Patriots scored all their points on three Adam Vinatieri field goals and two touchdowns by Martin, who scored on running plays of three and two yards.

Martin turned in another outstanding effort on November 24, when he helped lead the Patriots to a 27-13 victory over the Colts by rushing for 141 yards and one touchdown.

However, Martin saved his finest performance of the season for the Patriots' meeting with Pittsburgh in the opening round of the playoffs. Accounting for nearly half of New England's total offense on the day, Martin carried the ball 19 times for 166 yards, made 2 receptions for another 9 yards, and scored 3 touchdowns, in leading the Patriots to a resounding 28-3 victory. Martin scored his touchdowns on runs of 2, 78, and 23 yards, with his 78-yard TD scamper proving to be the longest of his career.

Martin had the biggest rushing day of his Patriots career on September 14, 1997, when he helped the Pats defeat his future team, the New York Jets, 27-24, by carrying the ball 40 times, for 199 yards and one touchdown. The following week, during a 31-3 win over the Bears, Martin recorded the longest regular-season touchdown of his career when he carried the ball into Chicago's end zone from 70 yards out.

NOTABLE ACHIEVEMENTS

- Rushed for more than 1,000 yards three straight times (1995–97).
- Surpassed 1,400 yards from scrimmage three straight times (1995–97).
- Scored at least 15 touchdowns twice (1995 & 1996).
- Surpassed 40 receptions twice (1996 & 1997).
- Led AFC with 1,487 yards rushing in 1995.
- Finished third in NFL with 1,487 yards rushing and 14 rushing touchdowns in 1995.
- Finished second in NFL with 17 touchdowns in 1996.
- Ranks fourth in NFL history with 14,101 yards rushing.
- Holds Patriots single-season record with 1,758 yards from scrimmage in 1995.
- Ranks among Patriots all-time leaders in: rushing yardage (4th) and rushing touchdowns (5th).
- 1996 AFC champion.
- 1995 NFL Offensive Rookie of the Year.
- Two-time Pro Bowl selection (1995 & 1996).
- 1995 First-Team All-AFC selection.
- 1996 Second-Team All-AFC selection.
- Elected to Pro Football Hall of Fame in 2012.

41

Larry Garron

Larry Garron running with the ball at the 1964 All-Star Game.
(Courtesy Tales from the American Football League)

An outstanding all-around player who did whatever the Patriots asked of him during his time in Boston, Larry Garron proved to be the team's most versatile running back in the early days of the AFL. Excelling as a runner, blocker, pass receiver, and kickoff returner, Garron did a little bit of everything for the Pats his first two seasons, before establishing himself as their primary running threat in 1963, when he rushed for a career-high 750 yards and led the AFL with 1,884 all-purpose yards. Two years later, he further displayed his versatility and sense of selflessness by moving from fullback to halfback to accommodate Jim Nance, who went on to lead the league in rushing in both 1966 and 1967, due, at least in part, to the blocking ability of Garron. Although Garron, who quarterback Babe Parilli called, "one of the best backs at catching passes I have ever played with," remains largely forgotten by recent generations of Patriots fans, his peers acknowledged the tremendous overall contributions he made to the success of the team during the 1960s by electing him to four Pro Bowls and one All-Pro Team. Garron also eventually earned a spot on the Patriots' 1960s All-Decade Team.

Born in Marks, Mississippi, on May 23, 1937, Lawrence Garron Jr. spent much of his youth in Argo, Illinois, moving there with his family shortly before his father became a police officer. While still just a youngster, Garron realized the importance of learning how to defend himself, recalling years later, "There was a Chinese laundry there, and my father got a call that some guy was trying to rob him. By the time he got there, the old gentleman had the guy tied up on the floor. My father asked him, 'Would you mind teaching my sons?'"

After graduating from Argo High School, Garron established himself as an outstanding all-around athlete at Western Illinois University, starring at running back for the school's football team, and also excelling in track and field, where he once defeated Wilt Chamberlain in a high jump competition. While playing his college ball for Lou Saban, Garron came to fully appreciate the lessons in self-defense he learned years earlier.

Recalling that Saban had received death threats from racist fans prior to a game against Arkansas State, Garron explained, "When you were playing Arkansas State, they would try to ride you off to the sidelines, and people would come out of the stands and trample you." Having returned the first kickoff for a touchdown, Garron subsequently found himself being forced out of bounds on his second return. He later recalled, "The people in the stands came down, and they were jumping on my legs. I didn't think I would ever walk again."

Fortunately, Garron survived that incident, after which he went on to pursue a career in professional football, even though he went undrafted by the NFL following his graduation in 1959. Recruited by Saban after his former college coach accepted the head coaching job in Boston, Garron signed with the Patriots prior to the 1960 season. However, he lasted only four games, being cut by the Pats early in the year after contracting tonsillitis. Garron spent the subsequent offseason working out feverishly, eventually adding 20 pounds of muscle onto his frame. Returning to the Patriots in 1961 in better shape than ever, Garron spent most of his first full season splitting time at fullback with Billy Lott, rushing for 389 yards and 2 touchdowns, on only 69 carries, en route to posting an outstanding average of 5.6 yards per rushing attempt. He also did an exceptional job coming out of the backfield, making 24 receptions for 341 yards and another 3 touchdowns. Garron further contributed to the Patriots on special teams, averaging 27.4 yards on 16 kickoff returns, amassing in the process a total of 1,168 all-purpose yards. Garron's solid all-around play earned him Second-Team All-AFL honors and the first of his four All-Star selections.

Garron had a similarly productive 1962 campaign, rushing for 392 yards and 2 touchdowns, making 18 receptions for 236 yards and 3 TDs, and finishing third in the league in kickoff return average for the second straight year, en route to accumulating 1,314 all-purpose yards. He followed that up by posting the best overall numbers of his career in 1963, earning a spot on the AFL East All-Star squad for the second time by gaining 750 yards on the ground and another 418 yards through the air, placing fourth in the league with 716 return yards, scoring 4 touchdowns, and topping the circuit with 1,884 all-purpose yards. Garron put up solid numbers again in 1964, earning his second consecutive trip to the Pro Bowl by amassing 1,133 all-purpose yards and scoring a career-high 9 touchdowns. However, he perhaps made his greatest impact at that year's AFL All-Star Game, helping to organize a boycott to protest the shabby treatment of black players by the host city of New Orleans that included refusing them rides at the airport and denying them service at local restaurants. Garron later recalled one particular incident that took place, revealing, "I remember this guy pulled a gun on Ernie Ladd and said, 'You are not coming in here to eat.'" The refusal of the black players to perform under such horrible conditions eventually prompted the league to move the game to Houston.

After leading the Patriots in rushing in each of the previous two seasons, Garron accepted a somewhat reduced role in 1965, when he shifted to halfback to make room in the backfield for rookie phenom Jim Nance. Yet, even though Garron rushed for more than 300 yards (319) just once more for the Pats, he remained an integral part of their offense his final four seasons, proving to be an excellent pass receiver coming out of the backfield, and doing a superb job of serving as lead blocker for Nance. Despite gaining only 163 yards on the ground and amassing another 670 yards on 30 pass receptions, Garron made the AFL East All-Star squad for the fourth and final time in 1967. Relegated to a backup role the following year, Garron announced his retirement at season's end, concluding his career with 2,981 yards rushing, another 2,502 yards gained on 185 pass receptions, 42 touchdowns, and a rushing average of 3.9 yards per carry. His 26 receiving touchdowns remain the most by any Patriots running back.

Following his retirement, Garron taught management, marketing, and economics at Bunker Hill Community College in Charlestown for nearly 20 years. He also spent one season serving as color commentator for Patriots preseason games. After studying various forms of martial arts while still playing for the Patriots, Garron ended up making his greatest mark in that sport, earning the highest degree attainable in World Martial Arts. Now more than 78 years of age, Garron continues to hold rank in Kenpō (fist law), Hakkō-ryū Jujutsu, Gōjū-ryū (hard soft system), Shintō Musō-ryū, Yoshitsune Jujitsu, and Taekwondo.

CAREER HIGHLIGHTS

Best Season

Garron had a solid all-around year in 1961, earning his lone Second-Team All-AFL selection by rushing for 389 yards and 2 touchdowns, catching 24 passes for another 341 yards and 3 touchdowns, and returning 16 kickoffs for 438 yards and 1 touchdown. His 1,168 all-purpose yards placed him ninth in the league rankings. Garron followed that up in 1962 by compiling career-high marks in rushing average (5.9) and kickoff return average (28.6), en route to finishing eighth in the AFL with 1,314 all-purpose yards. He again played well in 1964, when he rushed for 585 yards and established career highs with 40 receptions and 9 touchdowns. Nevertheless, there can be no doubting that Garron had his finest season in 1963, when he earned team MVP honors by leading the AFL with 1,884 all-purpose yards and placing among the league leaders with 750 yards rushing, 693 kickoff return yards, and 1,168 yards from scrimmage.

Memorable Moments/Greatest Performances

Garron had his breakout game for the Patriots on September 23, 1961, rushing for 90 yards on only 7 carries, catching 3 passes for 49 yards, and scoring on a 67-yard touchdown run during a 23-21 win over the Bills in Buffalo. Later in the year, on October 13, Garron returned a kickoff 89 yards for a TD during a 31-31 tie with the Houston Oilers. The very next week, Garron set a Patriots record that still stands by scoring on a touchdown run of 85 yards during a 52-21 home win over the Bills. Garron's TD jaunt remains the longest run from scrimmage in Patriots history. Displaying his usual modesty when asked about the play, Garron recalled, "It was two good blocks—one by Charlie Long and another by Gino Cappelletti—and I was gone. That's all there is to it." He finished the day with 116 yards on 10 carries.

Almost exactly one year later, on October 26, 1962, Garron rushed for a career-high 140 yards during a 26-16 victory over the Oakland Raiders. In an exceptional all-around effort, Garron gained those 140 yards on 13 carries, ran for a 41-yard touchdown, made 2 receptions for 21 yards, and completed a 39-yard pass to tight end Tony Romeo. The following week, during a 28-28 tie with the Bills, Garron returned a kickoff 95 yards for a touchdown. He also hauled in a 23-yard TD pass from quarterback Babe Parilli, concluding the afternoon with 51 yards on 7 carries, 49 yards on 3 pass receptions, and 2 touchdowns.

Garron again displayed his pass-catching ability on November 1, 1963, when he hooked up with Parilli on a 76-yard scoring play during a 45-3 pasting of the Oilers.

Garron had another big day on October 16, 1964, helping the Patriots forge a 43-43 tie with Oakland by scoring a career-high 3 touchdowns. Garron recorded all three TDs in the second half, scoring on a 10-yard TD pass from Parilli, a one-yard run, and an 11-yard pass from Parilli.

Garron, though, experienced his finest moment on December 28, 1963, in the 1963 AFL Eastern Division Championship Game against the Bills. Donning baseball shoes with rubber cleats to combat War Memorial Stadium's frozen field, Garron outmaneuvered Buffalo's defense all afternoon, leading the Patriots to a 26-8 victory by rushing for 44 yards and making 4 receptions for 120 yards and 2 touchdowns. The highlight of the game occurred midway through the first quarter, when Garron took a short swing pass from Babe Parilli near midfield, faked out a pair of Buffalo defenders, and took the ball the rest of the way, scoring from 59 yards out to extend Boston's lead to 10-0. Garron scored another touchdown in the fourth quarter, this time on a 17-yard strike from Parilli. Speaking of his teammate's performance, Parilli stated, "The guy that made the job a lot easier for me was Larry Garron. He was one heck of a guy coming out of the backfield. He made some good little swing passes, and he made people miss, and it was instrumental in us winning the game."

NOTABLE ACHIEVEMENTS

- Surpassed 1,000 yards from scrimmage once (1,168 in 1963).
- Caught 40 passes in 1964.
- Averaged more than 5 yards per carry twice (1961 & 1962).
- Returned two kickoffs for touchdowns.
- Led AFL with 1,884 all-purpose yards in 1963.
- Ranks among Patriots all-time leaders in rushing yardage (9th) and touchdowns scored (tied-9th).
- Holds Patriots record for longest run from scrimmage (85 yards vs. Buffalo on 10/22/61).
- 1963 AFL Eastern Division champion.
- Four-time AFL Pro Bowl selection (1961, 1963, 1964 & 1967).
- 1961 Second-Team All-AFL selection.
- Member of Patriots' 1960s All-Decade Team.

42

Russ Francis

An exceptional all-around athlete referred to by legendary sportscaster Howard Cosell as the National Football League's "All-World Tight End," Russ Francis served as a precursor to players such as Tony Gonzalez and Rob Gronkowski with his ability to stretch the field from his tight end position. Blessed with outstanding speed, the 6'6", 240-pound Francis ran as well as many wideouts, enabling him to gain nearly 3,000 yards through the air and average better than 15 yards per reception for the Patriots from 1975 to 1980, even though they remained predominantly a running team. Francis also excelled as a blocker, using his size and strength to help the Patriots amass an NFL-record 3,165 yards on the ground in 1978. Francis's rare skill set enabled him to earn three Pro Bowl selections and two All-Pro nominations over the course of his six seasons in New England, before he decided to leave the Patriots due to philosophical differences with the team's front office and the game of football in general.

Born in Seattle, Washington, on April 3, 1953, Russell Ross Francis grew up in Hawaii, where he attended Kailua High School on the island of Oahu. Urged by his family to spend time on a ranch in Oregon prior to his senior year at Kailua High, Francis ended up enrolling at Pleasant Hill High School, where he first displayed his extraordinary athletic ability by setting a new national high school record for the javelin throw (259 feet, 9 inches), while also competing in the decathlon. After nearly making the US Olympic team as a competitor in the first event, Francis received a track scholarship offer from the University of Oregon. While at Oregon, Francis began taking football seriously for the first time, making the varsity team as a sophomore. However, he spent just one full season playing for the Ducks, missing most of his sophomore campaign after breaking his ankle against

Oklahoma, and quitting the team his senior year to protest the firing of the head coach.

Yet, in spite of Francis's limited experience at the collegiate level, NFL scouts found it impossible to ignore his rare combination of speed, size, and strength, finding particularly appealing his 4.6 time in the 40-yard dash. Hall of Fame quarterback Dan Fouts, who graduated from Oregon two years earlier than Francis, described his former teammate as "just a phenomenal athlete," adding, "To have a tight end like that is so rare. Russ was the prototype tight end. When draft-nicks get together, they say, 'We have to get somebody like Russ Francis.'"

Eventually selected by the Patriots with the 16th overall pick of the 1975 NFL Draft, Francis wasted little time in establishing himself as one of the National Football League's best tight ends, making 35 receptions for 636 yards and 4 touchdowns as a rookie. Limited somewhat by injuries and the Patriots' heavy reliance on their running game, Francis made a total of just 42 receptions, for 7 touchdowns and fewer than 600 total yards, over the course of the next two seasons. Yet, he still managed to earn a spot on the AFC Pro Bowl roster in both 1976 and 1977. Francis also earned consensus Second-Team All-NFL honors in the first of those campaigns, before being awarded a spot on the Second Team by the Newspaper Enterprise Association the following year.

It was during the latter stages of that 1977 season that the free-spirited Francis began to grow somewhat disenchanted with professional football. After earlier being promised a bonus for making the Pro Bowl, Francis became upset when the Patriots reneged on the deal due to his inability to appear in the contest as the result of an injury he incurred during a motorcycle accident. Adding to the tight end's disillusionment with his chosen profession was an incident that took place during a 1978 preseason game with the Raiders in which Oakland safety Jack Tatum maliciously hit a defenseless Darryl Stingley after the Patriots wide receiver reached for a badly overthrown pass. Although Stingley, one of Francis' closest friends on the team, eventually regained limited movement in his right arm, he spent the rest of his life as a quadriplegic. Further angering Francis was the Patriots' subsequent attempt to cancel Stingley's medical insurance.

Although Francis never fully regained his earlier passion for football, he continued to perform well on the field for the Patriots in each of the next three seasons, averaging 40 receptions, nearly 600 yards, and 6 touchdowns from 1978 to 1980. After earning Pro Bowl honors for the third consecutive time in the first of those campaigns by making 39 receptions for 543 yards and 4 touchdowns, Francis established new career highs with

41 catches for 664 yards and 8 touchdowns in 1980. Francis' outstanding play throughout the period prompted Patriots head coach Ron Erhardt to suggest, "If you've got tight ends that can do the same things as your wide receivers, you're just more flexible."

Yet, in spite of the success he experienced in New England, Francis elected to announce his retirement prior to the start of the 1981 season, telling the media on July 21, 1981, "I've given this a lot of thought in the last few months. A career change is not something one does overnight. All I can say is that I am retiring because of personal reasons. I have to explore other avenues. I have found that at this point it is better to retire. . . . It's going to be difficult. It entails a lot of emotion. It's been fun. It's been a good game. I'm going to miss it."

Francis later admitted that he found it difficult to continue playing at times after watching his close friend Darryl Stingley suffer permanent paralysis as the result of an unnecessary hit delivered during a meaningless preseason game. He conveyed those feelings during a newspaper interview when he said, "I have problems with football. Philosophically, I mean. Why are people out there hurting each other? Why do human beings want to run into each other at full speed?" Francis also suggested that he considered it important to have his sight, to have the ability to walk, and to be able to awaken in a place like Hawaii every day.

Francis left the Patriots with career totals of 196 receptions, 2,996 receiving yards, and 28 touchdowns. In addition to his three Pro Bowl selections, he earned Second-Team All-NFL honors twice and Second-Team All-AFC honors three times.

Following his retirement, Francis took a broadcasting job with ABC Sports, for whom he earlier covered the 1980 Summer Olympics. Expecting to be offered a position in the *Monday Night Football* booth before long, Francis had a sudden change of heart after he interviewed 49ers head coach Bill Walsh at the 1981 Pro Bowl. Francis later revealed that Walsh told him following the interview, "This is the only time in your life that you'll be able to do this (play football). Your time is very narrow, and all of the guys on this team (the 49ers) are the best at what they do. I mean that. They are the best at what they do. That means you get better every day, instead of every week. If you want to find out how good you could be, then you need to come play with us."

After taking some time to consider Walsh's proposal, Francis chose to return to the NFL in 1982, becoming a member of the 49ers when they acquired him from New England for a draft pick that the Patriots eventually used to select future Hall of Famer Andre Tippett. Francis spent the next five-plus years with the 49ers, making another 186 receptions, for 2,105 yards and 12 touchdowns, and winning a Super Bowl championship with them in 1984. Waived by the 49ers late in 1987, Francis rejoined the Patriots, with whom he spent the remainder of the year and all of 1988 serving as a backup, before announcing his retirement at season's end. He concluded his career with 393 receptions, for 5,262 yards and 40 touchdowns.

Francis, the son of wrestling promoter Ed Francis, briefly competed in the American Wrestling Association and the National Wrestling Alliance after retiring from football, before eventually assuming a more sedate position as a radio talk-show host. He also served for a period of time as the sports coordinator for the Hawaii Tourism Authority.

PATRIOT CAREER HIGHLIGHTS

Best Season

Francis had an outstanding rookie season for the Patriots in 1975, making 35 catches for 636 yards and 4 touchdowns, en route to averaging a career-high 18.2 yards per reception. Although he compiled far less impressive numbers the following year, gaining only 367 yards and scoring just 3 touchdowns on 26 receptions, Francis made the Pro Bowl for the first of three straight times and earned unanimous Second-Team All-NFL honors. Francis, though, actually had his two best years in 1978 and 1980, posting his most impressive stat-line as a member of the Patriots in the second of those campaigns, when he made 41 receptions for 664 yards and 8 touchdowns. Francis failed to reach any of those marks in 1978, finishing the season with 39 catches for 543 yards and 4 touchdowns. Nevertheless, he played his best ball for the Pats that year, especially when it is considered that they ran the ball on 63 percent of their plays, en route to accumulating an all-time record 3,165 yards on the ground. Francis aided New England's running game by doing an exceptional job of blocking at the point of attack—a fact not lost on the members of the Associated Press and Newspaper Enterprise Association, who awarded him Second-Team All-NFL honors.

Memorable Moments/Greatest Performances

Francis helped the Patriots defeat San Diego 33-19 on November 9, 1975, by making 3 receptions for 81 yards, with his 48-yard hookup with quarterback Steve Grogan representing his longest gain of the year. Although the

Pats dropped a 45-31 decision to the Buffalo Bills two weeks later, Francis went over 100 yards for the first time in his career, catching 7 passes for 125 yards and one touchdown.

Francis earned the moniker "All-World Tight End" from sportscaster Howard Cosell with his brilliant performance against Pittsburgh on September 26, 1976, when he helped the Patriots defeat the defending world champions, 30-27, by making 6 receptions for a career-best 139 yards and 1 touchdown. In addition to hauling in a 38-yard touchdown pass from Steve Grogan, Francis connected with New England's quarterback on a pass play of 48 yards, which represented his longest gain of the year. Francis also performed extremely well during New England's 24-21 playoff loss to the eventual world champion Oakland Raiders nearly three months later, making 4 receptions for 96 yards and 1 touchdown.

Francis helped the Patriots gain a measure of revenge against Oakland on September 24, 1978, when he made 5 receptions for 126 yards and 1 touchdown during a 21-14 victory over the Raiders. During the contest, Francis hooked up with Steve Grogan on a 53-yard pass play, the longest of his career. Although the Patriots once again came up short in that year's playoffs, losing to the Houston Oilers 31-14, Francis turned in another huge effort, making 8 receptions for 101 yards and 1 touchdown.

Francis made 2 TD receptions in one game for the first time in his career on October 1, 1979, giving the Patriots all their points in a 27-14 Monday night loss to the Green Bay Packers at Lambeau Field. He finished the game with 5 receptions for 88 yards.

Francis had his last big game as a member of the Patriots on November 10, 1980, making 5 receptions for 86 yards and 2 touchdowns during a 38-34 loss to the Oilers in Houston.

NOTABLE ACHIEVEMENTS

- Caught more than 40 passes once (41 in 1980).
- Averaged 18.2 yards per reception in 1975.
- Finished eighth in NFL with 8 touchdown receptions in 1980.
- Ranks 10th in Patriots history with 28 touchdown receptions.
- Three-time Pro Bowl selection (1976, 1977 & 1978).
- Two-time Second-Team All-Pro selection (1976 & 1978).
- Three-time Second-Team All-AFC selection (1976, 1978 & 1980).

43

Stephen Gostkowski

(Courtesy Keith Allison)

Initially faced with the daunting task of trying to replace Adam Vinatieri as placekicker in New England, Stephen Gostkowski has given the Patriots everything they could have hoped for over the past nine seasons. In addition to surpassing Vinatieri as the Pats' all-time leading scorer, Gostkowski has set career and single-season franchise records for highest field goal percentage. Along the way, he has led the NFL in points scored four times, field goals converted three times, and extra points made twice, becoming in 2014 the first player since the AFL-NFL merger to lead the league in scoring in three consecutive seasons. An extremely accurate and reliable kicker, Gostkowski ranks third in NFL history in career field goal percentage, having also posted the highest career points per game average in league history (8.67). Gostkowski's deadly accuracy has helped the Patriots win three AFC championships and one Super Bowl, earning him three Pro Bowl and two All-Pro nominations in the process.

Born in Baton Rouge, Louisiana, on January 28, 1984, Stephen Carroll Gostkowski attended Madison Central High School in Madison, Mississippi, where he starred in baseball, football, and soccer, earning All-State honors in all three sports. Offered an athletic scholarship to play baseball at the University of Memphis, Gostkowski initially believed that his path to a career in professional sports lay in pitching, revealing years later, "There was a time when I thought about the major leagues. But I ran into a little arm trouble in college. I still started all four years, but it just became pretty apparent my junior year of college that I was going to have a better chance at football. I mean, if I would have played baseball year-round and quit everything else, I think I would have had a shot."

Fortunately for Gostkowski, he also spent his time in Memphis kicking for the Tigers football team, ending his college career with a school record 369 points—the 13th highest total in NCAA Division I-A history. Having earned First-Team All-Conference USA honors in both his junior and senior years, Gostkowski entered the 2006 NFL Draft, where the Patriots made him the first of just two kickers selected, tabbing him in the fourth round, with the 118th overall pick.

With Adam Vinatieri signing with the Indianapolis Colts as a free agent during the previous offseason, Gostkowski spent all of 2006 training camp competing with veteran kicker Martín Gramática for the starting job in New England. After warding off Gramática's challenge, Gostkowski went on to have a solid rookie campaign, converting 20 of 26 field goal attempts and scoring a total of 103 points, despite having to contend with having three different holders during the season. Although the Patriots ultimately came up short in their bid to make their third Super Bowl appearance in four years, losing to Indianapolis in the Conference Championship Game by a score of 38-34, Gostkowski acquitted himself extremely well in his first postseason, making all eight of his field goal attempts.

Gostkowski also performed well in his second year in the league, converting 21 of his 24 field goal attempts, en route to finishing third in the league with 137 points scored. He followed that up by leading the NFL with 148 points scored in 2008, cracking the 90 percent mark for the first time by making 36 out of 40 field goal attempts. In so doing, Gostkowski earned First-Team All-Pro honors and the first of his three Pro Bowl selections. Gostkowski had another good year in 2009, finishing sixth in the league with 125 points scored, before experiencing his first bit of adversity in 2010, when a torn quadriceps muscle kept him out of the Patriots' final eight games.

Healthy again by the start of the 2011 campaign, Gostkowski returned to top form, converting 28 of 33 field goal attempts, en route to finishing third in the league with 143 points scored. He subsequently began a string of three straight seasons in which he led the NFL in scoring, tallying 153, 158, and 156 points the next three years, earning in the process two more Pro Bowl selections and Second-Team All-Pro honors in 2014. Particularly effective the past two seasons, Gostkowski compiled a 92.7 field goal percentage in 2013 by converting 38 of 41 field goal attempts, before posting a career-high mark of 94.6 percent in 2014 by making 35 of 37 kicks.

The first player in NFL history to score 1,000 points in his first eight years in the league, Gostkowski believes that his pitching background helped prepare him for life as an NFL kicker, explaining:

> If you have a bad game in pitching, you don't get to just wake up the next day, pick up the bat and try to hit a home run. You've got to wait a whole week to pitch again. In football, I may miss a kick in the first quarter and not get another chance to make a kick, and then I've got to think about that the whole next week. Dealing with situations like, say, a full count, bases loaded and you have to throw a strike. That could be comparable to making a kick to win the game at the end of a game.

Gostkowski continued:

> You have the position players in baseball, and you have the offense and defense in football. Then you have the pitchers and the specialists. They are very important positions and they can play a very important role in the game, but the day-to-day grind that they go through isn't the same. The thing with pitching is you only get a few opportunities, maybe once a week, and you got to make the most out of that opportunity. It's the same thing in football. When you're kicking field goals you might only get one, two, three field goals in a game, and you have to make sure that you're ready to make the most of those opportunities.

Gostkowski has certainly made the most of his opportunities over the course of his first nine seasons, scoring a Patriots record 1,179 points, while also compiling a franchise record 86.8 field goal percentage that ranks as the third best in NFL history. With 243 field goals to his credit heading into the 2015 campaign, Gostkowski ranks second only to Adam Vinatieri in Patriots history.

Nevertheless, Gostkowski refuses to accept credit for the tremendous success he has experienced since joining the Patriots in 2006, stating, "It's cool. I have been put in a good situation, on a heck of a team with a great offense. I've been able to take advantage of my opportunities. I've been at the right place at the right time. Kicking field goals, you're only as good as the opportunities you're given. I try to take advantage of every one that I'm given. Thanks, Tom Brady, I guess."

CAREER HIGHLIGHTS

Best Season

Gostkowski earned First-Team All-Pro honors for the only time in his career in 2008, when he led the NFL in scoring for the first of four times by tallying 148 points, on 36 field goals and 40 extra points. However, while Gostkowski compiled a 90.0 percent field goal percentage that year, failing to convert four of his 40 attempts, he actually proved to be slightly more accurate in both 2013 and 2014, converting 92.7 percent of his kicks in the first of those campaigns, before proving to be successful on 94.6 percent of his kicks in the second. Gostkowski's league-leading 38 field goals and 158 points in 2013 both established new Patriots single-season records. However, he finished atop the league rankings in both categories this past season as well, converting 35 of his 37 attempts, while also making all 51 PATs, for a total of 156 points scored. Gostkowski's 94.6 field goal percentage established a new franchise record for kicking accuracy, making the 2014 campaign the finest of his career.

Memorable Moments/Greatest Performances

As a rookie in 2006, Gostkowski recorded the longest field goal in the history of Gillette Stadium when he connected from 52 yards out during a 17-13 victory over the Chicago Bears on November 26.

Gostkowski earned AFC Special Teams Player of the Month honors for the first time in his career in October 2008, when he went 9-for-10 on field goal attempts and 11-for-11 on PATs, compiling in the process a total of 38 points.

Gostkowski has kicked at least four field goals in a game on seven occasions, accomplishing the feat for the first time on December 17, 2006, when he connected from 36, 32, 31, and 21 yards out during a lopsided 40-7 victory over the Houston Texans. He duplicated that effort on September 14, 2008, helping the Patriots defeat the New York Jets, 19-10, by scoring 13 of their points, on four field goals and one PAT.

On December 21, 2008, Gostkowski amassed a then career-high 17 points during a 47-7 win over the Arizona Cardinals by kicking four field goals and five extra points. The four field goals gave him a total of 34 three-pointers on the season, breaking Tony Franklin's 1986 franchise record of 32.

Gostkowski helped the Patriots improve their record to 2-1 in 2009 by kicking four field goals during a 26-10 victory over the Atlanta Falcons. He again split the uprights four times during a 27-17 win over Miami six weeks later, earning in the process AFC Special Teams Player of the Week honors.

Although the Patriots lost their September 16, 2012, matchup with the Arizona Cardinals 20-18, Gostkowski had a huge game, hitting field goals from 46, 34, 51, and 53 yards out, with his last three-pointer breaking his own Gillette Stadium record for distance that he set six years earlier.

Gostkowski established personal career highs by kicking five field goals and scoring 19 points during a 43-17 pasting of the Cincinnati Bengals on October 5, 2014. His field goals came from 48, 19, 23, 47, and 35 yards out.

Gostkowski has also proven to be an outstanding clutch performer over the course of his career, kicking the Patriots to victory in the final moments of contests six times. In the 2006 Divisional Playoffs against San Diego, Gostkowski kicked a 31-yard field goal with only 1:14 remaining in regulation to give the Patriots a 24-21 victory that earned them a berth in the AFC Championship Game against Indianapolis. He also connected from 50 and 34 yards out earlier in the contest.

Gostkowski again came up big in the clutch on October 17, 2010, when, after tying the game with a 24-yard field goal late in the fourth quarter, he gave the Patriots a 23-20 win over Baltimore by converting a 35-yard field goal attempt with just two minutes remaining in overtime.

Gostkowski provided similar heroics on two other occasions, giving the Patriots overtime wins over the Jets on October 21, 2012 and the Broncos on November 24, 2013, by connecting from 48 and 31 yards out, respectively. He also gave the Pats a 23-21 victory over Buffalo in the 2013 regular-season opener by kicking a 35-yard field goal on the game's final play, before kicking two late 53-yard field goals that enabled New England to defeat Houston 34-31 later in the year.

NOTABLE ACHIEVEMENTS

- Has scored more than 100 points in eight of nine seasons, topping 150 points three times.
- Has converted at least 90 percent of field goal attempts three times.
- Has converted 450 of 451 PATs (point-after-attempts) over course of his career.
- Has led NFL in: points scored four times; field goals made three times; and extra points made twice.
- Holds Patriots single-season records for most points scored (158 in 2013) and highest field goal percentage (94.6 percent in 2014).
- Holds Patriots career records for most points scored (1,179) and highest field goal percentage (86.8 percent).
- Ranks second in Patriots history in field goals made (243).
- Ranks third in NFL history in career field goal percentage.
- Three-time AFC champion (2007, 2011 & 2014).
- Super Bowl XLIX champion.
- Three-time Pro Bowl selection (2008, 2013 & 2014).
- 2008 First-Team All-Pro selection.
- 2014 Second-Team All-Pro selection.

44

Deion Branch

(Courtesy Beth Hart)

An unheralded wide receiver who performed extremely well under pressure, Deion Branch served two tours of duty with the Patriots, playing for them from 2002 to 2005, and, then again, from 2010 to 2012. Although injuries kept Branch off the field for significant periods of time in five of his seven seasons with the Pats, he proved to be one of the team's most consistent offensive players, averaging nearly 50 receptions and just over 600 receiving yards during his time in New England. Taking his game up a notch during the postseason, Branch surpassed 10 receptions in back-to-back Super Bowls, earning in the process MVP honors of Super Bowl XXXIX. Meanwhile, even though Branch, who ranks among the Patriots all-time leaders in pass receptions and receiving yardage, never made the Pro Bowl, he earned the respect and admiration of head coach Bill Belichick, who said of the wide receiver, "He just gets it. He almost always does what the quarterback would expect him to do."

Born in Albany, Georgia, on July 18, 1979, Anthony Deion Branch Jr. attended Monroe Comprehensive High School in Albany, where he lettered in both football and track and field. After graduating from Monroe, he spent the next two years at Jones County Junior College in Ellisville, Mississippi, earning Second-Team All-American honors as a sophomore for his exceptional play as a wide receiver and kick-off/punt returner. Transferring to the University of Louisville prior to the start of his junior year, Branch helped lead the Cardinals to a 9-3 record and the Conference USA Football Championship by making 71 receptions for 1,016 yards and nine touchdowns, en route to earning First-Team All-Conference USA honors. A similarly productive senior year resulted in another Conference Championship for Louisville, and another First-Team All-Conference selection for Branch, who capped off his collegiate career by leading the 11-2 Cardinals to a 28-10 victory over BYU in the 2001 Liberty Bowl.

Subsequently selected by the Patriots in the second round of the 2002 NFL Draft, with the 65th overall pick, Branch started only seven games as a rookie, spending most of the year returning kickoffs and sharing time at wide receiver with Troy Brown and David Patten, before missing the final three games of the regular season with a leg injury. Nevertheless, Branch compiled solid numbers his first year in the league, concluding the campaign with 43 receptions, for 489 yards and two touchdowns. He also gained another 921 yards on special teams, giving him a total of 1,410 all-purpose yards.

Establishing himself as a full-time starter the following year, Branch gradually developed into quarterback Tom Brady's favorite receiver over the course of the campaign, leading the team with 57 catches and 803 receiving yards. Blessed with good speed and excellent instincts, the 5'9", 193-pound Branch proved to be particularly effective in keeping drives alive, recording first downs on 40 of his receptions, 24 of which came on third down. Commenting on the second-year wide receiver's ability to find holes in the opposing team's defense, head coach Bill Belichick noted, "He goes in there and has to make an adjustment, and you just are confident that he'll make the right one." Truly stepping to the forefront in that year's Super Bowl,

Branch made 10 receptions for 143 yards and one touchdown, in helping the Patriots defeat Carolina 32-29.

A leg injury suffered during New England's 23-12 victory over Arizona in the second game of the 2004 season limited Branch to only nine games, 35 receptions, and 454 receiving yards. However, after returning to the field in Week 11, Branch ended up having a fabulous postseason, scoring two touchdowns against Pittsburgh in the AFC Championship Game, and tying a Super Bowl record by making 11 catches during the Patriots' 24-21 win over Philadelphia in Super Bowl XXXIX. He followed that up by having his finest statistical season in 2005, making a career-high 78 receptions, for 998 yards and five touchdowns.

Seeking a huge salary increase following his outstanding 2005 performance, Branch became disenchanted with Patriots management when they offered him a three-year contract extension he considered unsatisfactory. After refusing to report to the team's mandatory June minicamp and holding out throughout training camp and the preseason, Branch received permission from the Patriots in August to seek a trade and negotiate a contract with other teams through September 1. With the Seattle Seahawks and New York Jets expressing interest in acquiring his services, the Patriots finally dealt the disgruntled wide receiver to Seattle on September 11, for a first-round selection in the 2007 NFL Draft. Branch subsequently signed a six-year, $39 million contract extension with the Seahawks.

Branch ended up spending four injury-riddled years in Seattle, experiencing moderate success. He had his best season for the Seahawks in 2006, when, appearing in as many as 14 games for one of only two times as a member of the team, he made 53 receptions for 725 yards and four touchdowns. Eager to return to New England by 2010, Branch saw his wish come true on October 12, when Seattle traded him back to the Patriots for a fourth-round pick in the 2011 NFL Draft, less than a week after New England traded Randy Moss to Minnesota. Appearing in the Patriots' final 11 games of the regular season, Branch finished the year with 61 receptions for 818 yards and six touchdowns, making 48 catches for 706 yards and five touchdowns as a member of the Pats. Branch spent the next two years in New England as well, recording 51 receptions for 702 yards and five touchdowns as a starter in 2011, before serving as a backup to Wes Welker and Brandon Lloyd the following season. Released by the Patriots at the conclusion of the 2012 campaign, Branch remained in involuntary retirement until January 6, 2014, when the Indianapolis Colts signed him to a contract just days before their playoff meeting with the Pats. After failing to appear in a single game for Indianapolis, Branch officially announced his retirement, ending his career with 518 receptions, 6,644 receiving yards, and 39 touchdowns. Over parts of seven seasons in New England, he made 328 receptions, for 4.297 yards and 24 touchdowns. Branch ranks eighth all-time on the Patriots in pass receptions and 10th all-time in receiving yardage.

In discussing the impact Branch made on the Patriots, Bill Belichick stated, "Deion had a great career here. . . . (He was a) very smart, professional player; great leader. One of the top guys we've had here in terms of off the field work ethic, leadership, intelligence, and preparation—all those things. He had some very productive seasons here. He's a tremendous person. He's had a great career."

PATRIOT CAREER HIGHLIGHTS

Best Season

Serving the Patriots as both a kickoff returner and a wide receiver in his rookie campaign of 2002, Branch accumulated a career-high 1,410 all-purpose yards. However, Branch made easily his greatest overall impact in 2005, when, in addition to scoring five touchdowns, he established career highs with 78 receptions and 998 receiving yards.

Memorable Moments/Greatest Performances

Branch scored the first touchdown of his career in his first game as a pro, hooking up with Tom Brady on a 22-yard scoring play during a 30-14 victory over Pittsburgh on September 9, 2002. He finished the contest with six receptions, for 83 yards and a touchdown. Branch continued his success against the New York Jets the following week, making three receptions for 65 yards and one touchdown during a 44-7 Patriots win. Branch's 49-yard scoring connection with Brady early in the fourth quarter ended up being his longest reception of the year and the last of the two touchdowns he scored as a rookie. However, Branch had his biggest game of the year in Week 4, making a career-high 13 catches for 128 yards during a 21-14 loss to San Diego.

Branch helped the Patriots defeat Denver 30-26 on November 3, 2003, when he hauled in a 66-yard scoring pass from Brady. Branch finished the game with three receptions, for 107 yards and a touchdown.

After missing the previous seven games due to a leg injury, Branch made his return to the playing field a successful one on November 22,

2004, making six receptions for 105 yards and scoring a touchdown during a 27-19 victory over the Kansas City Chiefs.

Branch had another big day in his first game back with the Patriots in 2010, making nine receptions for 98 yards and scoring a touchdown during a 23-20 overtime win over the Baltimore Ravens on October 17. Six weeks later, during a 45-24 Thanksgiving Day victory over the Detroit Lions, Branch made three receptions for 113 yards and two touchdowns, with his 79-yard third-quarter TD grab representing the longest reception of his career.

Nevertheless, Branch will always be remembered most fondly by Patriots fans for his exceptional postseason play. Branch first demonstrated his ability to rise to the occasion in Super Bowl XXXVIII, when he made 10 receptions for 143 yards and a touchdown during New England's 32-29 victory over the Carolina Panthers. Branch's 17-yard catch with only nine seconds remaining in regulation brought the ball down to Carolina's 23-yard line, putting Adam Vinatieri in position to kick the game-winning field goal moments later.

Branch turned in another clutch performance in the 2004 AFC Championship Game, earning NFL Offensive Player of Championship Sunday honors by making four receptions for 116 yards, rushing for another 37 yards, and scoring two touchdowns, in leading the Patriots to a 41-27 win over the Pittsburgh Steelers. After connecting with Tom Brady on a 60-yard scoring play in the first quarter, Branch scored New England's final TD of the game on a 23-yard run late in the fourth quarter. Two weeks later, Branch made 11 receptions for 133 yards against Philadelphia in Super Bowl XXXIX, earning game MVP honors. His 11 catches tied a Super Bowl record previously held by San Francisco's Jerry Rice and Cincinnati's Dan Ross.

Although the Patriots lost their 2005 Divisional Playoff matchup with the Denver Broncos 27-13, Branch turned in another outstanding effort, making eight receptions for 153 yards, including a 73-yard grab that represented the longest gain of his playoff career.

NOTABLE ACHIEVEMENTS

- Surpassed 50 receptions three times, topping 70 catches once (78 in 2005).
- Accumulated 998 receiving yards in 2005.
- Surpassed 1,000 all-purpose yards once (1,410 in 2002).

- Ranks among Patriots all-time leaders in: pass receptions (8th) and receiving yardage (10th).
- Three-time AFC champion (2003, 2004 & 2011).
- Two-time Super Bowl champion (XXXVIII & XXXIX).
- MVP of Super Bowl XXXIX.

45

Jim Colclough

Another native New Englander who went on to star for the Patriots during the early days of the AFL, Jim Colclough proved to be one of the new league's most dangerous offensive weapons. A true game-breaker, Colclough averaged better than 20 yards per reception twice for the Patriots, en route to posting a career average of 17.7 yards per catch that ranks as the third highest in league history. The speedy wide-out also made at least 40 receptions five times and scored at least 9 touchdowns in each of his first three seasons, making a career-high 10 TD grabs in 1962, when he earned his lone Pro Bowl selection. By the time Colclough left the Patriots at the conclusion of the 1968 campaign, he had compiled numbers that continue to place him among the team's all-time leaders in most pass-receiving categories, earning in the process a spot on the Pats' 1960s All-Decade Team.

Born in Medford, Massachusetts, on March 31, 1936, James Michael Colclough grew up in nearby Quincy, where he attended Quincy High School. A late bloomer, Colclough weighed only 115 pounds as a sophomore, preventing him from even making it into a junior varsity game. However, after growing five inches and adding 40 pounds the following summer, Colclough made enough of an impression on his high school coach to earn a starting spot at wide receiver on the varsity squad. Colclough subsequently played so well in his final two years at Quincy that he received a scholarship offer from Boston College, where he played both wide receiver and defensive back.

After having to wait until the 30th round of the 1959 NFL Draft to be chosen by the Washington Redskins, who selected him with the 353rd overall pick, Colclough elected to begin his professional career in the Canadian Football League, spending his time there playing defensive back for the Montreal Alouettes. But, with the formation of the American Football League shortly thereafter, Colclough decided to return to his roots, signing with his hometown Boston Patriots prior to the 1960 campaign.

Shifted by the Patriots to his preferred position of wide receiver upon his arrival in Boston, Colclough had an outstanding rookie season, placing among the league leaders with 49 receptions, 666 receiving yards, and 9 touchdown catches. Those figures placed him first on the Pats in all three categories. He followed that up by making 42 receptions, for 757 yards and a team-leading 9 touchdowns in 1961. Colclough subsequently established himself as one of the AFL's most dynamic offensive players in 1962, when he made 40 receptions, placed near the top of the league rankings with 868 receiving yards and 10 touchdowns, and topped the circuit with an average of 21.7 yards per reception, earning in the process a spot on the Eastern Division All-Star Team.

Colclough's performance over the course of his first three seasons made him one of the league's most feared wide-outs. A deep threat capable of going the distance every time he got his hands on the ball, the six-foot, 185-pound Colclough possessed outstanding speed, good moves, and exceptional hands. Although he starred for the Pats some 50 years ago, Colclough's teammate Tom Yewcic later suggested that the wide receiver had the kind of ability that would allow him to excel in any era.

Even though Gino Cappelletti became quarterback Babe Parilli's favorite target in subsequent seasons, Colclough remained the team's primary deep threat from 1963 to 1965, averaging 38 receptions, 675 yards, and nearly 4 touchdowns over that three-year stretch, and posting an average of 20.5 yards per reception in 1964 that placed him third in the league rankings. However, the emergence of young wide-out Art Graham prompted the Patriots to trade Colclough to the New York Jets following the conclusion of the 1965 campaign. Although the Pats reacquired him prior to the start of the 1966 season, Colclough found himself unable to regain his starting job, spending his final three years in Boston serving primarily as Graham's backup at the split end position. After making only 38 receptions for less than 700 total yards from 1966 to 1968, Colclough announced his retirement, ending his career with 283 catches, for 5,001 yards and 39 touchdowns. He also carried the ball 4 times for a total of 51 yards.

Following his playing career, Colclough partnered with Boston Bruins center Derek Sanderson and Jets quarterback Joe Namath, with whom he developed a close personal relationship during his brief stay in New York, in opening a sports bar in Boston's Park Square called *The Bachelors III*. He also went on to get a master's degree in education, enabling him to eventually land a job as head football coach at Boston State University (Division III), where he led his team to the league championship in 1978–79. Colclough later worked in the financial services field as well, authoring a Lotus program eventually purchased by New England Life. Colclough lived until May 16, 2004, when he died of complications from hepatitis C, at 68 years of age. Upon learning of Colclough's passing, Patriots owner Robert Kraft released a statement that said, "We are deeply saddened by the news of Jim's passing. Like so many of his teammates, Jim represented the Patriots with great dignity, both on and off the field, and proudly remained an active part of the New England community for more than four decades."

CAREER HIGHLIGHTS

Best Season

Colclough had an outstanding rookie season in 1960, making a career-high 49 receptions, for 666 yards and 9 touchdowns. However, there is little doubt that he had his best all-around year in 1962, when he made 40 catches and established career highs with 868 receiving yards, 10 touchdowns, and a league-leading average of 21.7 yards per reception, en route to earning his lone Pro Bowl selection.

Memorable Moments/Greatest Performances

Colclough had his breakout game for the Patriots on November 11, 1960, making 6 receptions for 85 yards and 2 touchdowns during a 38-21 win over the New York Titans. His TD scores came from 31 and 9 yards out. Colclough had another big day the following week, scoring another touchdown and making a season-high 9 catches during a 42-14 mauling of the Dallas Texans.

Colclough had the best day of his sophomore campaign on September 16, 1961, when he made 7 catches for 123 yards and 2 touchdowns during a 45-17 home win over the Denver Broncos, making his TD grabs from 14 and 18 yards out. Later during that 1961 season, Colclough helped the Patriots defeat the Buffalo Bills by a score of 52-21 by making a season-long 58-yard touchdown reception on a pass thrown by Butch Songin.

Colclough turned in a number of memorable performances over the course of his exceptional 1962 season, with the first of those coming on October 6, when he helped lead the Patriots to a 43-14 thrashing of the New York Titans by making 4 receptions for 142 yards and 1 touchdown, which came on a 63-yard hookup with Babe Parilli. Five weeks later, on November 11, Colclough caught 5 passes, for 123 yards and 2 touchdowns, during a 33-29 win over the Denver Broncos, with his scoring plays covering 7 and 67 yards. Later that month, on November 30, Colclough's fourth-quarter touchdown reception of 75 yards proved to be the difference in the Patriots' 24-17 victory over the Titans. He finished the day with 3 catches, for 127 yards and one TD.

Colclough amassed a season-high 137 receiving yards on November 17, 1963, by hauling in 9 passes during a 24-24 tie with the Kansas City Chiefs. He nearly matched that total one year later, making 6 receptions for 134 yards during a 24-14 loss to the Buffalo Bills in the 1964 regular-season finale, played on December 20.

Colclough had the last 100-yard receiving day of his career on November 7, 1965, when he made 4 receptions for 114 yards during a 23-7 loss to the Bills at Fenway Park.

NOTABLE ACHIEVEMENTS

- Caught at least 40 passes five times.
- Scored 10 touchdowns in 1962.
- Averaged more than 20 yards per reception twice.
- Led AFL with average of 21.7 yards per reception in 1962.
- Finished in top five in AFL in touchdown receptions three times.
- Ranks among Patriots' all-time leaders in: pass receptions (11th); receiving yardage (6th); touchdown receptions (6th); and touchdowns scored (tied-11th).
- Ranks third in AFL history in yards-per-reception average (17.7).
- 1963 AFL Eastern Division champion.
- 1962 AFL Pro Bowl selection.
- Member of Patriots' 1960s All-Decade Team.

46

Terry Glenn

Terry Glenn in Dallas Cowboys uniform
(Courtesy Matt Cordon)

Drafted by the Patriots over the objections of head coach Bill Parcells, who once referred to the team's first-round selection in the 1996 NFL Draft as "she," Terry Glenn spent six tumultuous years in New England, never quite fulfilling the enormous potential that enabled him to win the Fred Biletnikoff Award as the nation's top wide receiver in college. Plagued by injuries and the memories of a troubled past, Glenn experienced numerous personal problems during his time in New England that limited his playing time and affected his on-field performance, finally forcing the Patriots to part ways with him at the conclusion of the 2001 campaign. Yet, even though the circumstances under which Glenn left New England could hardly be described as ideal, he made significant contributions to Patriots teams that advanced to the playoffs four times, captured two conference championships, and won one Super Bowl. En route to earning a spot on the Patriots' 1990s All-Decade Team, Glenn surpassed 50 receptions four times, making a career-high 90 catches for New England's 1996 AFC championship club. Named *Sports Illustrated*'s 1996 NFL Rookie of the Year, Glenn amassed more than 1,000 receiving yards twice for the Patriots, appeared in one Pro Bowl, and earned First-Team All-AFC honors once.

Born in Columbus, Ohio, on July 23, 1974, Terrance Tyree Glenn grew up in poverty, wearing clothes donated to a local charity. The son of an alcoholic mother and a father he never knew, young Terry spent much of his childhood visiting his mother in the county jail; that is, when he wasn't watching her stumble down the neighborhood streets with a bottle of liquor in her hand. Looking back at the manner in which his unhappy home life affected his self-esteem, Glenn recalls, "The welfare thing didn't help. You're on food stamps. You're wearing 'charity-newsies,' and all those clothes would look the same. The pants all had a circle on the back pocket, and I'd try to remove the stitching so people couldn't tell. . . . Everybody knew if you had that, your parents didn't work, and you're basically nothing."

To escape his shame, Glenn turned to football, often donning his football uniform and riding his bicycle to the white side of Columbus, where no one knew him. Still, Glenn's frequent trips to the other side of town could only do so much for his injured psyche, since he knew what awaited him at home. Glenn noted years later, "Just my friends knowing that my mother was an alcoholic. I was the fastest guy in school, and you could see I had something in me. And then to have a family like that, it brought me down."

Glenn's situation changed dramatically shortly after he turned 13, when police found his mother beaten to death in an abandoned building. After spending the next year being shuttled between two aunts, each of whom he believed also drank too much, young Terry left home and moved in with Mary and Charles Henley, whose son played on the same little league football team as Glenn. Through the Henleys, Glenn eventually met a teacher named Georgia Hauser, who served as his mentor after he began attending Brookhaven High School. While in high school, Glenn expanded his athletic interests, lettering in football, basketball, track, and tennis.

From Brookhaven, Glenn moved on to Ohio State University, where he earned First-Team All-America honors and won the Fred Biletnikoff Award as a junior. Later selected by the Patriots with the seventh overall pick of the 1996 NFL Draft, Glenn experienced his first bit of controversy as a pro early in his rookie campaign when New England head coach Bill Parcells referred to him as "she" during a preseason press conference. Parcells, who would have preferred to take a defensive player with the team's first-round pick but ended up acquiescing to owner Robert Kraft's desire to select Glenn, grew increasingly impatient with the wide receiver as he sat out the entire preseason with a hamstring injury that the coach insisted was a mild strain. Asked about Glenn's condition one day at training camp, Parcells quipped, "She's making progress." Kraft subsequently admonished Parcells for his remark, informing the media that he told his coach, "That's not the standard we want to set. That's not the way we do things. It's just like there was a player last year that gave the finger to the crowd; He's not here anymore."

Following the initial period of uneasiness that existed between the two men, Glenn ended up endearing himself to Parcells with his play on the field. After missing the regular-season opener, Glenn started every remaining game for the Patriots, helping them capture the AFC East title by making a then-NFL rookie-record 90 pass receptions. He also amassed 1,132 yards through the air and scored 6 touchdowns, earning in the process First-Team All-AFC honors, recognition from the UPI as the AFC Rookie of the Year, and the honor of being named NFL Rookie of the Year by *Sports Illustrated*. Speaking of the relationship that eventually developed between him and Parcells, Glenn later revealed, "Coach pulled me aside and said, 'I think you're a 'he,' you know that.' He was a master motivator."

Glenn's real problems in New England actually began after Parcells left the Patriots following his rookie season. Limited to only nine games in 1997 by injuries to his ankle, hamstring, and collarbone, Glenn appeared in just 10 contests the following year after severely injuring his ankle midway through the campaign. Still, he ended up compiling respectable numbers in the second of those years, making 50 receptions, for 792 yards and 3 touchdowns.

However, it was during that 1998 season that Glenn began experimenting with marijuana for the first time. Unhappy over missing so much playing time and displeased with his role in new head coach Pete Carroll's offense, Glenn turned to marijuana to ease his sorrow, just as he had turned to football years earlier to hide his shame. A number of off-field incidents soon followed, sullying his reputation and prompting the New England front office to view him in a different light. On November 24, 1999, a woman claimed that Glenn groped her outside a nightclub. The very next day, police pulled Glenn over for speeding, causing him to be three hours late for practice. One month later, the Patriots suspended him for one game for skipping treatment for an injury. And, on December 19, 2000, Glenn and two of his teammates, Ty Law and Troy Brown, incurred the wrath of management by showing up late for team meetings in Foxboro after Law was arrested for possession of ecstasy while the three men entertained themselves at a Canadian strip club following a game in Buffalo.

Yet, in spite of his numerous indiscretions, Glenn continued to produce for the Patriots on the field. After earning his lone Pro Bowl selection in 1999 by making 69 receptions for 1,147 yards and 4 touchdowns, he caught 79 passes for 963 yards and 6 touchdowns the following year.

Nevertheless, Glenn's erratic behavior finally caused him to wear out his welcome in New England by the end of 2001. Shortly after being suspended by the NFL for the first four games of the regular season for violating the league's substance abuse policy, Glenn was arrested in May for shoving Kimberly Combs, the mother of his five-year-old son, Terry Jr. Subsequently diagnosed with clinical depression by an NFL psychologist, Glenn chose not to attend training camp after the Patriots withheld his signing bonus and elected to pay him the league minimum for violating a clause in his contract. After initially being suspended by the Patriots, Glenn returned to the team in Week 5 to make seven catches during a 29-26 overtime win over the San Diego Chargers. However, he appeared in only three more games and made just seven more receptions the rest of the year after claiming he had injured his hamstring. Doubting the word of Glenn, who hinted at his own lack of sincerity when he said during an interview on WBZ-TV, "I'm bothered by a hamstring right now, and I'm not getting paid. You do the math," New England head coach Bill Belichick deactivated the wide receiver prior to the start of the playoffs, forcing him to watch the Patriots' successful run to their first Super Bowl title from the comfort of his own home. Treated with disdain by team management from that point on, Glenn did not receive a championship ring with his teammates. Instead, the Kraft ownership group sent his ring by way of the US Postal Service.

Dealt to the Green Bay Packers for a pair of fourth-round draft picks at season's end, Glenn posted solid numbers in 2002, making 56 receptions for 817 yards and 2 touchdowns, before rejoining his former head coach Bill Parcells in Dallas the following year. Glenn spent his five remaining years in the league with the Cowboys, having his two best seasons for them in 2005 and 2006. After catching 62 passes for 1,136 yards and 7 touchdowns in the first of those campaigns, he made 70 receptions for 1,047 yards and 6 TDs in the second. Limited to just one game and no receptions in 2007 after undergoing arthroscopic knee surgery during the previous offseason, Glenn retired prior to the start of the 2008 campaign after being released by the Cowboys. He ended his career with 593 catches, for 8,823 yards and 44 touchdowns. Glenn also carried the ball 20 times, for 139 yards and one TD. In his six years with the Patriots, Glenn made 329 receptions, for 4,669 yards and 22 touchdowns—figures that place him in the team's all-time top-10 in both receptions and receiving yardage.

Unfortunately, trouble has continued to follow Glenn since he retired from football. Early in 2009, police arrested him for public intoxication and marijuana possession. Glenn again found himself incarcerated in January 2010 on grand theft auto charges after he failed to return a rented car. Police arrested him again later that year for marijuana possession. And, on January 22, 2011, law enforcement officers in Denton County, Texas, arrested him for driving while intoxicated and possession of marijuana.

PATRIOT CAREER HIGHLIGHTS

Best Season

Glenn earned his lone Pro Bowl selection in 1999, when he made 69 receptions for 4 touchdowns and a career-high 1,147 yards for a Patriots team that finished the regular season with an 8-8 record. However, he made his greatest overall impact in New England as a rookie in 1996, finishing seventh in the NFL with 90 receptions, amassing 1,132 receiving yards, and scoring 6 touchdowns, in helping the Patriots capture their first AFC East title in 10 years. Glenn's 90 receptions established a new NFL record for rookies (later broken by Arizona's Anquan Boldin, who caught 101 passes for the Cardinals in 2003), earning him in the process First-Team All-AFC and NFL Rookie of the Year honors.

Memorable Moments/Greatest Performances

Although the Patriots lost their second game of the 1996 campaign to the Buffalo Bills 17-10, Glenn played extremely well in his NFL debut, making 6 receptions for 76 yards and one touchdown, with his score coming on a 37-yard hookup with Drew Bledsoe in the third quarter. However, Glenn had his first truly big game for the Patriots nearly two months later, on November 3, when he made 10 receptions for 112 yards during a convincing 42-23 home win over the Miami Dolphins.

The rookie wide receiver turned in another exceptional effort in the 1996 regular-season finale, helping the Patriots overcome a 22-0 halftime deficit to the New York Giants by making 8 catches for one touchdown and a season-high 124 yards. Glenn's 26-yard TD reception from Bledsoe early in the fourth quarter trimmed New York's lead to 22-10, providing much of the impetus for the Pats to score another two times, en route to coming away with a 23-22 victory that enabled them to claim the AFC East title.

Limited by injuries to only nine games in 1997, Glenn made a total of just 27 receptions over the course of the campaign. Yet, even though the Patriots lost their October 27 Super Bowl rematch with Green Bay 28-10, Glenn proved to be easily their most potent offensive weapon, making 7 receptions for 163 yards.

Despite missing a significant amount of playing time the following year as well, Glenn performed extremely well whenever he took the field for the Patriots. During a 27-16 home win over the Tennessee Oilers on September 20, Glenn caught 4 passes for 102 yards and one touchdown, giving the Patriots their first lead of the game when he hooked up with Drew Bledsoe on a 51-yard scoring play midway through the fourth quarter. Glenn again topped 100 receiving yards two weeks later, when he made 4 receptions for 105 yards during a 30-27 victory over the Saints in New Orleans. On November 29, in just his second game back after sitting out the previous five weeks with a badly injured ankle, Glenn made 8 receptions for 104 yards during a 25-21 win over Buffalo. Glenn played his best game of the year the following week against Pittsburgh, making 9 receptions for 193 yards and one touchdown, in helping the Patriots defeat the Steelers 23-9. Glenn's TD—an 86-yard connection with Drew Bledsoe—proved to be the longest reception of his career.

Glenn turned in the most prolific pass-receiving performance of his career on October 3, 1999, when he made 13 receptions for 214 yards and one touchdown during a 19-7 victory over the Cleveland Browns. He scored New England's only touchdown of the game on the final play of the third quarter when he hooked up with Drew Bledsoe from 54 yards out.

Glenn had his last big day as a member of the Patriots on November 19, 2000, making 11 receptions for 129 yards during a hard-fought 16-13 home win over the Cincinnati Bengals.

NOTABLE ACHIEVEMENTS

- Surpassed 50 receptions four times, making 90 catches once (1996).
- Topped 1,000 receiving yards twice (1996 & 1999).
- Gained more than 1,000 yards from scrimmage three times.

- Averaged more than 15 yards per reception three times.
- Ranks among Patriots all-time leaders in pass receptions (7th) and receiving yardage (7th).
- Two-time AFC champion (1996 & 2001).
- Super Bowl XXXVI champion.
- 1996 UPI AFC Rookie of the Year.
- 1996 *Sports Illustrated* NFL Rookie of the Year.
- 1996 First-Team All-AFC selection.
- 1999 Pro Bowl selection.
- Member of Patriots' 1990s All-Decade Team.

47

Tony Collins

Tony Collins receives the handoff from Tony Eason.
(Courtesy Mainline Autographs)

A speedy and powerful runner, Tony Collins spent seven years in New England, helping the Patriots advance to the playoffs three times. The Pats' leading rusher in each of his first three seasons, Collins became in 1983 just the third player in franchise history to rush for more than 1,000 yards in a season. An outstanding blocker and exceptional pass receiver as well, Collins surpassed 50 receptions and 500 receiving yards twice, making a total of 77 catches in 1986 that remains a Patriots single-season record for running backs. Unfortunately, an addiction to cocaine shortened Collins' career, preventing him from placing any higher in these rankings. Nevertheless, he accomplished enough in his seven years with the Patriots to earn a spot on this list.

Born in Sanford, Florida, on May 27, 1959, Anthony Collins grew up in upstate New York, where he attended Penn Yan Academy. After gaining notoriety in high school as the star running back on the 1976 New York State Class B Champion Penn Yan Mustangs, Collins enrolled at East Carolina University, where his outstanding play prompted the Patriots to select him in the second round of the 1981 NFL Draft, with the 47th overall pick.

After originally being slated for backup duties in his first year with the Patriots, Collins ended up starting 11 games as a rookie due to injuries sustained by the team's other running backs. Reflecting back on the way things unfolded his first year in the league, Collins recalled, "I was drafted to return kicks and was the third string running back. Vagas Ferguson was the starter the year before, and he had set the rookie rushing record. He was a Notre Dame guy, a Heisman Trophy candidate, and I got the opportunity to play because Vagas got hurt in camp. Horace Ivory was a good running back from Oklahoma, and then he got hurt and I got a chance to start the season."

Making the most of his opportunity, Collins had an exceptional rookie campaign, rushing for 873 yards, gaining another 232 yards on 26 pass receptions, and scoring 7 touchdowns for a Patriots team that finished the season just 2-14. Doubling as the team's primary kickoff returner, Collins accumulated another 773 yards on special teams, amassing a total of 1,893 all-purpose yards that placed him sixth in the league rankings. He followed that up by starting all nine games for the Patriots in the strike-shortened 1982 season, helping them advance to the playoffs as a wild card by rushing for a team-leading 632 yards, making 19 receptions for 187 yards, and scoring 3 touchdowns.

The focal point of New England's offense by 1983, Collins posted the best numbers of his career that season, earning his lone Pro Bowl selection by rushing for 1,049 yards, gaining another 257 yards on 27 catches, and scoring 10 touchdowns.

Coming off his finest season, Collins appeared to be ready to claim his place among the NFL's elite running backs. However, injuries and the installation of a new offense following the replacement of Ron Meyer with Raymond Berry as head coach midway through the 1984 campaign resulted in less playing time for Collins, who started just 5 games and rushed for only 550 yards, although he still managed to score 5 touchdowns.

Returning kickoffs for the first time since his rookie season, Collins also gained another 544 yards on special teams, enabling him to surpass 1,000 all-purpose yards (1,194) for the third of five times.

Concerns over losing his starting job prompted Collins to turn to pain medication as a means of keeping him on the field as he battled through injuries throughout much of the 1984 season. But, when the medication made him nauseous, a teammate suggested that he use marijuana to ease his discomfort. Before long, Collins moved on to cocaine, to which he soon became addicted.

Yet, in spite of his dependence on drugs, Collins performed well for the AFC champion Patriots in 1985, gaining 657 yards on the ground, another 549 yards on 52 pass receptions, and scoring 5 touchdowns. He also did an exceptional job of blocking for backfield mate Craig James, helping the fullback rush for a career-high 1,227 yards.

A consummate team player, Collins looks back at the Patriots' championship campaign of 1985 with great fondness, stating, "The biggest memory was all of us got along so well. Raymond (Berry) came in and taught us how to win . . . he turned it around in one year."

Deriving particular pleasure from New England's 31-14 victory over the Miami Dolphins in the AFC Championship Game, Collins recalls, "We really put a spanking on them. That was really our Super Bowl. It was a great ride that year, a great run; but the biggest thing was the camaraderie we felt that season."

Collins had another good year in 1986, when, serving as New England's primary pass-catching threat coming out of the backfield, he made 77 receptions for 684 yards, rushed for 412 yards, and scored 8 touchdowns. Nevertheless, his reputation took a major hit prior to the start of the campaign when a report surfaced that he was among a dozen players that tested positive for illegal drugs the previous season.

Collins lasted just one more year in New England, rushing for 474 yards, making 44 receptions for another 347 yards, and scoring 6 touchdowns in 1987, before being suspended for one year due to his involvement with drugs. Many years after almost losing his life from a drug overdose, Collins described the nadir of his existence in the opening paragraph of his book, *Broken Road*: "I don't remember every detail about that awful morning in Indianapolis, but the guy in black is burned into my memory. I was on the grass outside my apartment complex, having convulsions, flopping up and down. There was this big wide field nearby, and I saw a man walking toward me, dressed in all black. I said to myself, 'I don't want to die like this.'"

Although Collins attempted a brief comeback with Miami in 1990, the Dolphins released him after only one game when he found himself unable to overcome his drug addiction. Collins ended his career with 4,647 yards rushing, 261 pass receptions for 2,356 yards, 1,365 kickoff return yards, 44 touchdowns, and a rushing average of 3.9 yards per carry. He continues to rank among New England's all-time leaders in rushing yardage, rushing touchdowns, and total touchdowns scored.

Collins remained addicted to drugs another 13 years before he finally regained control of his life. He eventually began educating high school athletes and their families on the college recruiting process as an educational speaker for the National Collegiate Scouting Association. Having learned from his earlier mistakes, Collins also became a motivational speaker who travels the country trying to influence the nation's youth to make the right choices in their own lives. In addressing the positive impact he tries to make in the lives of others, Collins says, "I talk about opportunity and choices, and I tell them they get the choice to study hard or be a class clown; to work hard at your sport, or whatever interests you, and the older you get, the more difficult the choices become."

Collins adds, "I used to think that my purpose in life was to play in the NFL, but that was part of it; the purpose of my life now is to let these kids, or whoever else wants to listen, know that there is life. If you make a mistake, you don't have to stay down; you can get back up and get back up to the top."

PATRIOT CAREER HIGHLIGHTS

Best Season

Collins had an outstanding first year in New England in 1981, scoring 7 touchdowns and establishing a new Patriots rookie record by rushing for 873 yards. He also gained another 232 yards on 26 pass receptions and accumulated 773 yards returning kickoffs, en route to amassing a career-high 1,893 all-purpose yards that placed him second only to San Diego's James Brooks (2,093) in the AFC. Collins also performed extremely well in 1985 and 1986, totaling 2,302 yards from scrimmage over the course of those two seasons, scoring 13 touchdowns, and making a total of 129 pass receptions. However, Collins made his greatest overall impact in 1983, earning Pro Bowl and Second-Team All-AFC honors for the only time in his career by establishing career highs in rushing yardage (1,049), yards from scrimmage (1,306), touchdowns (10), and rushing average (4.8), with the last figure placing him fifth in the league rankings.

Memorable Moments/Greatest Performances

Collins turned in an outstanding all-around effort in his first game as a pro, carrying the ball 15 times for 81 yards, making 3 receptions for 48 yards, and accumulating another 65 yards on 3 kickoff returns during a 29-28 loss to the Baltimore Colts in the opening game of the 1981 regular season. Looking back at his first pro start, Collins says, "It was a great experience. While I was pleased with the performance, I believe we did lose that game. But it was exciting—something you dream about as a kid, playing in the NFL."

Collins rushed for more than 100 yards for the first time in his career on October 25, 1981, carrying the ball 22 times for 103 yards and a touchdown during a 24-22 loss to the Redskins in Washington.

Collins had the biggest day of his career on September 18, 1983, leading the Patriots to a 23-13 home win over the New York Jets by carrying the ball 23 times for 212 yards and 3 touchdowns. His extraordinary effort, which set a new club record for most yards rushing in a game, proved to be the AFC's top rushing performance all year. Collins scored 18 of New England's 23 points with TD runs of 39, 7, and 23 yards.

Collins had another big day a little over one month later when he rushed for 147 yards and one touchdown during a lopsided 31-0 victory over the Buffalo Bills on October 23. Collins scored his touchdown on a season-long 50-yard scamper. He also made 4 receptions for 45 yards during the contest.

Collins surpassed 100 rushing yards for the final time in his career on November 6, 1983, when he carried the ball 21 times for 100 yards and a touchdown during a 21-7 win over the Bills.

NOTABLE ACHIEVEMENTS

- Rushed for more than 1,000 yards once (1,049 in 1983).
- Scored 10 touchdowns in 1983.
- Surpassed 50 receptions twice, making more than 70 catches once (77 in 1986).
- Averaged better than 4.5 yards per carry once (4.8 in 1983).

- Surpassed 1,000 yards from scrimmage four times and 1,000 all-purpose yards five times.
- Ranks among Patriots all-time leaders in: rushing yardage (3rd); rushing touchdowns (tied 5th); and total touchdowns scored (7th).
- 1985 AFC champion.
- 1983 Pro Bowl selection.
- 1983 Second-Team All-AFC selection.

48

Corey Dillon

(Courtesy Marc and Kelly Sebes)

By the time Corey Dillon joined the Patriots in 2004 he had already established himself as the most prolific running back in Cincinnati Bengals history, setting a franchise record by rushing for 8,061 yards in his seven years with the team. Dillon gained more than 1,000 yards on the ground in each of his first six seasons in Cincinnati, posting two of the top 10 single-game rushing performances in NFL history during his time there. However, while playing for the Bengals, Dillon also developed a reputation as a selfish malcontent who cared little about his team or his teammates. After arriving in New England, though, Dillon changed the overall perception that others held towards him by proving to be an exceptional leader and an outstanding teammate. Fueled by an intense desire to win, the enigmatic running back thrived in an environment in which he found himself surrounded by like-minded people, supporting the contention he made when he said, "My thing has always been, sit down with me for an hour and base your judgments off that. That's all I ask. Don't go by what you read in the paper or hear in the streets." Dillon also excelled on the field for the Patriots, leading them in rushing in each of his three seasons in New England. After scoring 13 touchdowns and rushing for a franchise-record 1,635 yards in 2004, Dillon totaled 26 touchdowns and more than 1,500 yards on the ground over the course of the next two seasons, en route to helping the Pats win three division titles, one AFC Championship, and one Super Bowl. Even though Dillon spent just three years in New England, he ranks among the Patriots' all-time leaders in rushing yardage, rushing touchdowns, total touchdowns scored, and rushing average.

Born in Seattle, Washington, on October 24, 1974, Corey James Dillon grew up in a single-parent household in the depressed Capitol Hill district of Seattle. Raised by his mother, young Corey experienced numerous problems with the law as a teenager, being charged with seven different offenses in juvenile court, the most serious of which came after he turned 15, when he was arrested and convicted for conspiracy to sell cocaine to an undercover cop. Introduced to football by his two older brothers at the age of seven, Corey actively participated in sports as a youth, often using the playing field to escape the harsh realities of life in the ghetto.

An outstanding all-around athlete, Dillon starred as a running back on the gridiron and a power-hitting outfielder on the baseball diamond while attending Franklin High School, earning First-Team All-State and All-Metro Player of the Year honors in football. Meanwhile, Dillon's speed and power made such a strong impression on the San Diego Padres that they selected him in the 1993 MLB Draft. Believing that his future in professional sports lay in football, Dillon instead chose to attend college, although he failed to meet the NCAA's minimum academic requirements coming out of high school. Furthermore, his earlier run-ins with the law scared off most of the nation's top programs. As a result, Dillon spent the next two years trying to improve his grades and his reputation at various community colleges, experiencing numerous setbacks along the way, including quitting one school and being kicked out of another for skipping classes and fighting. After landing at Dixie College, in St. George, Utah,

Dillon finally demonstrated the initiative to make something of himself, prompting the University of Washington to accept him in 1996. Dillon spent just one year at Washington, starring in the Huskies' backfield, before deciding to turn pro.

Selected by the Bengals in the second round of the 1997 NFL Draft, with the 43rd overall pick, Dillon spent the first half of his rookie campaign backing up former Penn State star Ki-Jana Carter, before supplanting him as the starter at running back. Although Dillon started just six of Cincinnati's 16 games, he ended up rushing for 1,129 yards and 10 touchdowns, with his finest performance coming against Tennessee on December 4, when he rushed for 246 yards and four touchdowns during a 41-14 victory over the Oilers. Dillon's 246-yard effort established a new single-game NFL record for rookies, surpassing the 40-year-old mark of 237 yards previously held by Jim Brown.

Dillon had similarly productive years in 1998 and 1999, rushing for 1,130 and 1,200 yards, respectively, while scoring a total of 11 touchdowns. Yet, even as Dillon ascended into NFL stardom, he began to run afoul of the law, just as he had done as a teenager. Arrested on suspicion of drunken driving in March of 1998, Dillon pleaded guilty to negligent driving and driving with a suspended license, forcing him to spend a day in jail and attend an alcohol information program. Some 17 months later, just weeks before the start of the 2000 NFL season, Dillon was charged with fourth-degree assault on his spouse, Desiree, who he had married six months earlier.

Nevertheless, Dillon refused to let his personal problems affect his on-field performance. En route to earning Pro Bowl honors for the second of three straight times by rushing for 1,435 yards and seven touchdowns in 2000, Dillon set a new single-game NFL record (since broken) by gaining 278 yards on the ground against Denver. He also performed extremely well in 2001 and 2002, surpassing 1,300 yards rushing each year, while scoring a total of 20 touchdowns.

In spite of his outstanding play, Dillon shared a somewhat contentious relationship with the local media, his coaches, and even some of his teammates. Upset over playing for a team that consistently finished with one of the league's worst records, Dillon often expressed his dissatisfaction to the press, telling a Cincinnati radio station on one particular occasion that he would rather flip burgers for a living than continue to play for a losing team.

With the Bengals having finished the 2002 season with a record of just 2-14, Dillon grew increasingly disenchanted with his situation in

Cincinnati. Things only worsened when an injury slowed him during the early stages of the 2003 campaign, prompting new head coach Marvin Lewis to replace him in the starting backfield with Rudi Johnson, who went on to lead the team with 957 yards rushing. Although the Bengals finished the year with a record of 8-8, reaching the .500-mark for the first time since 1996, an unhappy Dillon spent most of the season campaigning to be traded, alienating in the process his teammates and coaching staff. After Dillon further angered team management during the subsequent offseason by appearing on national TV in an Oakland Raiders jersey, the Bengals granted his wish, trading him to the Patriots in April 2004 for a second-round draft pick.

Feeling emancipated upon leaving Cincinnati, Dillon nonetheless kept a low profile in the Patriots locker room at first since he expected his new teammates to view him with a certain amount of suspicion. In discussing the attitude he brought with him to New England, Dillon stated, "I'm just going about my business. Am I going to bend over backwards to assure everybody that I'm a good guy? No, I'm not going to do it." However, with everyone in the organization keeping an open mind towards him, Dillon soon gained acceptance among his teammates, who came to admire and respect his intensity and desire to win.

Linebacker Mike Vrabel said of Dillon, "He brings a toughness and an attitude here. I think he's very happy to be part of our team."

Offensive lineman Matt Light noted, "The guy's a workhorse. You need people like that on your team."

Tight end Christian Fauria suggested, "Having him is just a plus, because he plays with so much heart and effort, and it's just contagious."

Head coach Bill Belichick also praised Dillon's work ethic, commenting, "Corey works hard. Football is important to him. He is attentive. He's into it."

Meanwhile, in discussing Dillon's running style, Belichick noted, "He's a powerful guy who can break tackles. And, when he gets in the open field, you don't see him get run down a lot."

Dillon did indeed possess good speed and excellent acceleration. However, with a powerful 6'1", 225-pound frame, he often used his strength to run over people. Never one to shy away from contact, Dillon tended to seek out defenders, preferring to run over them, rather than run away from them. He also had soft hands and a nice feel for soft spots in the defense, making him a good safety valve for Patriots quarterback Tom Brady.

Dillon's addition further strengthened the Patriots' offense, helping the defending Super Bowl champions increase their scoring output by nearly

90 points over the mark they posted in 2003. For his part, Dillon carried the ball 345 times for 1,635 yards, breaking in the process by almost 150 yards Curtis Martin's nine-year-old single-season franchise rushing record. Dillon also scored 13 touchdowns, en route to earning the last of his four Pro Bowl selections. With the Patriots finishing first in the AFC East with an exceptional 14-2 regular-season record, Dillon expressed the euphoria he felt over finally playing for a winning team when he said, "I laugh every day because I can't believe I'm in this situation."

Dillon continued, "It's relaxing here. I can just play football. I think any athlete wants to do his job and not worry about carrying the whole organization. . . . I'm now just an extra ingredient to this big pie—and it's sweet."

Meanwhile, in addressing the somewhat questionable reputation that Dillon brought with him to the team, Tom Brady commented, "He's really been a great leader. I don't care what someone's reputation is. Corey had a great attitude coming in, and it's only gotten better."

Dillon continued to make significant contributions to the success of the Patriots during the playoffs, rushing for 292 yards, catching nine passes for 53 yards, and scoring two touchdowns in the postseason, which culminated with a 24-21 victory over Philadelphia in Super Bowl XXXIX.

Although Dillon also performed well in each of the next two seasons, the 2004 campaign proved to be easily his best in New England. Plagued by injuries for much of 2005, Dillon appeared in only 12 games, finishing the year with just 733 yards rushing. Yet, he still managed to place among the league leaders with 13 touchdowns, scoring 12 of those on the ground. Sharing playing time with rookie running back Laurence Maroney the following season, Dillon rushed for 812 yards and scored another 13 touchdowns.

With Dillon approaching his 33rd birthday and Maroney showing great promise, the Patriots decided to release the veteran running back during the subsequent offseason. After briefly considering playing for another team, Dillon elected to announce his retirement, ending his career with 11,241 yards rushing, 244 pass receptions for another 1,913 yards, 89 touchdowns, and a rushing average of 4.3 yards per carry. In his three years with the Patriots, Dillon rushed for 3,180 yards, gained another 431 yards on 52 pass receptions, scored 39 touchdowns, and averaged 4.2 yards per carry, earning in the process a spot on the Pats' 2000s All-Decade Team.

Unfortunately, trouble continued to follow Dillon after he left the game. In early May of 2010, less than one month after Dillon's wife filed for divorce, police arrested him on suspicion of assaulting her at their home in Calabasas, California.

PATRIOT CAREER HIGHLIGHTS

Best Season

Although Dillon also played well for the Patriots in 2005 and 2006, rushing for more than 700 yards and scoring 13 touchdowns in each of those years, he had easily his best season for them in 2004, when he established a single-season franchise record by gaining 1,635 yards on the ground. In addition to finishing third in the NFL in rushing, Dillon placed among the league leaders with 13 touchdowns, 1,738 yards from scrimmage, and a rushing average of 4.7 yards per carry. By rushing for 1,635 yards, he became the first player in the 45-year history of the Patriots to surpass the 1,500-yard mark.

Memorable Moments/Greatest Performances

Dillon turned in a number of exceptional performances over the course of the 2004 campaign, with the first of those coming on September 19, when he carried the ball 32 times for a season-high 158 yards during a 23-12 win over the Arizona Cardinals. He had another big game five weeks later against the Jets, rushing the ball 22 times for 115 yards, in helping the Patriots defeat New York 13-7. During the contest, Dillon broke off a 44-yard run that proved to be his longest of the year.

Dillon also had a huge day against the Buffalo Bills on November 14, leading the Patriots to a 29-6 victory by rushing for 151 yards on 26 carries.

Named AFC Offensive Player of the Month for December 2004, Dillon totaled 398 rushing yards and five touchdowns in the Patriots' four games, with his top efforts coming against Cleveland on December 5, when he carried the ball 18 times for 100 yards and two touchdowns, and Miami on December 20, when he rushed for 121 yards and scored two touchdowns.

Dillon continued his outstanding play in the New Year, rushing for 116 yards on just 14 carries and scoring a touchdown during New England's 21-7 victory over San Francisco in the regular-season finale.

However, Dillon turned in his most memorable performance of the year in the opening round of the playoffs, rushing for 144 yards and gaining another 17 yards on five pass receptions, in leading the Patriots to a 20-3 win over Peyton Manning and the Colts on a snowy day in Foxboro. Dillon's runs of 42 yards in the second quarter and 27 yards in the fourth quarter proved to be the key plays in a pair of New England scoring drives.

Dillon followed up his exceptional effort against Indianapolis by rushing for 73 yards and one touchdown during the Patriots' 41-27 victory over Pittsburgh in the AFC Championship Game, before gaining 75 yards on the ground, catching three passes for another 31 yards, and scoring a touchdown against Philadelphia in the Super Bowl.

NOTABLE ACHIEVEMENTS

- Rushed for more than 1,000 yards once (1,635 in 2004).
- Surpassed 1,700 yards from scrimmage once (1,738 in 2004).
- Scored 13 touchdowns three straight times (2004–2006).
- Finished third in NFL with 1,635 yards rushing in 2004.
- Holds Patriots single-season record with 1,635 yards rushing in 2004.
- Ranks among Patriots all-time leaders in: rushing yardage (8th); rushing touchdowns (3rd); rushing average (tied-2nd); and touchdowns scored (tied-11th).
- 2004 AFC champion.
- Super Bowl XXXIX champion.
- 2004 Pro Bowl selection.
- Member of Patriots' All-2000s Team.

49

Jerod Mayo

(Courtesy Keith Allison)

An intense on-field competitor, Jerod Mayo established himself as a force on defense almost as soon as he arrived in New England, winning NFL Defensive Rookie of the Year honors his first year in the league. Since joining the Patriots in 2008, Mayo has led the team in tackles five times from his inside linebacker position, doing so in each of his first five seasons, before having each of his last two campaigns shortened by injuries. During that time, he has surpassed 100 tackles five times, leading all NFL players with 175 stops in 2010. Along the way, Mayo has earned two Pro Bowl selections and one First-Team All-Pro nomination, helping the Pats capture two AFC championships and one Super Bowl title in the process.

Born in Hampton, Virginia, on February 23, 1986, Jerod Mayo spent most of his formative years being influenced primarily by his mother and grandfather. Having lost contact with his father at an early age, Mayo gives most of the credit for his solid upbringing to his mother and granddad, stating, "My mother was a huge influence in my life. She always worked at least two jobs, and never let us know how tough it was. My grandfather, a master sergeant in the Air Force, was always there for us. I have always had great conversations with him about life in general."

Mayo attended Kecoughtan High School in Hampton, where he spent three years starring at linebacker and running back. After earning First-Team All-District, All-Area, and All-Region honors as a junior, Mayo capped off his high school football career by recording 110 tackles and two interceptions on defense, while also rushing for 1,245 yards and 13 touchdowns on offense. Rated as one of the nation's top recruits at linebacker, Mayo subsequently enrolled at the University of Tennessee, choosing that institution over a number of other suitors that included North Carolina State, Purdue, Virginia, and Virginia Tech. Splitting his three years at Tennessee between weak-side outside linebacker and middle linebacker, Mayo earned two Second-Team All-American selections and one First-Team All-Southeastern Conference nomination, before declaring himself eligible for the 2008 NFL Draft.

Described by the *Sporting News* as a "perfect fit to play one of the inside spots in a 3-4 defense," the 6'2", 230-pound Mayo ended up being selected with the 10th overall pick in the first round, by the New Orleans Saints, who then traded him to the Patriots in a deal that involved four selections in that year's draft. Subsequently signed by New England to a five-year contract worth $18.9 million, including $13.8 million in bonuses and guarantees, Mayo proved to be worth every cent the Patriots invested in him, earning a starting job in their 3-4 defensive scheme by the end of training camp. Starting at left-inside linebacker between veteran backers Mike Vrabel and Tedy Bruschi, Mayo led the team with 126 tackles (98 solo), earning in the process AP Defensive Rookie of the Year honors in a near-unanimous vote that saw him named on 49 of the 50 ballots cast (Cincinnati Bengals linebacker Keith Rivers received the other vote).

After being named a defensive captain prior to the 2009 campaign, Mayo made 103 tackles (70 solo), despite missing virtually all of the first four games with a sprained MCL in his knee suffered during the regular-season opener against the Buffalo Bills. He followed that up in 2010 by making a career-high 175 tackles (114 solo)—a figure that led all NFL players. Mayo's exceptional performance earned him First-Team All-Pro honors and the first of his two Pro Bowl selections.

Although Mayo's ascension to team captain in just his second season might seem a bit premature to some, it really should come as no surprise to anyone familiar with his work ethic. Known as someone who typically shows up early, stays late, watches film extensively, practices hard, and puts himself through a grueling workout regimen, Mayo quickly earned the respect of his teammates with his positive attitude and unassuming manner, which Michael Holley discussed in his book *War Room*:

> Mayo had been a top ten pick who didn't act like one. On draft day, when the best of the best are invited to New York, often wearing made-for-occasion tailored suits, Mayo had been home in Virginia with his family raking leaves. He was a worker there and a worker in Foxboro. In the offseason, he'd come to the stadium and watch film, even when there were no coaches to be found. He loved the game, and it could be seen by the way he played middle linebacker, never turning down the opportunity to plug a hole or run sideline to sideline.

Mayo further ingratiated himself to his teammates with his humility and willingness to share the spotlight with others. Quick to credit others for his success, Mayo frequently praises his coaches and teammates, suggesting, "Tedy Bruschi, Mike Vrabel, and Junior Seau taught me how to be a professional. They taught me how to study an opponent and prepare year-round for life in the NFL."

Mayo continued to perform well in 2011, making 102 tackles (59 solo), even though he missed three games due to injuries. Healthy again in 2012, Mayo led the Patriots in tackles for the fifth straight year, making a total of 147 stops (87 solo), en route to earning his second Pro Bowl selection and First-Team All-NFL honors from *Pro Football Focus*.

Unfortunately, Mayo proved to be less productive in each of the next two seasons, appearing in just six games in both 2013 and 2014 before being placed on injured reserve. After making 55 tackles (35 solo) in the first six contests of 2013, Mayo sat out the remainder of the year with a torn pectoral muscle he suffered during a come-from-behind 30-27 victory over the New Orleans Saints in Week 6. He experienced a similar fate this past season, missing the final 10 games of the regular season and the entire postseason after tearing his patellar tendon during a 37-22 win over the Buffalo Bills that ironically also took place in Week 6. The 53 tackles Mayo made in the season's first six contests gave him a total of 761 stops (500 solo) for his career. He has also recorded 10 quarterback sacks, intercepted three passes, defended 18 passes, forced 8 fumbles, and recovered 7 others.

Even in his absence from the playing field, Mayo impacted the Patriots in a positive way over the course of the 2014 championship campaign, serving as a mentor to the team's young linebacking corps that includes Dont'a Hightower and Jamie Collins. Speaking of the influence Mayo has had on him, Hightower revealed, "He's meant a lot. Before the injury, he was still a coach on the field to us. He's been a really good partner . . . helping me and Jamie see things on the sidelines and giving us adjustments. (Defensive coordinator) Matt Patricia has a big job on the sideline talking to Bill (Belichick), so Mayo's really helped that front seven, just as far as seeing things from the sideline."

Hightower added, "He's helped me a lot. I feel like I have a pretty decent football IQ, but Mayo's is on a different level. Whenever I'm able to pick his brain about anything, it really means a lot. I really feel like he can come up with a game plan on his own if you gave him the time of day. He's really smart. He's helped me learn the game, he's helped me help myself as far as understanding things to make myself better—playing downhill, getting out in space—some of the things he's good at."

Asked about the impact he may have had on his fellow linebackers, Mayo responded in typical unassuming fashion, "You may have to ask them. But they are smart guys, and if they can learn from me what I learned from Tedy, Mike, and Junior, then we will be a better team."

CAREER HIGHLIGHTS

Best Season

Mayo had an outstanding all-around year for the Patriots in 2012, earning Pro Bowl honors for the second time by making 147 tackles (87 solo), recording a career-high 3 sacks, intercepting a pass, and forcing 4 fumbles. But he had his best season in 2010, when he led all NFL players with 175 tackles (114 solo), sacked opposing quarterbacks twice, forced one fumble, and recovered three others, en route to earning his first Pro Bowl selection and his lone First-Team All-Pro nomination.

Memorable Moments/Greatest Performances

Mayo turned in one of the finest performances of his rookie campaign on November 2, 2008, spearheading a Patriots defense that surrendered just 47 yards on the ground to Indianapolis running backs by making a team-leading 11 tackles during an 18-15 loss to the Colts.

Although the Patriots lost their Thursday night matchup with the New York Jets two weeks later 34-31 in overtime, Mayo recorded a career-high 20 tackles (16 solo) during the contest.

Mayo turned in another exceptional effort on December 27, 2009, when he made 15 tackles during a lopsided 35-7 victory over the Jacksonville Jaguars.

Mayo turned in a number of outstanding performances over the course of his brilliant 2010 campaign, recording 13 tackles during a 38-24 win over Cincinnati on September 12, making 16 stops during a 41-14 victory over Miami on October 4, and making a season-high 18 tackles during a 23-20 overtime win over Baltimore on October 17. He also recorded 14 tackles during a 28-18 victory over Minnesota on October 31, made 15 stops during a 31-28 win over Indianapolis on November 21, and made 16 tackles during a 31-27 victory over Green Bay on December 19.

Mayo recorded the first interception of his career on December 4, 2011, picking off a Dan Orlovsky pass during a 31-24 win over the Indianapolis Colts. He made his second interception the very next week, picking off a Rex Grossman pass during a 34-27 victory over the Washington Redskins.

Although the Patriots ended up losing Super Bowl XLVI to the Giants 21-17, Mayo played extremely well, leading both teams with 11 tackles.

Mayo helped the Patriots get off to a good start in 2013 by making a team-leading 15 tackles during their 23-21 win over Buffalo in Week 1. He also had a big game in the 2014 regular-season opener, recording a sack, recovering a fumble, and making 11 tackles during the Patriots' 33-20 loss to Miami.

NOTABLE ACHIEVEMENTS

- Has surpassed 100 tackles five times, topping 140-mark twice.
- Has led Patriots in tackles five times.
- Led NFL with 175 tackles in 2010.
- Two-time AFC champion (2011 & 2014).

- Super Bowl XLIX champion.
- Two-time Pro Bowl selection (2010 & 2012).
- 2010 First-Team All-Pro selection.
- 2008 AP NFL Defensive Rookie of the Year.
- 2008 ESPN.com NFL Defensive Rookie of the Year.
- 2008 *Sporting News* All-Rookie Team selection.

50

Rodney Harrison

(Courtesy Aaron Frutman of DGA Productions)

The fact that injuries forced Rodney Harrison to miss a significant amount of playing time in four of his six seasons with the Patriots prevented him from finishing higher in these rankings. Various ailments limited the hard-hitting safety to just 63 starts between 2003 and 2008, keeping him out of the Patriots' lineup for the other 33 regular-season contests they played during that period. Nevertheless, Harrison earned a spot on this list due to the tremendous overall impact he made whenever he found himself able to take the field. Fully healthy in each of his first two seasons in New England, Harrison led all NFL defensive backs in tackles both years, totaling 266 stops over the course of those two campaigns. A key contributor to three AFC championship teams and two Super Bowl champions during his time in New England, Harrison made All-Pro twice and All-AFC once as a member of the Patriots, earning in the process a spot on their 50th Anniversary Team. An outstanding big-game player, Harrison posted more career playoff interceptions (7) than any other player in Patriots history. Harrison's exceptional ability and aggressive style of play earned him the respect and admiration of his peers, even though he also developed a reputation among them as being one of the league's dirtiest players.

Born in Markham, Illinois, on December 15, 1972, Rodney Scott Harrison attended Marian Catholic High School in nearby Chicago Heights, before enrolling at Western Illinois University in 1991. While at Western Illinois, Harrison spent three seasons starring on the gridiron, setting a school record during that time for most tackles in a career (345) and in a single game (28). After being named to the All-Gateway Football Conference Second Team as a freshman, Harrison earned First-Team honors in his sophomore and junior years. The Associated Press also accorded him Second-Team All-American honors as a sophomore, before naming him to its First Team the following year.

Subsequently selected by the San Diego Chargers in the fifth round of the 1994 NFL Draft, with the 145th overall pick, Harrison spent most of his first two seasons playing on special teams, although he also assumed the role of a fifth defensive back in his sophomore campaign of 1995. Harrison finally earned a starting job in San Diego's defensive secondary in 1996, a season in which he led the Chargers with five interceptions from his strong safety position and finished second only to Junior Seau on the team with 125 tackles (105 solo). After recording 132 tackles (96 solo), two interceptions, and four sacks the following year, Harrison earned Pro Bowl, First-Team All-AFC, and consensus First-Team All-Pro honors in 1998 by making 114 tackles (89 solo), three interceptions, and four sacks for a Chargers team that finished just 5-11. Injured for much of the ensuing campaign, Harrison returned to top form in 2000, finishing the year with a career-high six sacks and six interceptions, as well as a team-leading 127 tackles (101 solo). He followed that up by earning Pro Bowl and First-Team All-AFC honors for the second time in 2001 with a performance that netted him 107 tackles (90 solo), two interceptions, and 3 ½ sacks.

Yet, in spite of Harrison's outstanding play during his time in San Diego, the Chargers decided to release him after his production fell off somewhat in 2002 due to an assortment of injuries that limited him to 13 games. Seeing an opportunity to strengthen their defensive secondary, the Patriots signed Harrison to a six-year deal just two weeks later, in the hope that they might pair him with fellow safety Lawyer Milloy. However, when the Pats and Milloy failed to come to terms on a new contract, the team released the seven-year veteran, leaving Harrison to team up with rookie free safety Eugene Wilson instead.

Upon his arrival in New England, Harrison's teammates immediately named him a defensive co-captain, an honor they bestowed upon him in each of the next three seasons as well. Starting every game for the Patriots for the first of two straight times, Harrison had an exceptional 2003 campaign, leading all NFL defensive backs with 126 tackles (92 solo). He also recorded three interceptions, three sacks, two forced fumbles, and one fumble recovery, en route to earning First-Team All-AFC and First-Team All-Pro honors. Harrison again led all league DBs in tackles in 2004, bringing down opposing ball-carriers a total of 138 times, making 94 of those stops by himself. He also intercepted two passes, recorded three sacks, and forced three fumbles, earning in the process Second-Team All-Pro honors.

Harrison finished among his team's leading tacklers virtually every season due to his size, strength, and aggressive style of play. Standing 6'1" and weighing 220 pounds, Harrison looked as much like a linebacker as he did a safety, and he made good use of his solid frame to dole out punishment to opposing running backs and wide receivers who dared to cross the middle of the field. Although not a great one-on-one defender, he also possessed superior ball-hawking skills, as can be evidenced by his 34 career interceptions. Making Harrison even more of a factor on defense was his ability to apply pressure to opposing quarterbacks via the pass rush. In addition to his 34 picks, Harrison compiled a total of 30 ½ sacks, making him one of just two players in NFL history to surpass the 30-mark in both categories (Ray Lewis was the other). Harrison's 30 ½ sacks represent a league record for defensive backs.

Still, in spite of the respect Harrison garnered throughout the league for the strength of his all-around game, he also drew criticism from some quarters for what many considered to be his overly aggressive style of play. Voted the "dirtiest player" in the NFL by his peers according to a 2004 poll conducted by *Sports Illustrated*, Harrison again proved to be the top vote-getter in 2006. Two years later, NFL coaches awarded the title to Harrison in an anonymous poll conducted by ESPN. Harrison's penchant for delivering late or illegal hits resulted in numerous fines and suspensions by the league office, with perhaps the most notable of those coming in 2002 after he delivered a helmet-to-helmet hit on Oakland's Jerry Rice.

The physicality Harrison displayed on the playing field finally began to take its toll on him in 2005, when his season ended after only three games due to torn anterior cruciate, medial collateral, and posterior cruciate ligaments in his left knee. He missed another six games the following year after injuring his right shoulder while making a tackle on Marvin Harrison during New England's November 5 meeting with the Indianapolis Colts. Harrison subsequently found himself suspended for the first four games of the 2007 regular season after admitting to federal investigators that he knowingly obtained and used human growth hormone. While Harrison stated to the media that he used "a banned substance" for the purpose of "accelerating the healing process from injuries sustained playing football, and never to gain a competitive edge," it also surfaced that he received a shipment of HGH, with his name on it, just days before Super Bowl XXX-VIII in February 2004.

After suffering a season-ending thigh injury just six games into the 2008 campaign, Harrison elected to announce his retirement during the subsequent offseason. Shortly thereafter, he accepted a position with NBC Sports, where he continues to serve as an analyst for the station's *Football Night in America* program. In addition to recording 34 interceptions and 30 ½ sacks, Harrison made 1,197 tackles (911 solo), forced 15 fumbles, recovered nine others, and scored two defensive touchdowns. Over parts of six seasons with the Patriots, he recorded 441 tackles (312 solo), intercepted eight passes, registered nine sacks, and forced seven fumbles. Upon hearing of Harrison's decision to retire, Patriots head coach Bill Belichick called him one of the best players he had ever coached.

PATRIOT CAREER HIGHLIGHTS

Best Season

Harrison performed brilliantly in each of his first two seasons in New England, leading the Patriots and all NFL defensive backs in tackles both years. After recording 126 tackles (92 solo), three sacks, and three interceptions in 2003, Harrison made a career-high 138 tackles (94 solo), registered three sacks, and picked off two passes in 2004. Although either one of those campaigns would make an excellent choice, I ultimately settled on 2004 because Harrison proved to be one of the most significant contributors to the success the Patriots experienced during the postseason, en route to winning their second consecutive Super Bowl. Not only did Harrison intercept four passes during the playoffs, but he returned one of them 87 yards for a touchdown, in helping the Patriots defeat Pittsburgh by a score of 41-27 in the AFC Championship Game.

Memorable Moments/Greatest Performances

Harrison played exceptionally well during New England's 38-30 victory over Tennessee on October 5, 2003, recording a team-leading 11 tackles. He followed that up by making nine tackles and intercepting two Kerry Collins passes, in leading the Patriots to a 17-6 win over the New York Giants on October 12. Harrison turned in another solid effort the following week against Miami, leading the Pats with 11 tackles and recovering a fumble during a 19-13 overtime win over the Dolphins. Harrison came up big against Miami again on December 7, helping the Patriots shut out the Dolphins 12-0 by recording 10 tackles and a sack. Harrison equaled his season high the following week, when he recorded 11 tackles during a 27-13 victory over Jacksonville.

Harrison also turned in a number of outstanding efforts in 2004, with the first of those coming in Week 2, when he recorded two sacks and three tackles during a 23-12 win over the Arizona Cardinals. Harrison registered double-digit tackles for the first time that season when he brought down opposing ball-carriers 10 times during a 30-20 victory over the Seattle Seahawks on October 17. Although the Patriots lost their October 31 matchup with the Pittsburgh Steelers 34-10, Harrison turned in an epic performance, making a career-high 18 tackles (12 solo) during the contest.

Known as an outstanding big-game player throughout his career, Harrison experienced several of his most memorable moments in the postseason, particularly during New England's successful runs to consecutive championships at the conclusion of the 2003 and 2004 campaigns. After intercepting a Steve McNair pass during the Patriots' 17-14 divisional playoff win over the Tennessee Titans on January 10, 2004, Harrison provided more heroics against Indianapolis in the AFC Championship Game the following week when he ended a Colts' drive late in the first quarter by picking off Peyton Manning in the New England end zone. Harrison also forced a fumble and recorded a team-leading 10 tackles during the contest, which the Patriots won 24-14. Harrison continued his outstanding play against Carolina in Super Bowl XXXVIII, helping the Patriots defeat the

Panthers 32-29 by registering a sack and eight tackles, before fracturing his arm late in the fourth quarter.

Harrison performed even better during the 2004 postseason, recording four interceptions in the Patriots' three games. After beginning his exceptional playoff run by making a team-leading 11 tackles (9 solo), forcing a fumble, and picking off a Peyton Manning pass during New England's convincing 20-3 victory over Indianapolis in the first round of the postseason tournament, Harrison helped lead the Patriots to a 41-27 win over Pittsburgh in the AFC Championship Game by intercepting a Ben Roethlisberger pass late in the second quarter and returning it 87 yards for a touchdown that put the Pats ahead 24-3. He also recorded nine tackles during the contest. Harrison subsequently proved to be a thorn in the side of Donovan McNabb and the Philadelphia Eagles in Super Bowl XXXIX, picking off two McNabb passes, recording a sack, and making seven tackles during New England's 24-21 victory. After keeping the game scoreless late in the first quarter by intercepting a McNabb pass at the New England four-yard line, Harrison sealed the victory by picking him off at the Philadelphia 28-yard-line with only nine seconds remaining in the game.

Nevertheless, Harrison will always be remembered equally for the role he played in one of the most infamous moments in Patriots history, since he was the man that David Tyree victimized when he made his miraculous "helmet catch" in the closing moments of Super Bowl XLII. Tyree's reception, which he made with Harrison draped all over him, proved to be the critical play in a New York Giants scoring drive that ended with a 13-yard touchdown pass to Plaxico Burress with only 39 seconds remaining. The score gave New York a 17-14 win, ending in the process the Patriots' hopes for a perfect season.

NOTABLE ACHIEVEMENTS

- Surpassed 100 tackles twice.
- Led Patriots in tackles twice.
- Led all NFL defensive backs in tackles twice.
- Holds Patriots team record for most career playoff interceptions (7).
- Holds NFL record for most sacks by a defensive back (30 ½).
- One of only two players in NFL history to record at least 30 sacks (30 ½) and 30 interceptions (34).
- Three-time AFC champion (2003, 2004 & 2007).

- Two-time Super Bowl champion (XXXVIII & XXXIX).
- 2003 First-Team All-Pro selection.
- 2004 Second-Team All-Pro selection.
- 2003 First-Team All-AFC selection.
- 2006 Ed Block Courage Award winner.
- Member of Patriots' 2000s All-Decade Team.
- Named to Patriots' 50th Anniversary Team in 2009.

Summary and Honorable Mentions: The Next 25

Having identified the 50 greatest players in New England Patriots history, the time has come to select the best of the best. Based on the rankings contained in this book, the members of the Pats' all-time offensive and defensive teams are listed below. Our squads include the top player at each position, with the offense featuring the two best wide receivers, running backs, tackles and guards. A third wide receiver and third-down back have also been included. Meanwhile, the defense features two ends, two tackles, two inside linebackers, a pair of outside backers, two cornerbacks, and a pair of safeties. Special teams have been accounted for as well, with a placekicker, punter, kickoff returner, punt returner, and special teams performer also being included. The punter and special teams performer were taken from the list of honorable mentions that will soon follow.

OFFENSE:

Player:	*Position:*
Tom Brady	QB
Sam Cunningham	RB
Jim Nance	RB
Kevin Faulk	RB-3RD DOWN
Ben Coates	TE
Gino Cappelletti	WR
Stanley Morgan	WR
Troy Brown	WR
Bruce Armstrong	LT
John Hannah	LG
Jon Morris	C

DEFENSE:

Player:	*Position:*
Bob Dee	LE
Jim Lee Hunt	LT
Houston Antwine	RT
Larry Eisenhauer	RE
Tom Addison	LOLB
Steve Nelson	LILB
Nick Buoniconti	RILB
Andre Tippett	ROLB
Ty Law	LCB
Lawyer Milloy	S
Rodney Harrison	S

OFFENSE:

Player:	*Position:*
Logan Mankins	RG
Matt Light	RT
Adam Vinatieri	PK
Raymond Clayborn	KR

DEFENSE:

Player:	*Position:*
Mike Haynes	RCB
Rich Camarillo	P
Wes Welker	PR
Mosi Tatupu	ST

Although I limited my earlier rankings to the top 50 players in Patriots history, many other fine players have worn a Pats uniform over the years, some of whom narrowly missed making the final cut. Following is a list of those players deserving of an honorable mention. These are the men I deemed worthy of being slotted into positions 51 to 75 in the overall rankings. Where applicable and available, the statistics they compiled during their time in New England are included, along with their most notable achievements while playing for the Patriots.

51. Chris Slade (LB; 1993–2000)

Patriot Numbers: 51 Sacks, 642 Tackles (435 solo), 3 Interceptions, 2 Touchdowns.
Notable Achievements: Surpassed nine sacks three times.
Topped 100 tackles once (105 in 1994).
Led Patriots in sacks three times.
Ranks third all-time on Patriots in career sacks.
1996 AFC champion.
1997 Pro Bowl selection.
1997 First-Team All-AFC selection.
1997 Second-Team All-Pro selection.
Member of Patriots 1990s All-Decade Team.

52. Don Webb (DB; 1961–62, 64–71)

Career Numbers: 21 Interceptions, 366 Int. Return Yards, 4 Touchdowns.
Notable Achievements: Led Patriots in interceptions twice.
Led AFL with four non-offensive touchdowns in 1961.
Finished third in AFL with 153 interception return yards in 1961.

Ranks 11th all-time on Patriots in career interceptions.
1969 Pro Bowl selection.
1967 Second-Team All-AFL selection.
Member of Patriots 1960s All-Decade Team.

53. Ron Hall (DB; 1961–67)

Patriot Numbers: 29 Interceptions, 476 Int. Return Yards, 1 Touchdown.
Notable Achievements: Led Patriots in interceptions twice.
Set Patriots record by intercepting 11 passes in 1964.
Finished second in AFL with 11 interceptions and 159 interception return yards in 1964.
Recorded longest interception return in AFL in 1966 (87 yards).
Tied for third all-time on Patriots in career interceptions.
1963 Pro Bowl selection.
1964 First-Team All-AFL selection.
1963 Second-Team All-AFL selection.
Member of Patriots 1960s All-Decade Team.

54. Ted Johnson (LB; 1995–2004)

Career Numbers: 11 ½ Sacks, 758 Tackles (527 solo), 1 Interception.
Notable Achievements: Surpassed 100 tackles twice.
Led Patriots in tackles twice.
Ranks fifth all-time on Patriots in career tackles.
Four-time AFC champion (1996, 2001, 2003 & 2004).
Three-time Super Bowl champion (XXXVI, XXXVIII & XXXIX).
Member of Patriots 1990s All-Decade Team.

55. Fred Marion (DB; 1982–91)

Career Numbers: 29 Interceptions, 457 Int. Return Yards, 1 Touchdown.
Notable Achievements: Led Patriots in interceptions four times.
Led NFL with 189 interception return yards in 1985.
Finished fourth in NFL with 7 interceptions in 1985.
Tied for third all-time on Patriots in career interceptions.

1985 AFC champion.
1985 Pro Bowl selection.
1985 Second-Team All-AFC selection.
Member of Patriots 1980s All-Decade Team.
Named to Patriots' 50th Anniversary Team in 2009.

56. Leon Gray (OT; 1973–78)

Notable Achievements: Two-time Pro Bowl selection (1976 & 1978).
1978 First-Team All-Pro selection.
1978 First-Team All-AFC selection.
Two-time Second-Team All-AFC selection (1976 & 1977).
Member of Patriots 1970s All-Decade Team.

57. Asante Samuel (CB; 2003–07)

Patriot Numbers: 22 Interceptions, 313 Int. Return Yards, 3 Touchdowns.
Notable Achievements: Led Patriots in interceptions three times.
Led NFL with 10 interceptions in 2006.
Intercepted five passes and scored three touchdowns in postseason.
Ranks 10th all-time on Patriots in career interceptions.
Three-time AFC champion (2003, 2004 & 2007).
Two-time Super Bowl champion (XXXIII & XXXIX).
2007 Pro Bowl selection.
2007 First-Team All-Pro selection.
Member of Patriots 2000s All-Decade Team.

58. Don Blackmon (LB; 1981–87)

Career Numbers: 29 ½ Sacks, 5 Interceptions.
Notable Achievements: Led Patriots with 4 ½ sacks in 1982.
Led NFL with two safeties in 1985.
1985 AFC champion.
1986 Second-Team All-AFC selection.
Member of Patriots 1980s All-Decade Team.

59. Tony Eason (QB; 1983–89)

Patriot Numbers: 58.4 Completion percentage, 10,732 Passing Yards, 60 TD Passes, 48 Interceptions, 80.6 Quarterback Rating, 6 Rushing Touchdowns.
Notable Achievements: Completed more than 60 percent of passes three times.
Threw for more than 3,000 yards twice.
Threw more than 20 touchdown passes once (23 in 1984).
Compiled quarterback rating in excess of 90.0 once (93.4 in 1984).
Finished third in NFL with 93.4 passer rating in 1984.
Finished fourth in NFL with 61.6 completion percentage in 1986.
Ranks among Patriots all-time leaders in: pass completions (5th); passing yardage (5th); completion percentage (2nd); touchdown passes (6th); and quarterback rating (2nd).
1985 AFC champion.

60. Tom Neville (OT; 1965–74, 76–77)

Notable Achievements: 1966 Pro Bowl selection.
Member of Patriots 1960s All-Decade Team.

61. Brian Holloway (OT; 1981–86)

Notable Achievements: 1985 AFC champion.
Three-time Pro Bowl selection (1983, 1984, 1985).
1985 Second-Team All-Pro selection.
Two-time First-Team All-AFC selection (1983 & 1984).
1985 Second-Team All-AFC selection.
Member of Patriots 1980s All-Decade Team.

62. Jim Whalen (TE; 1965–69)

Patriot Numbers: 153 Receptions, 2,487 Receiving Yards, 17 TD Receptions.
Notable Achievements: Surpassed 40 receptions once (47 in 1968).

Topped 700 receiving yards once (718 in 1968).
Averaged more than 17 yards per reception twice.
Led Patriots with 47 receptions in 1968.
1968 First-Team All-AFL selection.
Member of Patriots 1960s All-Decade Team.

63. Charlie Long (OL; 1961–69)

Notable Achievements: Two-time Pro Bowl selection (1962 & 1963).
Two-time Second-Team All-AFL selection (1962 & 1963).
Member of Patriots 1960s All-Decade Team.

64. Craig James (RB; 1984–88)

Career Numbers: 2,469 Rushing Yards, 4.2 Yard Rushing Average, 11 Rushing Touchdowns, 81 Receptions, 819 Receiving Yards, 2 TD Receptions.
Notable Achievements: Rushed for more than 1,000 yards once (1,227 in 1985).
Surpassed 1,500 yards from scrimmage once (1,587 in 1985).
Averaged more than 4.5 yards per carry twice.
1985 AFC champion.
1985 Pro Bowl selection.

65. Ray Hamilton (NT; 1973–81)

Notable Achievements: Scored one defensive touchdown.
Member of Patriots 1970s All-Decade Team.

66. Sam Adams (OG; 1972–80)

Notable Achievements: Appeared in 113 out of a possible 118 games between 1973 and 1980.
Member of Patriots 1970s All-Decade Team.
Named to Patriots 35th Anniversary Team in 1994.

67. Ronnie Lippett (CB; 1983–91)

Career Numbers: 24 Interceptions, 420 Int. Return Yards, 2 Touchdowns.
Notable Achievements: Led Patriots in interceptions three times.
Led NFL with two interceptions returned for touchdowns in 1987.
Finished fifth in NFL with 8 interceptions in 1986.
Tied for eighth all-time on Patriots in career interceptions.
1985 AFC champion.
1986 First-Team All-AFC selection.
1987 Second-Team All-AFC selection.
1987 Patriots UNSUNG Hero Award winner.
Member of Patriots 1980s All-Decade Team.

68. Dan Koppen (C; 2003–11)

Notable Achievements: Started 79 out of 80 possible games between 2006 and 2010.
Four-time AFC champion (2003, 2004, 2007 & 2011).
Two-time Super Bowl champion (XXXVIII & XXXIX).
2007 Pro Bowl selection.
2007 Second-Team All-Pro selection.
Member of Patriots 2000s All-Decade Team.

69. Johnny Rembert (LB; 1983–92)

Career Numbers: 16 Sacks, 7 Interceptions, 2 Touchdowns.
Notable Achievements: 1985 AFC champion.
Two-time Pro Bowl selection (1988 & 1989).
1988 Second-Team All-AFC selection.
Member of Patriots 1980s All-Decade Team.

70. Ty Warren (DL; 2003–10)

Patriot Numbers: 20 ½ Sacks, 375 Tackles (253 solo), 1 Safety.
Notable Achievements: Recorded career-high 7 ½ sacks in 2006.
Surpassed 80 tackles once (84 in 2006).

Led Patriots defensive linemen in tackles five times.
Three-time AFC champion (2003, 2004 & 2007).
Two-time Super Bowl champion (XXXVIII & XXXIX).
2007 Pro Football Writers First-Team All-Pro selection.
Member of Patriots 2000s All-Decade Team.

71. Roland James (DB; 1980–90)

Career Numbers: 29 Interceptions, 383 Int. Return Yards, 1 Safety, 1 Punt Return TD.
Notable Achievements: Tied for Patriots team lead with 4 interceptions in 1988.
First Patriots player to intercept three passes in one quarter (third quarter of 31-0 win over Buffalo on 10/23/83).
Recorded 75-yard punt return TD in 1980.
Tied for third all-time on Patriots in career interceptions.
1985 AFC champion.
1983 Second-Team All-AFC selection.
Member of Patriots 1980s All-Decade Team.

72. Sam Hunt (LB; 1974–79)

Patriot Numbers: 7 Interceptions, 189 Int. Return Yards, 1 Touchdown.
Notable Achievements: Returned interception 68 yards for touchdown during 31-14 win over Tampa Bay on 12/12/76.
Member of Patriots 1970s All-Decade Team.
Named to Patriots 35th Anniversary Team in 1994.

73. Julian Edelman (WR, PR; 2009–Present)

Career Numbers: 266 Receptions, 2,742 Receiving Yards, 14 TD Receptions, 24 Rushing Attempts, 177 Rushing Yards, 7.4 Yard Rushing Average, 1,620 Punt Return Yards, 4 Punt Return Touchdowns, 563 Kickoff Return Yards, 5,102 All-Purpose Yards.
Notable Achievements: Has surpassed 90 receptions twice, topping 100 catches once (105 in 2013).

Has surpassed 1,000 receiving yards once (1,056 in 2013).
Has led Patriots in receptions twice and receiving yards once.
Led NFL with five fumble recoveries in 2013.
Finished second in NFL with 15.3 punt return average in 2010.
Finished fourth in NFL with 105 pass receptions in 2013.
Holds Patriots franchise records for most punts returned for touchdowns (4) and longest punt return (94 yards).
Holds highest punt return average (12.3) among active NFL players.
Two-time AFC champion (2011 & 2014).
Super Bowl XLIX champion.

74. Mosi Tatupu (RB, ST; 1978–90)

Patriot Numbers: 2,415 Rushing Yards, 3.9 Yard Rushing Average, 18 Rushing Touchdowns, 96 Receptions, 843 Receiving Yards, 2 TD Receptions, 56 Kickoff Return Yards, 3,314 All-Purpose Yards.
Notable Achievements: Averaged more than 5 yards per carry three times.
Led NFL with 5.5 yard rushing average in 1983.
Ranks fourth in Patriots history in games played (194).
1985 AFC champion.
1986 Pro Bowl selection.
1986 First-Team All-AFC selection (special teams).
Member of Patriots 1970s All-Decade Team.
Member of Patriots 1980s All-Decade Team.
Named to Patriots 35th Anniversary Team in 1994.
Named to Patriots 50th Anniversary Team in 2009.

75. Rich Camarillo (P; 1981–87)

Patriot Numbers: Averaged 42.6 yards per punt; Career long: 76 yards.
Notable Achievements: Averaged better than 42 yards per punt five straight seasons, posting average in excess of 43 yards three times.
Recorded longest punt in NFL in three different seasons.
Finished second in NFL with punting average of 44.6 in 1983.
1985 AFC champion.
1983 Pro Bowl selection.
1983 Second-Team All-Pro selection.

1983 First-Team All-AFC selection.
Member of Patriots 1980s All-Decade Team.
Named to Patriots 35th Anniversary Team in 1994.
Named to Patriots 50th Anniversary Team in 2009.

Glossary

ABBREVIATIONS AND STATISTICAL TERMS

C. Center.

COMP %. Completion percentage. The number of successfully completed passes divided by the number of passes attempted.

INTS. Interceptions. Passes thrown by the quarterback that are caught by a member of the opposing team's defense.

KR. Kickoff returner.

LCB. Left cornerback.

LE. Left end.

LG. Left guard.

LILB. Left inside linebacker.

LOLB. Left outside linebacker.

LT. Left Tackle.

NT. Nose tackle.

P. Punter.

PK. Placekicker.

PR. Punt returner.

QB. Quarterback.

RB. Running back.

RCB. Right cornerback.

RE. Right end.

RG. Right guard.

RILB. Right inside linebacker.

ROLB. Right outside linebacker.

RT. Right tackle.

S. Safety.

ST. Special teams.

TD PASSES. Touchdown passes.

TD RECS. Touchdown receptions.

TDS. Touchdowns.

TE. Tight end.

WR. Wide receiver.

Sources

VIDEOS

Greatest Ever: NFL Dream Team. Polygram Video, 1996.

WEBSITES

Biographies, online at *Hickoksports.com* (http://www.hickoksports.com/hickoksports/biograph).
Biography from *Answers.com* (www.answers.com).
Biography from *Jockbio.com* (www.jockbio.com).
CapitalNewYork.com (www.capitalnewyork.com).
CBSNews.com (http://www.cbsnews.com).
ESPN.com (http://sports.espn.go.com).
Hall of Famers, online at *profootballhof.com* (http://www.profootballhof.com/hof/member).
Inductees from *LASportsHall.com* (http://www.lasportshall.com).
LAYTimes.com (http://articles.latimes.com).
Newsday.com (www.newsday.com).
NYDailyNews.com (www.nydailynews.com/new-york).
NYTimes.com (www.nytimes.com).
Patriots.com (www.patriots.com).
Pro Football Talk from *nbcsports.com* (http://profootballtalk.nbcsports.com).
RememberTheAFL.com (www.remembertheafl.com).
SpTimes.com (http://www.sptimes.com).
StarLedger.com (www.starledger.com).
SunSentinel.com (http://articles.sun-sentinel.com).
TalesFromTheAFL.com (www.talesfromtheamericanfootballleague.com).

The Players, online at Profootballreference.com (http://www.pro-football-reference.com/players).
TwinCities.com (http://www.twincities.com).
YouTube.com (www.youtube.com).